The Great Decision

By

JAMES T. SHOTWELL

NEW YORK
THE MACMILLAN COMPANY
1944

321.041
S559g

Copyright, 1944, by
THE MACMILLAN COMPANY.

All rights reserved—no part of this book may be reproduced in any form without permission in writing from the publisher, except by a reviewer who wishes to quote brief passages in connection with a review written for inclusion in magazine or newspaper.

FIRST PRINTING.

A WARTIME BOOK
THIS COMPLETE EDITION IS PRODUCED IN FULL COMPLIANCE WITH THE GOVERNMENT'S REGULATIONS FOR CONSERVING PAPER AND OTHER ESSENTIAL MATERIALS

June 26, 1944
Gen.

PRINTED IN THE UNITED STATES OF AMERICA
AMERICAN BOOK–STRATFORD PRESS, INC., NEW YORK

THE GREAT DECISION

THE MACMILLAN COMPANY
NEW YORK · BOSTON · CHICAGO
DALLAS · ATLANTA · SAN FRANCISCO

MACMILLAN AND CO., LIMITED
LONDON · BOMBAY · CALCUTTA
MADRAS · MELBOURNE

THE MACMILLAN COMPANY
OF CANADA, LIMITED
TORONTO

Foreword

THE argument of this book is that our victory over the Axis powers can be made a victory over war itself, if we bring to the support of peace the same kind of realistic strategy which we devote to war. We have now to decide whether this will be done or whether as an inescapable alternative we must prepare for a possible third world war. It is a hard choice and one for which we are not ready. But there is no escape from it. Science has seen to that. This newest thing in human history has already changed the arts of peace and now is revolutionizing the technique of war. The transformation thus begun is not a mere interlude in the history of mankind but, on the contrary, will go on with increasing power throughout all the future. Its bearing upon the theme of this study is fundamental. From now on all war will be total war and therefore the preparation to meet it will also have to be total. This means that so long as the war system lasts it will not only denature the economic life of nations but will endanger all the freedoms within them. Isolation can no longer provide the safety of the past. No single nation can adequately protect itself against a force which is bound more and more to conquer nature and thus change the whole basis of national security. To live well and prosperously in a world under the constant threat of war waged under these conditions is simply impossible. But on the other hand, the organization of peace is the most difficult task that has ever been envisaged by human intelligence.

The pages which follow deal with this problem. The solution which is proposed is one which already rests upon the experience of history. It is not offered in the spirit of dogmatic insistence that it is the one and only solution; but it does reject as unrealistic both the do-nothing policies and half-measures of the past and those theories of world peace which at a single leap would merge the sovereign nations of today under some form of world government. International peace must be safeguarded by institutions not unlike those which have shaped and maintained domestic peace. But, while the community of nations must be strong enough to end the threat of anarchy, it must be so designed as not to overturn but rather strengthen the institutions of freedom within each state.

Keeping these fundamental things in mind, we turn to the world of today and tomorrow, confident that sooner or later international relationships will be adjusted to a system which, leaving behind the law of the jungle, will be based upon that moral order which has so long been recognized in home affairs. The first step in this emancipation from the persisting savagery of force and violence is the complete and utter defeat by war itself of those nations which have made it their fetish and used it for the oppression of others. Until this is fully accomplished all plans for world peace are idle dreaming.

But peace is not merely negative; it is more than policing against violence. In proportion as its institutions develop under the regime of science, its benign influence must find expression in substitutes for war designed to help get rid of conditions which no self-respecting people can endure. War, which was the oldest argument of kings, will not disappear from the world of freedom unless there is provision for justice among nations.

It is at this point that the skeptic registers his doubt, expressed in the time-worn phrase that human nature will not change, and that as wars have been with us from the beginning of time they will be with us as long as human nature remains what it is. This argument seems all the stronger because it appeals to history for its support. But it is a mistaken reading of history as well as a superficial judgment upon the nature of man, for which our school books have been largely to blame. The splendor of Greece lay not in the anarchy of its warring states but in its conquest of the mind. The contribution of Rome which made its influence eternal was less the exploits of its generals than the magnificence of its system of law. And it would be a complete misreading of Western civilization to claim that the teaching of Jesus had not changed the outlook of succeeding centuries. The moral forces of history are not dead; on the contrary they are gaining new life with the development of human intelligence. The one field in which that intelligence has been laggard hitherto is this with which we must at all costs deal effectively now. Science, by making the world interdependent in peace, has made it interdependent in war, and thus brings to the support of morals the greatest force in the determination of the daily life of men and nations.

These generalizations have now to be put into practice. The study which follows deals with ways and means for achieving this. It was begun as a summary of the conclusions of the Commission to Study the Organization of Peace which, during the last four years, has been engaged upon an analysis of the technical as well as the political problems involved in the elimination of war as an instrument of national policy. To his colleagues on the Commission, who worked with such devotion upon these plans, the author would express his sense of deep appreciation.

J. T. S.

Contents

	PAGE
FOREWORD	v

PART I
THE WAR AND ITS LIQUIDATION

I. THE NATURE AND CONSEQUENCES OF TOTAL WAR	3
II. THE PROBLEM OF LIQUIDATION	16
III. SMALL POWERS AND GREAT	25
IV. THE BEGINNINGS OF THE UNITED NATIONS	44
V. THE MOSCOW CONFERENCE	51
VI. SOVIET RUSSIA PREPARES FOR THE POSTWAR WORLD	67

PART II
FUNDAMENTALS OF THE ORGANIZATION OF LASTING PEACE

I. THE SECURITY OF NATIONS	85
(a) Definition	85
(b) Isolation	89
(c) Nationalism	90
(d) Cooperative or Collective Security	93
II. THE PACIFIC SETTLEMENT OF DISPUTES	100
(a) The Test of Aggression	100
(b) Political Settlement of Disputes	101
(c) Justice and the Law	109
(d) Arbitration	114
(e) A World Court	116
III. THE ENFORCEMENT OF PEACE	123
(a) The Obligations of Enforcement	123
(b) Land, Sea and Air Power	126
(c) Teachings of the Christian Churches	132

		PAGE
IV.	THE REDUCTION AND CONTROL OF ARMAMENTS	136
	(a) General Statement	136
	(b) Disarmament Conferences Between the Two World Wars	142
	(c) The Inspection of Armaments	149
V.	LIVELIHOOD AND WELFARE	152
	(a) General Statement	152
	(b) The International Labor Organization	162
	(c) The United Nations Conference on Food and Agriculture	166
	(d) The United Nations Relief and Rehabilitation Administration	171
	(e) International Monetary and Financial Organization	175
VI.	HUMAN RELATIONS	183
	(a) International Cultural Relations	183
	(b) The Safeguards of Freedom	192
VII.	THE POLITICAL ORGANIZATION OF THE UNITED NATIONS	200
	(a) General Statement	200
	(b) Central Political Organization	207
	(c) Regional Organizations: Graded Responsibilities	214
VIII.	THE UNITED STATES IN WORLD ORGANIZATION	218
	(a) General Statement	218
	(b) Security	225
	(c) Justice	227
	(d) Livelihood	228
	(e) Central or Political Organization	230
	(f) The Constitution and World Organization	231

APPENDICES

THE ATLANTIC CHARTER	235
SECTION VII OF THE LEND-LEASE AGREEMENT	236
THE THREE-POWER CONFERENCE AT MOSCOW	236
JOINT COMMUNIQUE ON CAIRO CONFERENCE	241
THE TEHERAN DECLARATION	242
INDEX	245

PART I

THE WAR AND ITS LIQUIDATION

I

The Nature and Consequences of Total War

THERE are few who remember now, or care to remember, the scene of August, 1928, when in a beflagged Paris a document was signed which purported "to outlaw war." The Paris Peace Pact, commonly known as the Briand-Kellogg Pact, was never taken seriously by the nations which it sought to restrain by the moral force of public opinion and a code of laws not yet in existence. History will not deal so harshly with that event, for it was a pioneering episode, a gallant gesture. Nevertheless, the fact remains that today the only sounds which reach the deserted hall of the French Foreign Office, in which the Pact was signed, are the tramp of enemy troops along the Quai d'Orsay and the rumble of gun carriages; while peace-loving nations, which have been enslaved by conquest, are still facing the terror of brute force before their liberation. It is clear that the great reform envisaged ten years after the entry of America into the first World War still confronts the world with an unanswered challenge.

There are many reasons why the civilized world reverted to barbarism in the years between the wars, but one of the most important reasons was the failure of the peace movement to understand the nature of war. There was far too much wishful thinking in place of solid analysis of the facts which had to be faced if war were to be set aside and no longer used as the final argument, the *ultima ratio*, of nations. For war is not only as old as history; it is older. It is also a comprehensive name for many different things—as comprehensive in its way as peace and as miscellaneous in its content. When, therefore, we say that we are going to get rid of war we need to know definitely what kind of war we are getting rid of. Is it police within a nation or many nations? Is it defense? Is it plans for security in case of possible violations of the peace? Is it economic as well as military mobilization? Or is it only that kind of war which is resorted to by governments to force their will upon other countries either in violation of peacetime commitments or because in the consciousness of overwhelming power they plan for empire? In other words, is it the aim of the peace movement to eliminate all use of force from the processes of politics by a single revolutionary act which would not draw any distinction between the support of justice and the commission of crime; between the maintenance of liberty and its violation; between the defense of civilized life and the attack upon it? If that is the aim of the peace movement it is clearly an immoral aim. If, on the other hand, by the elimination of war we mean the elimination of aggression, if the outlawry of war means the outlawry of aggressive war, we have a program which aims both to rid the world of the crime of war and to build at the same time the structure of enduring peace. Viewed in the light of history and of common sense it is aggressive war which the peace movement must concentrate upon, for if we can get rid of that we can get rid of all war by making defense a cooperative police action under the international agreement which would then really "outlaw war."

But at once we come upon the stumbling block which has divided the peace movement and confused it so much as to nullify its effectiveness: How can we distinguish the wars of aggression from other kinds of war? While this problem never came to the fore until our own time, because until now war has always been regarded as inevitable, nevertheless as far back as ancient Greece statesmen and philosophers argued that a war was unjust if it was waged without previous resort to conference and diplomacy. In ancient Rome there was the same sense that it was wrong to go to war except after the formalities prescribed by religion and law. In modern time, especially with the growth of an enlightened public opinion, it has become increasingly imperative for statesmen to justify the wars which they are intent upon waging by offering proof that they have previously exhausted every effort at peaceful settlement before resorting to force. No one was more conscious of this need than the man who used war most deliberately as the instrument of his policy, Bismarck. It was natural, therefore, that on summing up this long history the test of aggression should be found where it had been plainly evident to statesmen in the past, that is, in the acceptance or refusal of pacific means of settlement provided and agreed upon beforehand. This was the test of aggression proposed by an unofficial committee of Americans at Geneva in 1924, and subsequent events have shown that both in theory and in practice this test clarifies the issue and offers a program with clear and definite objectives. In defining aggressive war as that kind of resort to violence which ignores the procedures of peace, it follows that the peace movement must first of all strengthen those procedures so as to make the choice between them and war not only open and aboveboard but one that presents real possibilities of reaching a just settlement. The renunciation of war cannot in the nature of the case make any permanent progress as long as it leaves nations facing the blank alternative of a status quo if they do not resort to force to secure desired changes in international relations.

The distinction between aggressive war and other kinds of war is not the result of vague and wishful thinking, but is positive and practical. Fortunately the test of aggression can be applied without delaying over refinements of definition. It may be difficult to distinguish precisely between aggressive and other kinds of war but the problems of international law, real as they are, may be left largely for academic discussion. We must concentrate upon the initial task of securing adequate substitutes for the age-old method of decision by the sword. This is a case where progress can be made almost without our knowing it. For example, the same British government which refused to accept the formal definition of aggression offered at Geneva in the Protocol of 1924 unconsciously built the Treaty of Locarno around that very definition. That Treaty (in Article 5) provided for British intervention if either France or Germany went to war while refusing to resort to the pacific means of settlement which had been accepted either in the Covenant of the League of Nations or in the Treaty of Locarno itself. None of the negotiators of Locarno bothered about theories or definitions. They were concerned to strengthen the methods of peace in place of the method of war for settling the disputes between Germany and France. This was an instance of war outlawry in actual practice. Its validity has not been lessened by the fact that one of the signatories, Germany, later tore up the treaty by an act of force, any more than the laws of a country are rendered invalid by acts of crime. Unfortunately the initial success of the aggressor in this case, as also the initial successes of Japan in Asia and Italy in Africa, seemed to many people at the time to be convincing proof that the whole movement to eliminate war was inherently fallacious and that the efforts to erect standards of international justice calling for pacific procedures would be forever faced by defeat when strong nations were determined to have their way. This disillusionment would have been justified if it had turned out that the militarists of today had really in their grasp the master forces of our time, if the Hitlers and Mussolinis had been right in contending, as they did, that war and not peace is the fundamental condition of government.

The immediate answer to this challenge must be the defense of democracies by the same methods as those used by their attackers, namely, war itself. Aggression must be met and overcome if peace is ever to have a foothold in the world of reality. That foothold cannot be gained by surrender to the attacker nor by retreating to an attitude of indifference under the pretext of neutrality. Peace cannot prosper if there is no defense against its violation. But defense is also war, the application of force against force. Permanent peace must reach beyond such temporizing efforts to hold back attack or invasion. It must grapple with a far more fundamental problem; namely, Is war what the militarists think it to be, the most effective instrument for achieving a nation's purpose? If it is the one supreme method for overcoming the obstacles that lie in a nation's pathway, there is hardly any doubt that it will be used in the future as in the past, and at no matter what cost. Moreover, the greater the forces of destruction which science offers to the governments of today, the greater will be the effort to mobilize them to secure national ends. In short, the final answer to the peace problem is to be found in a further analysis of the nature of war. Is it what the militarists claim for it, or is it destined to be an outworn instrument, invalid because incapable of achieving its ends?

It is a strange fact that although war is as old as history there has never until our own day been any thorough-going effort to understand it as a technique and instrument of politics. It was the German military expert, Clausewitz, who, in the first half of the nineteenth century, first pointed out the relation between politics and war, making the point that war is the continuation of policy, using another language and another medium than in the peacetime dealings of one nation with another. International law as well as the practice of nations accepted this use of war as legitimate. Indeed, an important part of the international law deals with the conditions under which war is carried on, the limitations imposed by agreements with reference to neutrality and the like, all of which are based upon the presupposition that war is a legitimate instrument of national policy. This is but an interpretation in terms of law of the practice of nations which follow politics of power.

While this theory has always been opposed on moral grounds by at least a section of the peace movement, it was never attacked until the closing years of the nineteenth century on the practical ground that war, under modern conditions, cannot be counted upon to achieve the aims for which it is waged. In 1898, a treatise of the Russian, Jean Bloch, on the future of war influenced Czar Nicholas II profoundly. This was one of the reasons why that ill-fated monarch issued the call for the disarmament conference at The Hague. The thesis of M. Bloch was that war was bound ultimately to become impossible because of its increasing cost in both lives and property. Three years later, Norman Angell published the *Great Illusion,* an eloquent argument against the validity of war not only because of its suicidal nature but also because, owing to the ever-growing interdependence of nations, it was bound to cost the victorious nation more than would be gained in its victory. The example of the Franco-Prussian War of 1870 was a case in point, showing the unsuspected benefits to France and the difficulties encountered by Germany in spite of the brilliance of Germany's military achievement.

The first lessons drawn from the World War seemed to disprove this line of reasoning. At least it was evident that the governments of Europe, in spite of their protestations, were paying very little attention to any such seemingly altruistic conclusions. War was still regarded as the dominant instrument of politics and the German Chancellor, Bethmann-Hollweg, was right in his defense when called in to testify before the Reichstag after the war was over, when he stated that no one in power in 1914 questioned the legitimacy of the ultimate appeal to the arbitrament of arms. It was by concentrating their power on the field of battle that the nations of Europe would achieve those aims which seemed to them necessary or valid.

During the course of the war, however, it became evident that the results of military action were not the measure of the total effects of the war effort. Wars fought under the regime of science are necessarily totalitarian, because the scientist can make war supplies of practically everything in the world, and to do this he needs the labor, or at least the cooperation, of practically everybody. This was first clearly seen by the industrialist, Dr. Walther Rathenau, the head of the German electrical industry, who in the early days of August 1914 organized the Division of Raw Materials for the Ministry of War. To Rathenau's trained and experienced mind, it was clear that war had passed into the era of mass production just as definitely as peacetime economy had substituted the factory for hand labor. Alongside the marching columns of troops from the Rhine to the Belgian and French frontiers, he saw stretching over the horizon an unending line of tall chimneys belching the smoke of battle above German cities, battle prepared at home but to be fought on a front hundreds of miles

NATURE AND CONSEQUENCES OF TOTAL WAR

away. To support this vast organization all Germany and all the territories conquered by Germany would have to be reconstructed for the purposes of war. In short, war itself had entered upon its industrial revolution.

The vision of Rathenau was treated by the Ministry of War more like that of a visionary than of an industrial organizer. He was given one small room at the back of the Ministry with a single secretary. But war is the unrelenting test of realities, and by 1918 the Division of Raw Materials of the German War Office had spread over several blocks of buildings almost overshadowing the rest of the War Office itself. The fact that the German General Staff had not foreseen the changing nature of war in the industrial era of modern science is too important to be passed over as a mere incident of history; for in the years preceding the outbreak of the World War military preparedness had been a constant preoccupation, not only of Germany, but of all the great powers of Europe. The court of the Emperor William II was dominated by militarism. Even Bismarck wore a uniform most of the time. The race in sea power with Great Britain which produced the Dreadnoughts was but one chapter in the story of militarism in Europe at the turning of the century. It was military considerations which lay primarily behind the grouping of the European powers into the Triple Alliance of Germany, Austria and Italy, and the Entente of France, Russia and Great Britain. In the chancelleries of Europe, Prussianized Germany—of which Nazism was only its variation in fortissimo—was symbolized by the mock wars of the yearly maneuvers, to which the French and the Russian armies replied in kind, rather than by the prodigious growth of industry and the increased production of wealth. The militarists still clung to the idea set forth at the dawn of modern history by Machiavelli, that soldiers and not treasure measure the power of a nation. This rigidity of the mind of militarists which kept the science of warfare in a compartment of its own, distinct from the processes and interests of peace, was disguised by the fact that the military technicians also used the inventions of the engineer. But not until the first World War did the soldiers finally make the complete adjustment necessary for a conflict waged by the massed forces of industry instead of by the hand labor of fighting men. Moreover, this enlarged conception of the nature of war, which had steadily grown in the War Office in Berlin during the first two years of the war was not accepted by the Allied Powers until the end of 1916, when it was forced upon them by the terrible wastage of man power at the battlefront. "Business as usual," which had been the British slogan in 1914, was seen to be a blind acceptance of a way of fighting which resulted only in the mass murder of Allied soldiers, ill provided with munitions. It was not until a year and a half of this tragedy had dragged along that the slow-moving democracies awoke to the fact that war as an engineering operation could be won only by transforming the whole structure of economic life. Once awake, however, the democratic peoples moved fast and showed more resiliency than those peoples whose efficiency had been regimented by bureaucracies. This is a fact of great importance which was to be seen more clearly in the second World War.

It was at this stage of the first World War that the United States became a belligerent, bringing the great weight of its resources into the balance before it was organized for actual combat. The fact that our guns and airplanes were late in arriving in Europe did not prevent American participation in the war from turning the scale. The trenches were outflanked, not only at Ypres and Verdun, but also in mill and shipyard and in the wheatfields of Kansas.

Total war cannot be fought without far-reaching disturbance to the whole economic life not only of the belligerents but of all the countries with which they do business. This means the entire civilized world. The total effect of the first World War was the sum total of the impact of this disturbance upon the normal activities of all the nations concerned. It was to clarify these issues that the Carnegie Endowment for International Peace decided to make a comprehensive analysis of the War, especially in Europe. This survey, begun in 1918, ultimately took shape in the one hundred and fifty volumes of the *Economic and Social History of the World War*. It is too vast and too technical for the general reader; but the fundamental conclusion of the whole work supports the thesis just set forth: namely, that with the progress of modern science the nature of war has undergone a change fully as revolutionary as the peacetime activities of nations. The purely military part of war, the actual test of strength in battle, is by no means final. Total war, which covers the whole of national life, not only economic but moral, intellectual and political as well, is even fought in the future as well as in the present, through continuing dislocation in a world of credit. Seen in this, its time perspective, it is by no means the sharp-edged "instrument of national policy" which the statesmen of the past turned over to soldiers to use in order to attain some definite end.

This conclusion, drawn from the body of the first World War, immediately implies another. If war is no longer a directable and controllable instrument of national policy, then it should be renounced. By a supreme paradox, the very extension of war to cover all the activities of life and to threaten all lives in the warring countries, is the chief reason for the otherwise almost incredible conclusion that the time has come to get rid of war itself. As long as it was a limited technique affecting only a fraction of the population and making profits possible for the members of a ruling class, profits in which many others might hope to share, it could be maintained as a gambler's chance by nations which did not regard the spoliation of others as a violation of the moral law, because the others might do it when their turn came. The use of war for these purposes, while always involving risks, was nevertheless much more under control and its consequences much more calculable when it was a technique limited to the highly specialized profession of arms than is the case with total war. All this has now changed. The organization for war, by including all the activities and resources of economic life along with the incalculable element of scientific invention, has ended for all time that military science which rested upon the nice calculations of a General Staff composed of officers who in their hearts despised the peacetime operations of a humdrum world. Totalitarian war is another kind of thing than that conducted by drill masters or captains of sailing ships whose services were at the ready disposal of the governments which employed them. In total war the profession of arms has become only the last operation in a vast transformation of national life, a transformation which extends throughout the whole world economy. It is not by chance, but in the nature of the case, that any major war from now on must tend to become a world war.

If, while the soldier is achieving his goal, the nation behind him is traveling, perhaps unconsciously, in another direction, then this oldest of all the instruments of politics should be discarded as inadequate and outworn. As a political device, war has become as capricious as a machine gun out of control, raining death and destruction on combatant and civilian alike. The conclusion is not unlike that of M. Bloch or Sir Norman Angell, but it has more definite reference to the implications of science. For, if in these first years of the scientific era, war has already begun to change its nature, the inevitable advance of science in the years to come will bring greater and greater change in the same direction; war will be less and less applicable to the pursuit of definite aims of governments, because it will more and more escape control and involve consequences that do not lie in the orbit of military action.

The first statement of this general conclusion drawn from the *Economic and Social History of the World War* was made in the address which I delivered in Berlin in the presence of the German government in March, 1927. At that time, it was accepted by the successors of Bismarck and Von Moltke as embodying a political and military axiom.

It was this reasoning which, a few weeks later, brought from M. Briand his challenging letter to the American people inviting America to join with France in renouncing "war as an instrument of national policy." By this phrase, as was clearly indicated in his letter, M. Briand was referring to aggressive war, having in mind the Covenant of the League of Nations and the treaties of Locarno.[1] Unfortunately, Secretary Kellogg, following Senator Borah and his friends, refused to accept any distinction between aggression and defense in the proposed treaty, which should "outlaw all war" as an institution. History, both before and since the Paris Peace Pact which resulted from these negotiations, has abundantly shown the fallacy of this generalization. War is not one institution but several. The wars of imperialism may be, and often are, quite different from those of disputes over "honor" or "vital interest"; but, above all, defense, although war in the fullest sense of the word, is in a different category from aggression. This is not the place to discuss the Peace Pact, except to note that in its final form it did not embody the lesson of the World War which was recognized as valid by soldiers as well as by statesmen. Instead of building upon the solid ground of the proved failure of totalitarian war to accomplish the limited objectives for which it is waged, a purely practical argument against the attempt to use war "as an instrument of policy," the negotiations shifted to the basis of humanitarianism and became lost in confusion of thought.

The issue as presented in 1927 was not settled then. Nor has it been settled by the apparent violations of the Peace Pact in succeeding years. The heart of the problem is and remains: what is the effect of science upon war as an instrument of politics—that is to say, upon aggressive war. If, in view of the far reach of the interdependence of nations under the regime of science, war is no longer a pertinent political instrument, then the statesmanship of the future will find the way to get rid of it. If, on the other hand, it is still an instrument of politics which can be used by nations to secure what they hope to gain by it, it will not only defy the whole peace movement but will increase in the years to come because of the increased capacity for destruction, offering no hope of escape. There is no possibility of blinking this supreme challenge of scientific militarism; for the language in which it is couched is that of bombing terror by night, lurking destruction in the Seven Seas, and a Gestapo operating in homes

[1] See *International Conciliation*, October, 1928, No. 243.

of peace. If the laws of history are those of war, this is what awaits us all.

This conclusion of despair has been the first reaction of disillusioned public opinion to the present war. The reasoning as to the character of modern war, which had been based upon the study of the War of 1914-18, was apparently disproved by the Nazi conquest of France and other countries. Never did war seem more under the control of its makers. Clausewitz seemed justified. Scientific war could be directed as definitely as in the prescientific days, when war was carried on by small forces for visible objectives, such as the seizure of land, booty or slaves. Naturally many of those who watched these events with poignant interest came to the conclusion that the militarists are still the great realists, in whose hands are the final decisions of history. Indeed, throughout the black months of the summer of 1940, it looked to many observers as though Machiavelli had been right even if his current exponent, Mussolini, might be going a little far in stating that war, not peace, is the fundamental basis of human society.

Had there been no miracle at Dunkirk, had Great Britain not held out, alone and unsupported, against the forces of militarism, this first impression of the nature of war today, falsifying, apparently, the lesson of the first World War, might have remained unchallenged for many years to come. It is a sobering fact, that, because of its seeming success, the Romans never understood the effects of the war system upon their own empire, nor did historians understand it until recently. The obvious and direct effect of the Roman Wars was the empire itself, a supreme embodiment of power, a great political creation. Yet the final effect was that war gutted the structure of the State which it had built. The instrument of victory which the Caesars had at their command was destined to undo the prosperity that depends upon the arts of peace, until at last the Roman Empire fell, not because of the strength of barbarian invaders—there were never very many of them—but because of its own weakness. The day of reckoning was long delayed, but inevitable. Time runs faster now than in antiquity and it might not require centuries to show what would be the final results of a new Roman Empire, with Nazi legions overrunning Europe.

Fortunately, we did not have to await the long processes of history, for Great Britain's heroic defense turned the imperialist raids of Germany into a kind of world civil war between the champions of freedom and those of oppression. Time was gained for science to catch up with war, as the unprepared peace-loving nations matched preparations with the dictatorships. Every day that passed made the second World War more and more like the first. The most reluctant isolationists in the United States were forced to accept the effect of war upon their country and themselves up to the very threshold of military involvement. The aims originally sought by the German General Staff or by their Leader are no longer achieved without upsetting so much of the routine of civilized life as to leave in doubt or falsify the ultimate result. That is not to say that battles of this war have not had far-reaching effects—perhaps even more far-reaching than those of the first World War—but, like the latter, they are sure to have other consequences than those intended.

Here is a fundamental basis for the peace movement. It is a conclusion which rests not only upon the nature of war, but also upon that of a vastly more important force—science itself. The increasing mastery of time and of space and of human conditions makes us more and more dependent upon each other; and this process will go on increasingly from now until the end of time. But science has only just begun its great career. For a long time yet there will be nations which will be tempted to risk wars which they will hope to "localize" either by a quick decision or by diplomatic maneuvers. The growth of law and order among nations will not be uniform or without interruption, any more than has been the case within the State. But the danger of the spread of such disturbance of the peace cannot any longer be ignored by the community of nations. The following pages deal with the immediate setting and the long-range solution of this problem.

II

The Problem of Liquidation

WHILE the paradox holds true that the very extent and scope of total war has become the prime reason for getting rid of it, this broadening of the war effort has rendered the process of war liquidation infinitely more difficult. The vast upheaval and destruction which has been wrought is not the only obstacle to recovery, there will also be an immensely increased confusion in the processes by which law and order and the necessities of life may be restored. This problem of administration during the war and in the period immediately following is not the subject of this study, but it stands so strongly in the foreground that it cannot be passed by without a hurried survey of its nature and scope.

At the very beginning it is necessary to distinguish between the organizations necessary for the prosecution of the war and those for the maintenance of peace after the war is over. Organizations must be planned with reference to their functions and in spite of all the civilian activities of the belligerent nations, there is a world of difference between the functions of a coalition which is primarily military in purpose and those of a political association of nations devoted to the furtherance of peaceful relations. The United Nations organized for war have one fundamental purpose, which is to destroy the power of their enemies. On the other hand the chief purpose of the peacetime cooperation of the United Nations is the welfare and security of nations as well as individuals. The distinction is not clear-cut, for, even while the armies are in the field, organizations of relief and rehabilitation must begin to operate, partly to strengthen military action in the war as well as to extricate civilization from its consequences. Practical common sense dictates that these constructive measures should take account not only of immediate needs but also of the more distant future. They, therefore, bridge the gulf between techniques of war and peace, serving to lessen the economic hardships and to prevent the spread of disease in the civilian population and the occupying troops, and to shorten the time of occupation.

We are now witnessing this dual activity of wartime: the unrelenting destruction of everything which can be used by the enemy for military purposes and the re-establishment of law and order in the occupied territories. Alongside the army as the visible symbol of power and authority, or under its control, there is a kindlier administration, which, in spirit if not in law, belongs with the technique of peace, being helpful where such activities are most needed. The permanent organization of peace should be so shaped as progressively to take over and continue under appropriate auspices such of these activities as may be necessary in future years.

However, while the wartime structure of the United Nations includes important elements which must be retained in the permanent peacetime structure, the organization for war is temporary in proportion as it is successful. It lasts until the enemy states are completely reduced and pacified. It cannot relax its vigilance or authority immediately upon their surrender, but must continue as long as martial law will be necessary to furnish the basis for a revival of civil government. During this period of transition to normal international relationships, the United Nations must maintain the military coalition of the great powers and their fighting allies and associates. They have an immediate work to do in preventing a state of anarchy or minor wars arising out of the world war. This will be a most difficult task and cannot be carried through without the exercise of authority based on the right of the conqueror. It is an authority against which the defeated powers will have no power of resistance after their unconditional surrender. This applies as well to the civilian administrations which will be set up in conformity with the principles of the United

Nations, as is evident in the plans already adopted for the government of the areas liberated from Fascist or Nazi rule by the expeditionary forces. These regimes will, in the course of events, be modified from time to time and varied from district to district, in what may outwardly look like a whole series of experiments in international government. But in one important respect, at least, they cannot furnish models for the organs of the permanent international organization of the future. In the very nature of the case, they must take over essential parts of the government of the occupied countries, purposely curtailing their sovereignty and dominating their life, but that is the very kind of action to be avoided, as far as possible, in the permanent organization.

Let us be quite clear upon this point. The organization of the United Nations for war has one primary purpose, that of defeating an enemy which is not only destroying the international structure of the past but the political institutions within states and the liberties of their citizens. In view of the nature of the war and of the issues involved in it, it must be carried through to complete and uncompromising victory, so that those nations which have resorted to war as the instrument of their policy will realize that such use of war is criminal folly. It is admittedly a hard and unwelcome task which the United Nations must carry out, but there is apparently no other way to free the world from the ruthless use of blood and iron by nations under militaristic control than to teach them by their own suffering what the suffering of their victims is like. This does not mean a war plan of mere vindictiveness and revenge, although it will be difficult and perhaps impossible to prevent some revenge. As far as control by the United Nations is concerned, it should be thought of rather as a curative surgery, by which the nations trained to use force and violence as a means for attaining their end can be saved from themselves to make the world safe for policies of peace in the future.

Just when the line will be drawn between war and peace cannot be determined beforehand. It will vary in different countries, according to the difficulties of the task of war liquidation and the degree of cooperation on the part of the occupied countries. It is very important, however, that all these activities should be considered as falling within the general sphere of total war. Otherwise misunderstandings are bound to arise as to where the ultimate authority lies for acts which will be necessary for general security but which will be met wth protest and sullen or overt opposition. The line between peace and war should be drawn at the end, not at the beginning of the period of occupation. For occupation, even under the best of conditions, implies servitude, which no nation, least of all proud nations like Germany and Japan, will accept as a formal part of the regime of peace. For that regime starts only when they are no longer compelled to obey by the presence of foreign troops or by the threat of their speedy return. Wherever or whenever that is the case, a nation is unfree to that extent; and the United Nations as a permanent body must be composed of free nations. Otherwise it is only a disguised imperialism.

In the preceding chapter we have referred to the fact that total war extends its operations in time as well as in space by the continuing disturbance which it sets going in the economic field. But its extension reaches farther than that. Total war is not over when the firing ceases, because the firing has only been a part of it, all citizens and all activities of the nation having been mobilized behind the front. The surrender of armies and navies is, therefore, only a part of that total surrender which the United Nations are this time going to exact. The war will not be ended this time by any armistice agreement limited to the fighting forces. The task of completely eradicating the basic military potential of the enemy will be greatly lessened if the Axis powers are not free to argue, as Germany did last time, that the maintenance of blockade after the armistice was illegal or at least illegitimate because, according to her, the war was over with the surrender at Compiègne. The bitterest complaints of the Germans, and more especially the liberal Germans, were directed against the maintenance of the blockade from the armistice in November, 1918, until the following March. There were strong protests at the time, not only by the Germans but among the Allies as well, against this protracted blockade throughout the hard winter of 1919. But, while the Allied protests were chiefly based upon the conviction that the measure was wholly unnecessary because of the change in government in Germany and, therefore, a political blunder of the first magnitude, involving the unjustified infliction of suffering, the Germans added to their protest a further grievance in their denial that we had any right to continue what amounted to a military operation after the armistice was signed. This was not a mere secondary grievance on the part of Germany. It nursed a long continued irritation and a sense of wrong which played into the hands of the militarist leaders and was kept before the German mind by Nazi demagogues as a grievance that touched nationalism to the quick. Whether justified or not such a continuing blockade is legally valid as an aspect of total war. That concept, however, was not wholly clear in 1919, because it was not wholly realized during the war. Now we can see more clearly that the revolution in warfare is bound to change the principles of international law. Total war can only be ended in a total peace, which means that the period of liquidation, while furnishing a transition from war to peace, does not call for the relinquishment of those measures of force which are necessary to insure compliance with the demands of the victors.

This recognition of the realities inherent in total war will seem to many liberals, schooled in the international law of the past, like a surrender to enlarged militarism. On the contrary it recognizes the necessity for the champions of law and order to be freed from the outworn categories of war and peace which might block the path to their greatest duty, that of the complete elimination of the danger of another major war. This is another place where policies of appeasement must yield to realities. Instead of palliatives making the consequences of war less to be dreaded there must be complete denial of the legitimacy of war itself as an instrument of national policy.

This fundamental purpose of the United Nations in the second World War must not be thwarted in the process of suppressing militarism, any more than in the rebuilding of post-war prosperity. The penalty for violating the peace of the world is not paid alone by the violators. It is being inflicted now upon peace-loving nations by the awful cost of the second World War, which is making suppression of war itself an unavoidable process of history. This still seems to many people too good to be true, which is certain to be the case so long as the nations which have relied upon militarism can still cherish the hope that they can use it again with safety for themselves. That is why the first step in the establishment of lasting peace is the complete and inescapable defeat of those who instinctively resort to war or the threat of it as an instrument of their policy. It can be brought home to the aggressor nations only by bringing the consequences of modern war home to all their citizens. Only then can the peace-loving nations limit their precautions against the recurrence of war to the safe proportions of relatively minor military establishments, for as long as there are any great nations which cherish a hope of the renewal of militarism after this war, the peace-loving nations cannot safely reduce their armaments, and the old dangers of the policies of power politics will still be dominant. The organization for war of the United Nations, therefore, has as its first task the inescapable duty of teaching the lesson of peace to those who only understand the language of power.

This problem of the liquidation of the war machine, vast as it is, is, however, less difficult in many ways than the positive measures which the United Nations must take for the restoration of peace. So great and so difficult are these that many people despair of their solution, and yet without it there can be no organization of enduring peace. Some of these problems are highly dangerous like unexploded time bombs in the tracks of retreating armies; indeed they are not unlike these weapons of ambush because they can create local disturbances which may spread disorder by preventing the coordinated effort necessary for success.

The discussion of these problems of relief and rehabilitation, important and pressing as they are, is not the subject of this study, which deals with plans for maintaining peace after it has been established. The problems of the transitional period which lies between actual warfare and the final settlement are the subject of separate studies. A whole year's work was spent upon them by the Commission to Study the Organization of Peace, the results of which were embodied in its Second Report, published in April, 1942. The mere listing of the problems left by the war forms a terrible indictment of our time.

First of all there is the danger of post-war epidemics which may in this case, as in that of previous wars, wipe out as many if not more lives than the weapons invented by man. Four wartime conditions contribute powerfully to the spread of disease: malnutrition and famine; movements of population; lack of hospitals and medical care; and the breakdown of ordinary community life. No catastrophe in history has ever happened to compare with the human misery created by this war, most of it due to the ruthless acts of Nazi Germany. There are as many refugees and transplanted people as there are inhabitants of a country as large as France. The Mongol invaders of Asia and the Huns in Europe created no such havoc in the lives of men.

To disease and civil disorder which are inevitable, will be added economic problems of greater magnitude than at any one time in the history of modern nations. And yet, with wisdom and foresight, much can be done to alleviate this suffering and to re-establish the conditions of normal life. The very magnitude of the "economic vacuum" caused by the ravages of war and by the wartime cessation of production for peacetime consumption, may render less difficult than would otherwise be the case the immediate problem of the reabsorption of soldiers into civilian life. The problem of unemployment will, however, not be fully met by this mere readjustment of the period of demobilization. Unless precautions are taken to establish business upon sound principles of international cooperation, there will be an economic collapse much greater than that which followed the first World War. This is less a matter for the interim period between war and peace than for long-term planning. But temporary measures of adjustment and recovery should be planned with reference to the future as well as to the immediate situation.

The problem of the uprooted peoples is perhaps the most difficult of all. Millions of them have been dragged from their homes as industrial slaves, thrown helter-skelter by the waves of war, kept ignorant of what is going on in the world, with children's lives distorted by an education of hatred. Unless these victims of invasion or oppression find their way back to their homes or are successfully fitted to new ways of life, hope for the future economic and political recovery will be rendered almost impossible in large sections of Europe. Similarly, many of the colonies and dependent areas will need immediate aid if native life is not to deteriorate and if government is not to break down. Under these conditions of social insecurity, both labor and capital will be confronted with proposals for extreme measures, some well-meant and some of sinister design. Unless these problems are frankly faced by international effort the high aim of freedom from want, set forth in the Atlantic Charter, may remain unrealized, to haunt the postwar period of the second World War with that sense of disillusionment which did so much damage in the decade following the first World War.

The mere enumeration of these problems might at first seem to justify counsels of despair. But history shows a surprising capacity in the recuperative powers of national life, a capacity increased to an undreamed-of extent by the scientific technique of mass production. What is needed is guidance and foresight, so that these recuperative forces may work out a design for living which will not permit the return of disasters like the present or others greater still in a third World War. The only real solution, we repeat once more, is one that is planned with an eye to the elimination of the causes of these evils and not simply to their temporary alleviation.

In short, the administration of the humane elements in post-war reconstruction, while carried out largely under martial law, should be planned for a long-term future as well as for the more immediate task of saving lives, restoring economic activities and establishing the guarantees of freedom. Without provision for continuance, these initial acts would constitute an even greater source of disillusionment than after the first World War. Viewed in this light, this study of the plans for the ultimate organization of peace is not an unreal exercise in political theory; it is a statement of definite aims for practical tasks from which there is no escape and for which the terms are already set by the nature of the liquidation of the war.

III

Small Powers and Great

As WE have just seen, the liquidation of the war brings us face to face with one of the most difficult of all the political problems in international organization, that of the relation of the great powers to the small and also of the great powers among themselves. Throughout all the history of the modern nations, their inequalities in size and power have been sources of instability which were often used to advantage by the larger states. With war continually in the offing alliances and counter-alliances built up that unstable equilibrium known as the balance of power, which in turn was challenged by the France of Louis XIV and Napoleon and by the Germany of the twentieth century, to mention only the more notable episodes in a history which seemingly was involved in an inextricable process. The small powers which maintained their independent existence, developed in the hard school of experience a sense of nationality fully as strong if not stronger than that of the great powers, and managed by playing off one great power against another to realize a degree of independence which they jealously guarded against the return of any such combination of the great powers as that of the Holy Alliance after Waterloo. The result was an international anarchy in which each nation played its own hand as best it could with the aid of temporary and more or less unreliable partners.

There were, of course, limits to this international anarchy. Rules were agreed upon from time to time and more or less observed. International law, as we shall see below, developed sets of accepted principles of conduct which could only be violated with impunity by the strongest powers and even then not without risk. One of these principles was that which asserted "the equality of states" great and small. It was a doctrine based to some degree upon the old Greek and Roman ideas of natural law, but it was also a practical doctrine of self-defense. When invoked by the smaller powers on the plea of the inviolability of sovereignty the great powers had to recognize it in principle as something which applied to themselves as well. But in practice both lawyers and statesmen underlined the difference between legal equality, which concerns the "status of the state as an international person," and the political equality, which concerns matters like representation in international bodies or on international tribunals. The former was readily granted but the latter as regularly denied. This distinction is especially important at the present time, when the Soviet Government is testing out the nature of the State.

We shall deal with these problems in due course in relation to the international organization of the future. Before coming to them, however, we must pause here to glance hurriedly over the political history of the relations of small and great powers in recent years. It is too large and complicated a subject to be covered adequately in a few pages, but at least a short survey of the main problems as they confront us at the present time is a necessary basis for the study of a future world organization.

First, with reference to the smaller powers. It cannot be too clearly stated that they have had a great responsibility for the maintenance of that very condition of international affairs which has been shown at last by the second World War to furnish them no real guarantee of independence or even autonomy. Nevertheless the spirit of freedom in which they have been nurtured is a precious thing and nowhere held in higher regard than in America. Throughout all our history there has been a constantly recurring note of sympathy for every nation, however small, whose liberties were imperiled by foreign aggression. In the nineteenth century our one and only formulated principle of foreign policy was the Monroe Doctrine. We were led into the War with Spain through sympathy for the oppressed Cubans, and on many occasions have taken steps only short of war to throw the weight of our influence on the side of the little peoples or the under-privileged. Nevertheless this sentiment in support of freedom, strong as it is, is too often played upon by nationalistic politicians. There is a widespread fallacy among liberals that nationalism is reprehensible only in the Great Powers. The politics of Europe during the 1920's are proof to the contrary. One might even generalize that the Great Powers have a wider area of adjustment of policies than the small ones, because of their world-wide interests and connections. Little things are important when they are all one has. And politics are necessarily backward where life remains almost untouched by the great current of world affairs.

The organization of the United Nations is, therefore, confronted at the outset by this disparity not only in the size but also in the outlook of its members. Fortunately we now have the experience of the League of Nations with its Assembly in which all nations had an equal voice and its Council in which the larger nations dominated. This kind of compromise points the way to the only kind of settlement of the problem which holds promise for the future. It has yet to be worked out in the new world organization, but fortunately the United Nations came to grips with it at once in the constitution of the first organization actually set to work by them, the United Nations Relief and Rehabilitation Administration. The first form of the constitution of that body was rejected by some of the smaller nations as giving too much control to the Great Powers. This difficulty was ironed out by a compromise which gave the Council the right to decide the most important issues and made the Director General an agent of all the interested powers. It was a good omen when the great powers yielded gracefully to the protestations of the smaller ones, led in this instance by the Dutch. In all this, however, there is nothing surprising to those who know the history of the League of Nations. With reference to the details of its procedure, there was upon the whole less grievance against League action or non-action on the part of the smaller powers than on the part of Great Britain, France and Germany. Much of the actual conduct of business takes place in committees where the issues are threshed out by qualified specialists. There is no reason to fear any undue subordination of any of the United Nations if the precedent set by the United Nations Relief and Rehabilitation Administration and the experience supplied by the League are duly followed in the shaping of other international organizations within that great complex of bodies which will be necessary for the adequate transaction of the international business of governments and peoples within the structure of the United Nations.

There will, of course, be many difficult problems in the adjustment of this miscellaneous body made up of all kinds of nations. The mere creation of an organization does not settle the problems of the future. It only provides a mechanism and sets a standard for their settlement. No one knows how well it will work, but it must be made to work efficiently if war is to be eliminated; for in the nature of the case there can be no other substitute. It is this major fact which can be counted upon to make the small powers loyal supporters of the international organization. Without a guarantee of peace, in which they can share by their corporate action in some kind of collective security, they are doomed.

No less difficult than this problem of the relation of great and small powers is that of the great powers among themselves. Fortunately for the future of the United Nations this is taking shape under the pressure of war needs. Initial difficulties and prejudices are giving way as the war progresses; and the battlefront is shared with equal heroism. Admiration for the miracle of Russia's victorious war has largely dislodged the former suspicion of an ulterior motive in the spread of communism through the world. No one can tell how long these ties of wartime association will last in their present form or how strong they will be once the danger of the war is over. But there is at least a newly laid foundation for cooperation for the winning of the peace—which means the holding of it as well as the winning of the war.

First of all a word should be said about the relations between the United States and Great Britain. Without a formal alliance the two nations have not only become inseparable associates in arms but their leadership in the councils of the global war has been accepted by others of the United Nations, while they share their leadership of the war in Europe with the Soviet Union. Thus the American-British entente became a closer coalition than that with Russia, partly because of America's vital interest in the war in the Pacific and Asia. This interest is felt more keenly in large sections of the country than the interest in the war of the Atlantic and Europe. America and Britain drew closer together also partly because Russia seemed until recently to maintain an attitude of aloofness which was variously interpreted in Great Britain and the United States. The relation of China to this wartime alignment of the Great Powers did not receive the attention which it deserved; but that was due to the exigencies of a war for which we were not prepared. China's position will undoubtedly become stronger when the theater of war shifts to the Orient. Soviet Russia and China—the latter in the longer future—are certain to share the leadership of the world. They occupy a major portion of the inhabitable globe, with almost unlimited resources in both material and manpower. But these potentialities are not so immediate as those which lie in the association of the United States with the British Commonwealth of Nations and with those other nations of Europe and the Americas in which the spirit of liberty found an early home.

The effect of this close association between the British and American peoples is felt in the forces in the field, as General Eisenhower has so definitely stated, as well as in the procurement of supplies. Yet the strength of any lasting association among nations lies not in expediency but in an agreement upon fundamentals in outlook and ideals. The extent to which these are shared in varying degrees among the nations of Western Europe and the Americas has been obscured by the fact that the very freedom which they cherish in common leads them to accentuate their differences. Independence, which is the political embodiment of liberty, tends to develop barriers against international understanding while it strengthens solidarity at home. The result has been that the freedom-loving nations of modern times have been as reluctant to unite in an effective political union as the freedom-loving cities of ancient Greece. Fortunately, however, there is a core of unity in the modern world which the Greeks lacked, for the leadership of the United States and Great Britain, unlike that of Sparta and Athens, has no possibility of future warring conflict. The implication of the happy fact that there has been peace between the English-speaking peoples for over a century and that its continuance is the surest of all things in international relations, has only recently been given outright expression in the United States. This is the significance of Walter Lippmann's book, *United States Foreign Policy*, in which is traced the history of our unconscious reliance upon the fact of British support for the Monroe Doctrine and other aspects of our interests abroad.

No lover of peace can consciously do anything to lessen the strength of this entente, so long as the ideals of the partnership are those which make for the extension of freedom and security from war throughout the world. Mr. Churchill was not overstating the case when he said, "If we are together, nothing is impossible. If we are divided, all will fail." But the basis of that unity must be not the mere self-aggrandizement of either partner in this great enterprise. The aims of the partners were stated by Mr. Churchill, in his Harvard address, in terms strikingly similar to those in which Woodrow Wilson invoked the moral support of the American people for the League of Nations:

> I therefore preach continually the doctrine of the fraternal association of our peoples, not for any purpose of gaining invidious material advantages for either of them, nor for territorial aggrandizement or the vain pomp of earthly domination, but for the sake of service to mankind and for the honor that comes to those who faithfully serve great causes.

Based on these principles, an understanding between the United States and the British Commonwealth of Nations could be an invincible force for the creation and preservation of an organization of peace which would ultimately include the whole civilized world.

The word *entente* has been used to describe the historic relationship which has existed between the United States and the British Commonwealth of Nations. It might be better for us to discard the use of that French translation of the good old Anglo-Saxon word "understanding" when the partnership is wholly of English-speaking peoples, especially because the one great entente in European history, that between Great Britain and France in the years preceding the first World War, has rightly or wrongly acquired the connotation of a binding force of an alliance. An understanding based on the principles set forth by Mr. Churchill is a different thing, a moral as well as a political force for the creation and preservation of the organization of peace which would ultimately include the whole civilized world. But this widening of the understanding between the United States and the British Commonwealth of Nations to include other like-minded, freedom-loving peoples, will not happen unless the other nations are invited in, not as beneficiaries of the generosity of power, but as nations sharing with each other the responsibility for the maintenance of a world of ordered freedom, while cherishing with undiminished ardor love for and devotion to their own countries.

Such are our ultimate aims in the second World War. To those who think only of the suffering which it brought and the anarchy which threatens to follow in its wake they will seem distant and unreal ideals. And such they will remain if the English-speaking peoples with their traditional love of freedom fail to meet the greatest challenge in their history, that of unity for the achievement of world order and justice. The starting point for this development has already been reached in the initial effort to create out of the organization for war the first beginnings of a lasting organization for peace

The reception of Mr. Churchill's speech in the United States shows how difficult is the creation of any real structure of international politics. While there was relatively little evidence of that traditional anti-British sentiment which has been kept alive in certain quarters, two obstacles were freely spoken of and therefore should be freely registered here. In the first place, there was the fear that Great Britain might draw us into the arena of European politics as a make-weight in the old game of the balance of power. In the second place, there was a widely shared feeling that we should not tie ourselves to Great Britain in a way which might strengthen the hand of reactionary and imperialist elements in the Empire, especially with reference to Asia. The answer to the first of these objections lies in the suppression of militarism and the speedy development of the United Nations in which neither Great Britain nor the United States would have more than its appropriate share of responsibility. This is the problem to which this study is directed. The second obstacle to the closer association of the English-speaking nations is one upon which a new start is certain to be made as a result of the war. It will probably be known in history as the problem of Asia for that is where it is presented in its most challenging form. It has to do with the relation between peoples which differ not only in history and political experience but in race and color, barriers older than history and deeper than reason.

This is not the place to deal with the grave issues which lie between East and West except in so far as they block the pathway to the organization of peace by those nations which must lead in its creation and direction. However, it should be pointed out that the old colonial system based on the principle of exploitation of the resources and labor of non-self-governing peoples is as much in disrepute in enlightened, forward-looking circles in Great Britain as it is in the United States. British opinion in labor and liberal circles is conscious of the responsibility for finding a solution which will work and which will not leave the Asiatic peoples at the mercy of their own native exploiters. The liberation which Gandhi would bring to India is opposed by those slaves of taboo, the millions of untouchables. American liberalism would follow a most perverse course indeed if its support of freedom for the Asiatics were guided by sentiment only, without fully measuring the consequences for peoples left to themselves before they have acquired experience in the art of government. This perversity would be much worse, however, if the support for the cause of Asiatic freedom were permitted to impede the movement for British-American cooperation in the effort to eliminate war among civilized nations. The best guarantee of freedom for the backward peoples as well as for those more advanced lies in the fullest possible achievement of this most immediate need of civilization.

The understanding between the British Commonwealth of Nations and the United States will be much stronger if it is not cast in the form of a treaty, for treaties can only cover those definite engagements which the United States Senate would be ready to ratify, and the result would probably be to impede instead of enlarge further freedom of action. Now that foreign affairs are debated throughout the country as widely as domestic matters, the fundamental support for an understanding lies in increased knowledge of each other's history and outlook. One reason that the problem of India has been so alive in the United States is that for most Americans it recalls their own colonial history as set forth in the Declaration of Independence. History as taught in the American schools until recently failed adequately to bring out the significance of the fact that Washington accepted the leadership of the colonial troops in order to fight for the liberties of an Englishman, trampled upon by the government of George III. The most eloquent endorsement of the justice of the American cause in the Revolution was that voiced in the English Parliament by the elder Pitt, Earl of Chatham. Had they not been schooled in freedom, the founders of the country which gave it new and glorious asylum would not have been so stirred as to pledge in support of it their lives, their fortunes and their sacred honor. The Bill of Rights in the Constitution is almost literally that of over a century earlier in English history. This ancient heritage of freedom which both countries share is now their sacred trust not only for themselves but for all the world.

If there have been obstacles to clear away from the pathway of understanding between Great Britain and the United States this is still more the case with reference to the relation of either of them with the Soviet Union. Suspicions of Russia's motives have had much deeper roots in British history than in our own, the result of a century-long contest on the Asian frontiers of the British Empire. British support of Turkey as a bulwark against the Russian drive for the Dardanelles, imperiling the British pathway to India, reached a climax twice in the nineteenth century, first in the Crimean War and twenty years later at the Congress of Berlin. It was voiced in the Kiplingesque suspicion of "the bear that walks like a man." In this nineteenth-century rivalry the United States had no part and took little interest. But we shared with liberal sentiment in Great Britain in detestation of the tyranny in the old regime in Russia and felt that the Muscovite was a stranger to our way of living and thinking.

When the Russian Revolution broke out in 1917 we hailed its first form, that of the Kerensky Government, as evidence that Russia was developing along the lines of our own history of freedom. At that time our elder statesmen joined with Elihu Root in attempting to link up Russia within the traditional framework of international law. The interlude was short, however, for before the war was really over there was American support for British forces fighting alongside the "White" Russians in a losing war against the newly established Communist Government of the Bolsheviks. The result of this episode was to strengthen the conviction of a section of the Communists that countries of free capitalism were as great a danger to them, if not greater, than those of a bureaucratic society like that of the Germans. Germany speedily took advantage of this situation and at the Treaty of Rapallo in 1922 secured an entente with Russia, as a result of which German technicians built up the Soviet war industry and instructed its officers in the military lessons to be learned from the first World War. Both countries reaped advantage from economic as well as political cooperation, although it was evident that neither one trusted the other. The entente culminated in April, 1926, in a treaty of mutual assistance between Germany and the Soviet Government.

The clue to this chapter of the history of Soviet foreign relations is to be found in the fact that Moscow maintained an attitude of cynical distrust of all the capitalist nations and that Germany was useful to it so long as French and British policies were chiefly directed toward securing fulfillment of the Treaty of

Versailles. When Germany entered the League of Nations in 1926, however, Moscow was left still more isolated than it had been in the past. It took occasion in that same year to reiterate the orthodox communist belief that under the capitalist system the League of Nations was a farce, existing simply to help imperalist States secure "spheres of influence, colonies and markets." In a highly charged, vituperative statement, it went on to say that capitalist society was based fundamentally upon war and that the League as an organization of those States was inherently impotent. In 1927, however, Trotsky and Zinovieff, the leaders of intransigent communist orthodoxy, were expelled from the Central Committee of the Party and the way was cleared for the complete triumph of Stalin. The obsession of a world-wide mission gave way to the practical conception of Russia as a "third power" outside of either the French-British coalition on the one side, or that which the Weimar Government of Germany was already beginning to dream of building in Central Europe. The Soviet position was still one of equal distrust of both "capitalist" policies, but events forced its hand. The fateful year 1933 witnessed the rise of Hitler to power in January, the Reichstag fire in February, the failure of the World Economic Conference in June and Germany's withdrawal from the League in October. By December of that year, therefore, the Soviet Government had changed its attitude toward the League and admitted that it at least "exercised a restraining influence upon those forces which are preparing for war." It was but a step from this to acceptance of membership in the League in 1934.

It was during this change in the orientation of Russia's foreign policy that the United States Government recognized the Soviet Union in 1933. Nevertheless, the barriers of distrust were still high enough to prevent resumption of wholly normal relations. This was evident in many ways. For example, when Litvinoff challenged the nations at Geneva to undertake general disarmament (a proposal made by the Soviets as long ago as the Conference of Genoa in 1922) the offer was discounted on all sides as not having been genuine and it did not dispel the lingering doubt as to whether the Soviet Union had any real intention to join in practical plans for world peace.

This situation was not helped by the three Moscow Treason Trials in 1936 and the two succeeding years. Although most of the victims of those trials had been the advocates of the extreme doctrine of world revolution and their treason consisted in the opposition to Stalin's rejection of it, the ruthless way in which the doctrinaire leaders were "liquidated" seemed, to western observers, to reveal an essentially Asiatic rather than European attitude toward human life, and brought back an echo of the old-time distrust of the Muscovite. The confessions of guilt were as puzzling as the outcome was tragic. One thing at least was clear to all Americans: this was not freedom or democracy.

Meanwhile, however, through this long story of internal controversy and international misunderstanding, one fact in Russian history began to emerge more and more clearly. As the Messianic dream of world communism faded, Russian communism took on the character of proud isolation; and that fact furnishes the key to the understanding of its policies throughout all the more recent period. It is impossible to trace here the way in which self-interest, henceforth identified with a great ideal, led the Soviet Government into a maze of contradictions, accepting with tongue in cheek the overtures of any government which at the time seemed to offer the greatest advantage. This, however, was more than a policy of pure expediency. There was method in it, for it was the practical expression of a new nationalism, as yet somewhat uncertain of itself but steadily growing in power and conviction. Political theorists have often pointed out that the nationalism of a communist country is bound to have more coherence and fanatic strength of purpose behind it than is the case in the countries of freedom; and Soviet Russia has proved this theory to be true.

The culmination of this trend came in the relations with Finland and the group of small republics along the Baltic Sea which began independent careers as sovereign States after the first World War. There is no doubt that Stalin is determined to incorporate into the Soviet Republic these little Baltic States, the old camping ground of the Teutonic Knights who have left there their impress of German culture, particularly in the form of a well-established landed gentry until the agrarian reforms at the beginning of the 1920's. If we knew more of the sufferings of Leningrad in its long and heroic defense, we might perhaps have a clearer sense of what is in Stalin's mind as he looks for a territorial buffer against any future German invasion of the north.[1] Undoubtedly to him these political settlements are primarily dictated by strategic needs, but the Soviet leaders have not forgotten that from the eighteenth century to 1917 the territories of these Baltic States lay within the frontiers of that great empire which at Kiev and Moscow had from time immemorial been known as "Holy Russia."

Finland presented a special problem to Russia both because of its past history and its belligerently anti-Bolshevik government. Moreover, its guns were little farther away from the approach to Leningrad than are the Atlantic Highlands from New York Harbor. From the standpoint of security the Soviet Government had therefore a real reason for insisting upon an adjustment, but when this led to war, the Russian attack upon Finland brought a practically unanimous condemnation from the outside world as the aggression of a Great Power against a small, freedom-loving people. This judgment was registered in an action taken by the League of Nations which was unparalleled in its history. It expelled Russia. In doing so it undoubtedly strengthened the Soviet conviction that the expulsion was due more to the innate dislike of the Communist State than to the policy in question. For the year was 1939, long after the failure of the League to take action in Spain or Abyssinia while it had allowed Japan at least the dignity of a voluntary withdrawal. No wonder, therefore, if the Soviet Government felt that it was unduly discriminated against. It remains to be seen in the coming months and years whether the memory of that act of Geneva will prevent the Government of Stalin from allowing "the general international organization,"

[1] It was out of these considerations that Russia concluded in September and October, 1939, special treaties with the three Baltic States concerning naval bases, airdromes, etc., to be possessed by Russia on their isles and territories.

agreed to in the Moscow Conference, to meet within the historic walls of the League of Nations, or even prevent it from wholehearted participation.

The war with Finland has thus left its scar on the face of Soviet policy. It accentuated the trend toward nationalism at the same time that it embittered relations with Great Britain and France in those fateful days of the first period of the second World War. It is impossible here to unravel that tangled skein of history, but the main facts are clear. As the shadow of the approaching war grew ominously darker, Stalin measured with a realistic eye the military unpreparedness and the diplomatic ineptness of the British and French Governments, and made a temporary deal with Germany while speeding up his munition factories and preparing his army to be in readiness for any eventuality. Whether he misjudged Hitler's intentions or not, his policy was wholly pro-Russian. Therefore, when he moved in upon the frontier of Poland after that country had been shattered by the German invasion, it was in pursuance of the same aim which had led him to invade Finland: the incorporation within the Soviet Union of a *cordon sanitaire* of independent republics instead of allowing that device of safety to develop outside it. To the outside world this scheme of extending the Soviet State over all the peoples on the western border bore the marks of Russian imperialism recognizable under the camouflage of voluntary acceptance of membership in the Soviet Union. This, of course, is not the way it looks from Moscow.

From the standpoint of the Kremlin, the best solution of the problem of security for the approaches to Leningrad is for the peoples of the Baltic States to accept membership within the Soviet Union. This argument is strengthened in Russian eyes by the historical fact that the Baltic States were a part of Russia prior to the first World War. The objection by the Western Powers to re-incorporation is therefore interpreted at Moscow, like the case of Finland, as being chiefly due to an inherent objection by the capitalist West to the nature of Soviet society which does not find equal expression in the case of other countries.

The problem of the Polish frontier is more complicated. The old kingdom of Poland was never an expression of Polish nationalism, but of conquest reaching out over the vast plains which later became Western Russia as far as the sword of Poland could reach. Yet within these far-flung frontiers, the solid Polish population which centers at Krakow and Warsaw has, throughout the tragedy of their country's history—its three partitions by Russia, Prussia and Austria and its final disappearance of 1795—nursed a glowing patriotism to an extent which is perhaps without parallel in any other country. When, therefore, the Paris Peace Conference restored the independence of Poland in 1919, the Polish patriots were not willing to accept the Eastern frontier which the geographers had tentatively traced for it, based chiefly on ethnographic data. This was subsequently known as the Curzon Line because of the support given to it by Lord Curzon, the British Foreign Minister. Its supporters claimed that it was one of the best ethnic frontiers in Eastern Europe, dividing Polish territory as well as could be done from that inhabited predominantly by White Russians on its northern sector and Ukrainians on the south. The ethnic problem, however, is complicated by the fact that there are many Poles scattered through the area, chiefly in the cities. The political problem is further complicated by the fact that many Polish magnates and army officers came from east of that line. Neither the Republic of Poland nor the Soviet Union accepted this Curzon Line. Instead the Bolshevik army invaded Poland up to the outskirts of Warsaw, and then Polish forces, fighting with French help, forced them back beyond Kiev. Poland, taking over the territory thus won by its surprising victory, claimed title to it as having been a part of the ancient kingdom of Poland. The Peace Treaty between Poland, Russia and Ukraine, signed at Riga on March 18, 1921, recognized the incorporation by Poland of territories lying far to the East of the Curzon Line. Thus things remained until September, 1939, when Hitler invaded Poland and occupied Western Poland and Warsaw. Then Stalin moved in from the East "to protect the White Russian and Ukrainian population," and in less than a week's time divided the whole country with Germany, accepting a line of demarcation very close to that of the Curzon Line. In the war with Germany which followed, the Polish frontier was apparently never forgotten by Stalin, for with the advancing Soviet armies in the winter of 1944 the old claim for the Curzon Line has become the unshaken policy of the Kremlin.

The Western frontier of the Soviet Union is not the only one that calls for settlement at the end of this war. That on the Far Eastern end of Siberia raises problems with Japan and also with China which evidently are being left for the future. But the century-old question of the outlet to the Persian Gulf has apparently been settled at Teheran, in the conference of Stalin with Churchill and Roosevelt. The guarantee given Iran (Persia) is of the utmost importance, not only for the settlement of an outstanding source of international discord, but also for the moral effect which it has in all the other countries which are Russia's neighbors. Turkey, especially, took note of the self-denying quality of Soviet diplomacy, which in the long run promises to be most advantageous to Russian interests. Wise statesmanship knows how rich are the returns on the policy of the good neighbor.

If this interpretation of recent history seems somewhat optimistic, there is a basis for it in the effect of the war upon Russia itself. The greatest victories in all the history of warfare are now to the credit of the Soviet Union, and this marvelous achievement cannot but strengthen in Russia the Soviet form of government which carried it through. At the same time it will serve to strengthen Stalin's interpretation of the Revolution as a peculiarly Russian event. The most compelling reason, however, for Russia's concentration upon its own problems in the post-war period is the vast and terrible extent of the devastation wrought by the invader. By far the most pressing need confronting Russia in the post-war period will be the rebuilding of its homes and cities and the recovery of its economic life. The liquidation of the war will present as great a challenge to the Soviet Government as that which it has met by victorious conduct on the field of battle. It will call for continued cooperation by the United States and Great Britain as well as by other members of the United Nations; and, if realism continues to reign at the Kremlin, the politics of the Soviet Government will be directed by its economic needs away from any adventurous course which would lessen sympathy for it or the desire to cooperate with it on the part of the other powers. Again this is an optimistic conclusion but it is the logical one under the circumstances.

Even more difficult than the problems of any of these powers which we have been considering is the case of France. It is perhaps more difficult than the problem of Germany itself, for the settlement of Germany can be imposed by an act of power while that of France must be negotiated in terms of sincere and unfailing friendship for the French people. Four years of oppression under the heel of the German conqueror will have left its scar not only upon the face of France but upon its soul. There is evidence that this has already happened to a section of that younger generation which should be the hope of a regenerated France. Who would not think in terms of force, when that has been the dominant thought for four years of war during most of which there seemed almost no hope of deliverance? American sympathy for the French people, caught as they have been in the grip of the German war machine, has been so strong as to evoke a movement of impatient protest against the cautious and seemingly slow-moving attitude of our government with reference to the strong and sometimes impetuous actions of General Charles de Gaulle and the other leaders of the Fighting French. The intricacies of this unhappy political situation, which everyone must deplore, lie outside the scope of this short survey. All that need be stated here is a reaffirmation of unshaken faith in the solid good sense of the French people, in whose hands the fate of their nation will be entrusted.[1] There is not the slightest reason for doubting that France itself will be

[1] France's unbroken will to freedom found its most heroic expression in the relentless activities of the French underground movement from the beginning of German occupation. These activities and especially the acts of sabotage give the best evidence that even under the danger of arbitrary executions and extermination the general will of the French people remains in full harmony with their traditional love for equality and human rights.

given the chance to choose its own form of government and that it will be reinstated in its proper place among the Great Powers, to continue its historic task of the clarification of thought and the furtherance of the ideals not only of justice and liberty but of the arts and sciences as well.

So far we have been dealing with the nations of the western world, but the priority given to the war in Europe over that of Asia must not blind us to the fact that unless adequate provision is made for the questions of the Orient in the post-war settlement it will not be a settlement at all. The vast and brooding East is awakening from its troubled sleep of the long centuries. It will be one of our first concerns to make sure that the new order in the Orient—for there will be a new order there—is not that of militarist Japan but that of the great pacific tradition of China. The link across the centuries that binds the teaching of Confucius with that of Sun Yat-sen is a real one. Although the Chinese Republic disowns the extreme conservatism of the philosophy that finds law and order in the observance of ancient precepts of ancestral wisdom, it maintains its ancient respect for the achievements of peace. Its chief ideal has remained that of Confucius, social justice. The link with the West was made by Sun Yat-sen in the shaping of this ideal into the form of the "Three Principles" of Nationalism, Democracy and Livelihood, principles now so deeply rooted in the thinking of contemporary China that no military leader can possibly displace them. It will not escape the critical reader that these Three Principles are practically identical with the three divisions of international organization under which the suggestions for world organization are classified in this study—security, justice and welfare. It is only fair to state, however, that the international organization has shaped itself in these terms from its own inherent needs and without reference to the political philosophy of Sun Yat-sen.

It may seem out of place to speak now of the liquidation of the war in the Orient while the end is not in sight and the disasters to be repaired are of appalling magnitude. It is, however, an essential part of this process that the spiritual outlook of China should not suffer from it, and this means our keeping in touch with those enlightened leaders of the Chinese people who through untold sacrifices maintain their faith in the Three Principles as a practical rule of conduct for the largest single nation in the world. The militant leadership of Chiang Kai-shek is one of the greatest in the history of war; but its great achievement must not blind us to the fact that another kind of regime will be needed in the years of peace. The Chungking Government has already given its promise to restore political freedom of discussion, the fulfillment of which will be welcomed as an act of genuine, forward-looking statesmanship.

Especially should we support such an inspiring movement as that of Mass Education, of which James Y. C. Yen is the founder and leader. Nowhere else in our time has there been anything to match the way in which the little group of enlightened educational leaders in an obscure corner of China transformed the life of the countryside and made their experiment in practical democracy a model for the transformation of the whole nation. There is a lesson in this for more than China. The new basis of society in this "people's movement" is the best of all possible guarantees against militarism or tyranny of any kind. It is the modern parallel to the democracy of the town meeting out of which sprang so much of both English and American political experience. Those who see the future only as a repetition of the past should study the inspiring story of contemporary China.

IV

The Beginnings of the United Nations

BEHIND all these problems of a military and quasi-military nature lies the political problem of the wartime administration of the United Nations themselves. Structurally this has been slow in forming. Until recently the only formal alliance created during the war has been that between Great Britain and the Soviet Union, signed in May, 1942, which was drawn to last for twenty years. The second alliance, that between the U.S.S.R. and Czechoslovakia, was held back until after the Moscow Conference. Upon the whole, the relationship of the United Nations has been little more than a coalition of leaders with relatively uncertain commitments, because the Atlantic Charter, which is the basis of the Declaration of the United Nations, is not a structural document but a program. So far as the United States is concerned, its chief formal relationship with the other United Nations has been through the Lend-Lease Agreements, which have enabled the "arsenal of freedom" to help in arming and feeding its comrades-in-arms. The fact, however, that Lend-Lease was in operation before the Pearl Harbor attack threw us into the war, indicates the tentative nature of our earlier relationship with the enemies of the Axis. The neutrality legislation of 1937 by its sincere but blundering efforts "to keep us out of the wars of other peoples" had technically made us the accomplices of aggressor nations because they had more ready access than some of their victims to our supplies. That, however, is now ancient history and is only recalled in this connection because of the anomalous position in which the United States found itself when the liberties of the world were imperiled by the initial victories of the Axis. The

Lend-Lease legislation, the repeal of the Neutrality Acts and the entry of the United States into the war still left this relationship to the other nations in somewhat the same position as it had been in the first World War, that of an associate rather than an ally. But it was not long before the iron pressure of events forced a closer tie in the actual conduct of the war, especially with Great Britain. Without a formal political alliance which would have required a treaty and opened the way to profitless debate, the resources of both countries were pooled in the hands of their Executives and their combined General Staffs while their fighting forces were linked up under joint command. This cooperation extended throughout the world and drew within its circle the defense forces of other peoples. Meanwhile Lend-Lease continued to function with ever greater efficiency under the stress of total war.

The one great step that was taken in this period of political formation of the United Nations was that of August, 1941, four months before Pearl Harbor, in the Atlantic Charter. So great was the need for such a clarification of purposes that this document was frequently spoken of as though it contained a formal commitment to an international organization. As a matter of fact it is only a declaration of general principles. The principles, accepted in January, 1942, shortly after our declaration of war, were those to which freedom-loving nations would give ready consent. In the Declaration of the United Nations, therefore, these principles became a political platform on which a working coalition could be based.[1]

Nothing further, however, was done along these lines for some months, and to many people the delay in the actual setting up of an organization of the United Nations seemed as unaccountable as it was to be regretted, but the conduct of the war in the perils of those critical months had the right of way so long as the associated powers worked well together on their military task. The argument against proceeding to build a permanent international organization in wartime was that these military preparations

[1] The texts of the Atlantic Charter and the Declaration of the United Nations are given in the Appendix.

would be delayed and hampered by political debates which would almost certainly reveal disagreements among the associated governments. On the other hand the argument in favor of proceeding to form such a political organization was that there would be greater likelihood of agreement upon fundamentals during the war than in the post-war period, when nationalism would run rampant if there had been no provision made against it while the impulsion of a common purpose still prevailed. Counsels of caution prevailed and the practical applications of war aims were apparently left to be ironed out by diplomatic acts or the logic of events.

The doubt as to the extent of agreement among the United Nations was made evident by what happened at the first dress rehearsal for the conference of their representatives, that which met in Hot Springs, Virginia, in May, 1943, to consider the problem of food supply. The purpose of this meeting, as we shall see below, was not to deal with immediate food supplies but with a long-range program for improving the standard of nutrition and adjusting world agriculture. The more immediate matters of relief were left to the United Nations Relief and Rehabilitation Administration, which at that time had not been organized. While the program of the Conference on Food and Agriculture covered only a small, if vital, portion of international relations, there was doubt in the mind of some of its participants as to the wisdom of facing up to such questions in public while the war was on, a doubt which had much to do with official reluctance to allow the presence of journalists. Fortunately, all of these doubts and distrusts proved to be without foundation, for the conference was a real success, meeting its tasks with technical efficiency and a full sense of its political implications. Similar competence marked the discussions of experts on currency matters, dealing especially with the stabilization of international exchange. Although the same distrust of publicity marked its meetings, they also opened a field of potential controversy with happy results. Again, the same hesitancy to come squarely face to face with international problems was seen in the early phases of the planning for relief and rehabilitation; but ultimately all difficulties were overcome and the first real international organ of the United Nations was inaugurated by the signing of the draft agreement for the United Nations Relief and Rehabilitation Administration (U.N.R.R.A.) in the White House on the ninth of November, 1943, followed by the meeting of the Administration at Atlantic City. Such meetings have a double value, for in addition to the transaction of the necessary affairs on their agenda, they furnish the United Nations with experience in the technique of conference. Contrary to public opinion the successful conduct of an international conference is a difficult thing; all the more so if its program is to be carried out through an indefinite future.

The success of the initial attempts at conference by the United Nations should not be over-emphasized, however. Reference is made in a later chapter to a danger in this method of procedure by way of consultations in special fields, if it is carried out in such a way as to imply a failure to appreciate the interdependence of these various fields of international action or a distrust of wider political association among the United Nations. The connection between such matters as relief and finance is an obvious example of the way in which even the more technical aspects of international relations have to be worked out with relation to each other. Therefore the process of arranging for the detailed solution of international problems by the United Nations must before long result in their coordination, and this can only be done under the regime of freedom, by consultation of all concerned. The success—or even the fear—of these special conferences calls for the creation of a more general conference for which adequate provision must be made sooner or later. The only questions are when and how.

There could be no better indication of the way in which the organization of the United Nations is now taking shape than to recall the fact that this proposal for a conference of the United Nations was the only definite proposal which the Commission to Study the Organization of Peace felt justified in making in its Third Report of March, 1943. It is true that the conservatism of these reports did not fully register the thought of all members of the Commission but they did reflect the length to which informed public opinion at the time was ready to go in support of international organization.

Meanwhile vastly more important steps have been taken than would have seemed possible at the time; but it must be pointed out that they are steps taken by the executives of the major powers and have not sprung out of the exchange of views of all the United Nations in conference. This giving of priority to executive action has been justified by the great success of the Moscow Conference which achieved much more than could have been accomplished in any large deliberative body. It has been further justified by the successful conferences which followed at Cairo and Teheran. But it is a method to be followed only in time of crisis and for matters of urgency.

A general United Nations Conference in wartime could not be entirely sure of its constituency. Some of its members would represent governments-in-exile which cannot offer any guarantee that their action will be ratified by their countries when the war is over. Therefore its program would have to be limited to those activities concerning which, because of their unquestioned benefits, there would be little or no chance of subsequent disagreement or disavowal, or to those activities which the more powerful nations might reasonably insist upon as providing a minimum basis for security. This is a field for statesmanship in which sound judgment may achieve more if combined with courage than with that kind of discretion which keeps the door half open behind which misunderstanding and suspicion may lead to intrigue. These, however, are general principles which those in power will interpret in the light of more information than is vouchsafed to those who do not share the responsibilities of office.

Among the subjects excluded from discussion in a general conference held in wartime would be the actual conduct of the war. Even within the national state this is never the province of the legislative branch of government, but belongs to the executive. The same holds true in international affairs for still more obvious reasons. In the field of security, authority for action must be delegated to those who can act quickly and without undue regard for secondary considerations. Fortunately this is just the way in which the organization of the United Nations is taking shape. Dominant executive authority is in the hands of the Great Powers. It could not be otherwise for all questions related to war or the threat of war. The Great Powers have a major interest in the policies of security, because upon them will fall the final responsibility for the maintenance of peace. Their sacrifices in war, while relatively not greater than those of some of the smaller nations, total to such appalling dimensions that their right to assume the major direction of affairs in all that concerns the conduct of defense can hardly be questioned. In any case it will be exercised.

From what has just been said, it is clear that both logic and political necessity imply recognition on the part of the United Nations of a definite leadership by the Great Powers in all matters relating to war. There is no escaping this conclusion and anything to the contrary is wishful thinking on the part of those who do not recognize the great realities of history. But this does not mean that the smaller members of the United Nations surrender sovereignty to their powerful neighbors. The World War has shown that in regard to war those smaller nations are defenseless by themselves and that they cannot rely upon neutrality or isolation except in a few rare instances where they are strategically defended by nature and by their situation as are Switzerland and Sweden. Therefore they are not surrendering to the Great Powers a freedom of action which they do not possess. The one solution for the dilemma which confronts the small nations in the matter of security is to render all assistance in their power to the elimination of war as an instrument of national policy, for in that area of politics their sovereignty is a delusion. On the other hand they have every right to insist upon full equality in the politics of peace, in the assurance of justice and fair play among nations.

This is the true democracy of nations. Its realization, however, falls upon a generation wearied with effort, weighed down with anxiety and bitterly conscious of great wrongs for which justice has not yet been meted out. The liquidation of the second World War cannot be expected to proceed with a steady march of progress and to bring at once pacification and hope to all concerned. Too much blood has run in the streets of European cities. Too much cruelty has been inflicted for the immediate and ready acceptance of the renunciation of force among nations which have experienced nothing but force during the long years of the war. The Great Powers have already shown their sense of responsibility in this regard by the provision for the treatment of war criminals set forth in the Moscow Agreement. But none of the freedom-loving nations, least of all the United States, would wish to keep its citizen soldiers policing occupied territory for a stretch of years after the war is over. That, however, is a problem to be dealt with by the permanent organization of the United Nations and not merely a matter of wartime controls.

V

The Moscow Conference

THROUGHOUT the tragic months and years of the second World War the United Nations found themselves confronted with many unforeseen problems, concerning both the conduct of the war and its subsequent liquidation. Under the stress of the need for immediate action, little if anything could be done about them, or at least so it seemed to the governments concerned. Even relatively innocent questions, like those of food and agriculture, were handled delicately by foreign offices careful not to raise any political issues that might in any way impede action by the joint military staffs, while anything resembling outspoken criticism of foreign policy was disavowed by public opinion, and properly so, for its possible bad effect on the military effort.

Such was the situation after almost three years of war, a situation that left much to be desired in the clarification of ultimate war aims and the relation of the powers with reference to them. Then, on November 1, 1943, a date to remember, dawn broke over the world from the walls of the Kremlin, when the Tripartite Conference of the Foreign Secretaries of the United States, Great Britain, and Russia issued a communiqué which showed complete agreement on the major political problems of the postwar settlement, an agreement to which China adhered in the part that had to do with the planning of a post-war world. There was universal surprise at the wide reach of this agreement. Public opinion had not been prepared for it because the press in both England and America had made much of the fact that the Soviet Government would not meet at some more convenient spot in a relatively neutral territory like northern Africa or Egypt, but insisted upon having the delegates take the long journey to Moscow. It was thought by those who habitually distrusted Moscow that this was only a roundabout way of trying to prevent the conference from meeting, because Mr. Hull might not be able to stand the strain of the journey. Moreover, it was known that he had never been in an airplane and that his physicians warned him against the risk. Once more, however, experience showed that the way to test the reality of Soviet policy was to meet it frankly face to face and by personal contact dissipate the fog of distrustful surmise in people's minds. This is what took place in the last week of October as Mr. Hull, Mr. Eden and Mr. Molotoff with their technical advisers surveyed the whole vast field of world politics in which the three Great Powers would have such grave responsibilities in the future.

Few, however, even of those who had faced with courage the problems which the war was sure to leave upon a disordered world had dared to hope for anything so clear-visioned as the statesmanlike utterance of the Moscow Conference. The general public had little knowledge of the long and careful preparations which our State Department had made, and the few who remembered the declarations of post-war good intentions in the British-Soviet treaty of May, 1942, were inclined to regard them as diplomatic dust thrown in the eyes of the democracies. Therefore, there was a universal note of surprise that so much could be achieved in so little time, when the heads of the ministries of foreign affairs of the United States and Great Britain met with Soviet Commissar Molotoff in Moscow.

This element of surprise no longer enhances the drama of the Moscow Conference, and in the succeeding weeks two other conferences were held which were of such epochal importance that the Moscow Conference might very well have been completely overshadowed by them. But even the meetings of the heads of State in Cairo and Teheran, decisive as they have been for the conduct of the war and undoubtedly for political decisions as well, apparently have not unlocked the gates of the future with any such far-reaching program as that set forth at Moscow in the Four-

Nations Declaration. So far-reaching is this document in its reconstruction of the whole world of international politics that it would have been discounted from the very first by sober opinion in the United States if it had not been negotiated by so cautious and experienced a statesman as Mr. Cordell Hull. Moreover, from what we have learned of the proceedings at the other conferences, the fact seems to be established that Roosevelt and Churchill, with Chiang Kai-shek at Cairo and with Stalin at Teheran, built upon the foundations laid at Moscow, which thus remains—for the present at least—the determining event in the grand strategy of international politics for the post-war world.

There were, however, other reasons than the importance of the Moscow documents themselves for the universal acclaim which greeted their publication. It was not only against the background of the war that they stood out so strongly and so convincingly; it was also against the background of the long period of mounting doubt and cynicism which had developed as the structure of the League of Nations failed to provide an adequate bulwark against the world-wide conspiracy of militaristic governments. The disillusionment after the first World War had left a legacy of distrust which nullified the protestations of the governments of peace-loving peoples, as the tide of nationalism swelled throughout the world and tended to obliterate the institutions of international cooperation. To this constant undertone of doubt in the decade preceding the second World War were added the uncertainties created by the war itself. There were those in each nation who kept questioning whether the forces of freedom were really bound together by more than a common danger. Although the leaders of these nations had emblazoned the high ideals of international freedom and justice on their oriflamme of battle there was as yet no clear assurance of their fundamental harmony with the ultimate aims of the war.

In spite of the military need for unity of purpose, there were still many points of possible misunderstanding among the three Great Powers. There was a persistent trend of public opinion in the United States which distrusted the fundamental motives of the British and held back the fullest measure of cooperation with them because of a fear of British imperialism in the Orient. In Great Britain there was fully as strong a current of doubt as to whether the United States could be counted upon to make good in the post-war period its wartime protestations that it supported a structure of world cooperation. We have already spoken of the mutual distrust between the Western Powers and the Soviet Government which even extended to the military effort itself. It was not to be wondered at that the Axis Powers counted upon these underlying difficulties as affording the chance of a political division from which Germany could profit either during the war or in the post-war settlement. If the only thing which held this loose alliance together was war against a common enemy, German diplomacy ought not to find impossible its task of separating the Allies on the two major questions of when and how the war should come to an end. In short, the political front was by no means impregnable so long as the basis of interallied relations was not cleared of misunderstanding.

As months passed into years without any further implementation of the Atlantic Charter or the Declaration of the United Nations than the tentative beginnings outlined in the previous chapter, public opinion in the United States began to call rather definitely for something more tangible either in the form of an international organization or some statement by the three or four Great Powers in the United Nations of their ultimate war aims. It was evident that American public opinion was swinging definitely away from its isolationist background. Measurements like those of the Gallup poll taken every few months throughout 1941 and 1942 showed a steady increase in the number of those favoring a post-war international organization "with power to maintain peace." These polls finally registered between 75 and 80 per cent of acceptance of the very kind of international obligation which had kept the United States out of the League of Nations.

Naturally the trend in public opinion was a matter of interest to the leaders of the great political parties, but more especially to the Republicans because it might portend a division in their ranks. Consequently their leaders met in conference at Mackinac in Northern Michigan the first week in September, and speedily adjusted themselves to the new outlook. Although the resolution which they passed still paid the accustomed homage to national sovereignty, it opened the door to the support of policies of international cooperation, strengthened and stabilized in international organization.

Without reviving the old controversies of 1919, it was clear that the country was reconsidering its attitude on the fundamental principles of Woodrow Wilson. Study groups, both national and local, began to shape these ideas once more in terms of programs, platforms or draft resolutions for the United Nations. One of the last of these to shape its ideas in a definite but comprehensive statement was the Commission to Study the Organization of Peace. After four years of careful study it finally produced, in November, 1943, a document entitled "Fundamentals of the International Organization," covering the main points of the organization of peace, and accompanied it with a general statement which summarized in a few pages the argument of this volume.

Meanwhile events had taken place in Congress. The Chairman of the Committee on Foreign Affairs of the Senate, Senator Connally of Texas, revealed the fact that he and some of his colleagues had been working on a resolution setting forth the principle that the United States accepted a responsibility for the maintenance of peace among nations to be exercised by the cooperation of the United Nations. Before the text of this resolution was hammered into shape, however, a far-sighted Congressman, Mr. J. W. Fulbright of Arkansas, had introduced a resolution in the House of Representatives which literally swept Congress off its feet.

The Fulbright Resolution read as follows:

Resolved by the House of Representatives (the Senate concurring), that the Congress hereby expresses itself as favoring the creation of appropriate international machinery with power adequate to establish and to maintain a just and lasting peace among the nations of the world, and as favoring the participation by the United States therein.

The vote on this Resolution on September 21, 1943, was 360 to 29. The strength of this Resolution lay in its simplicity. It left to the Executive the planning of the details of the post-war organization and to the Foreign Relations Committee of the Senate to criticize the proposals when giving its advice and consent in accordance with the provisions of the Constitution. There were, therefore, no thorny details to thresh out in debate, the kind of detail upon which such major proposals are often defeated. As its author stated, it was only a first step in the development of post-war foreign policy. But it told the world that the United States now "recognizes that any organization for peace must be based upon power adequate to enforce peace," and that "the United States will share both in supplying that power and in the responsibility for the exercise of it." He went on to say that

> The art of government has not kept pace with the physical sciences. But the lesson of history is that the unit of government will in time proceed to the international level. The question is: Do we have the intelligence to do it now or must we wait one hundred or five hundred years to achieve that goal?

This challenging proposal of Congressman Fulbright and the surprisingly large majority for it in the House of Representatives, led to strenuous efforts on the part of some Senators to bring the Connally Resolution out of Committee and to make it stronger in its commitments. But it was not until after the publication of the Moscow Agreement that the Resolution was finally, on November 5, adopted by the Senate by 85 to 5. Those who wanted a more definite commitment accepted the Resolution as a basic statement of principles which, after all, would be helpful to the Executive in framing more definite proposals. The text of the Resolution is as follows:

RESOLVED, That the war against all our enemies be waged until complete victory is achieved.

That the United States cooperate with its comrades-in-arms in securing a just and honorable peace.

That the United States, acting through its constitutional processes, join with free and sovereign nations in establishment and maintenance of international authority with power to prevent aggression and to preserve the peace of the world.

That the Senate recognizes the necessity of there being established at the earliest practicable date a general international organization, based on the principle of the sovereign equality of all peace-loving states, and open to membership by all such states, large and small, for the maintenance of international peace and security.

That, pursuant to the Constitution of the United States, any treaty made to effect the purposes of this resolution, on behalf of the Government of the United States with any other nation or any association of nations, shall be made only by and with the advice and consent of the Senate of the United States, provided two-thirds of the Senators present concur.

Analysis of the votes on these two Resolutions showed that the principles set forth in them had substantial support in all but a few sections of the country. Over 90 per cent of the total membership of Congress voted their adherence to the principle of collective security. Moreover, when the votes were classified geographically, it was found that in the representation of thirty-four of the forty-eight states not a single vote in Senate or House was cast against either of these Resolutions and in eleven other states there were only one or two opposed. Equally important was the fact that the vote was non-partisan in character. For the time being at least, the great issue of constructive planning for world peace was taken out of the arena of domestic politics by the joint action of political leaders conscious of their responsibility to the country as a whole.

But all of this movement in Congress would have been of no avail had the Executive not been conscious of its duty in the preparation of plans for the future and negotiations to make those plans real. Little if anything of this was known to the country, however, until the summer and autumn of 1943. Later on, in January, 1944, the State Department in a nation-wide broadcast revealed the fact that during all those months it had been busily at work studying the post-war situation and that experienced staffs within the State Department had been aided by experts in an advisory capacity on all manner of questions in the preparation for the post-war settlement. In this work the former Undersecretary of State, Mr. Sumner Welles, had taken an important part. Secretary Hull himself, however, presided over the most important of these consultations, those dealing primarily with political questions. Mr. Hull also realized that there must be consultation with leaders in Congress on post-war planning, for the one thing most constantly in his mind was the memory of how the plans at the end of the first World War were frustrated by the conflict between the Senate and the Executive. From his long experience in public life he realized also that it would be a mistake for the Executive to go too fast and too far, making promises or holding out hopes that could not be fulfilled unless Congress also was committed to them. This policy of caution was unfortunately mistaken in certain quarters for conservative stagnation, a charge which Mr. Hull was unable at the time to refute publicly, because the conduct of foreign affairs cannot be carried on by public pronouncements to one's own countrymen during negotiations with the other nations involved. For example, the Department of State could not disclose its preparations for the Moscow Conference until that Conference had concluded its meetings and the other Governments had passed upon our proposals. Prior announcement of what we want from a conference might make it extremely difficult for the other nations to accept even those points upon which they were in agreement if it would seem as though they had been imposed upon them. The first principle of successful diplomacy is to offer to the other partners in the negotiations the chance to make the propositions their own. The subtle flattery involved in this technique is, after all, only human nature in action, and the masters of diplomacy have always been those who have been able to read the minds of their opponents by sympathetic understanding. On more than one occasion Mr. Hull has shown that he is a master of diplomacy. The result, however, of this whole situation, was that until the closing week of October, 1943, when the Moscow Conference was in session, the State Department kept silent on its major plans and the Senate had not yet voted on the Connally Resolution. The need for a forthright, unequivocal statement as to the nature of the organization of peace was so great that Mr. Hull's long journey to Moscow was watched with almost breathless anxiety by those interested in the organization of peace. When the news of its success was made public, cool-headed, competent observers even estimated the moral value of the agreement as the equivalent of at least one whole army at the front. The *New York Times,* commenting upon the statesmanship shown at the conference in the Kremlin, remarked that it constituted nothing less than the first peace conference for the settlement of the second World War. That these statements did not seem extravagant at the time was borne out by the reception given to Mr. Hull by Congress when, in an incident unique in American history, the Secretary of State told what happened at Moscow to the members of both Houses of Congress, in a joint session especially arranged for the purpose. The significance of this meeting, especially in view of the universal acclaim with which Mr. Hull was greeted, is hardly less than that of the Moscow Conference itself. Two weeks before, the Senate had finally voted the Connally Resolution, and now it listened to the calm, unemotional statement of one in whose judgment everyone had confidence, that a revolutionary change in the conduct of international affairs was in the making. A new international organization was to be "for the maintenance of peace and security," the foundation stone of which would be the recognition of the "principle of the sovereign equality of all peace-loving nations, irrespective of size and strength. . . . As the provisions of the four-nation declaration are carried into effect, there will no longer be need for spheres of influence, for alliances, for balance of power, or any other of the special arrangements through which, in the unhappy past, the nations strove to safeguard their security or to promote their interests." Cheers greeted the statement that "in Moscow their four Governments pledged themselves to carry forward to its fullest development a broad and progressive program of international cooperation. This action was of world-wide importance."

This high moment in the history of our foreign relations did not, however, mislead for a moment so experienced a statesman as Mr. Hull. Both then and afterwards he emphasized the fact that it was only a beginning which had been made at Moscow and that the great work of stabilizing and maintaining peace involved much more than agreement upon a single formula. Subsequent events soon justified this sober conclusion that one must not mistake the dawn which broke over Moscow for the day which is to follow, a day in which high promise will be tested by realities. Clear thinking and devoted effort will be needed on the part of everyone, not governments alone, if an enduring structure of peace is to be reared upon the foundations provided by the Four-Power Agreement. No one has been more eloquent than Mr. Hull in insistence upon the fact that governments alone cannot guarantee peace by authoritative utterances or even by treaty agreements. The people themselves are guardians of their own safety. This, as he has repeated on more than one occasion, is true of all countries, which is one added reason for faith in democracy, because in it the people have a voice in the settling of major questions.

The full texts of the documents of the Three-Power Conference at Moscow include declarations regarding Italy and Austria and a statement on war atrocities, each of which is of great importance in its own field. But prefacing these definite statements of policy, there is a still more important Joint Four-Nation Declaration which the Chinese Ambassador at Moscow signed along with the three Foreign Secretaries on behalf of their governments. In this declaration the four Great Powers jointly affirmed their steadfast purpose to carry the war through to the utter defeat, surrender and disarmament of the enemy, and then went on to outline the structure of an enduring peace. In this supremely important part of the Declaration the Four Powers jointly declare:

4—That they recognize the necessity of establishing at the earliest practicable date a general international organization, based on the principle of the sovereign equality of all peace-loving States, and open to membership by all such States, large and small, for the maintenance of international peace and security.

5—That for the purpose of maintaining international peace and security pending the re-establishment of law and order and the inauguration of a system of general security, they will consult with one another and as occasion requires with other members of the United Nations with a view to joint action on behalf of the community of nations.

6—That after the termination of hostilities they will not employ their military forces within the territories of other States except for the purposes envisaged in this declaration and after joint consultation.

7—That they will confer and cooperate with one another and with other members of the United Nations to bring about a practicable general agreement with respect to the regulation of armaments in the post-war period.

In the Introduction to this Four-Nation Declaration it was definitely stated that "provision is made for the inclusion of all other peace-loving nations, great and small, in this system." Then it outlined the provisional steps taken to give reality to the principles of international cooperation by the United Nations. An Advisory Commission was to be set up in London to study the questions which were bound to arise in connection with the erection of this international organization and the maintenance of peace. This Commission would not have any authority to act but only to make joint recommendations to the three Governments, which would also use "the existing diplomatic channels." This General Advisory Council was to be distinguished from another Advisory Council to be established for matters relating to Italy, on which there would be not only representatives of the three Great Powers but also of the French Committee of National Liberation and ultimately of Greece and Yugoslavia.

No matter what comes of it in the future, the Joint Four-Nation Declaration will rank among the great state papers of history. Nevertheless it covers only a part of the wide field of international relations. It is limited to the problems of security and does not deal with those of economic and social welfare or international justice. These are left for future consideration, and properly so, because the establishment and maintenance of peace is the indispensable condition for progress in all other matters. It would be absurd to imagine that Mr. Hull, or for that matter Mr. Stalin, should even for a moment lose sight of those dynamic forces which both of them, although from different standpoints, believe to be the fundamental element of both national and international life. The fact that they limited themselves in this pronouncement to the maintenance of security was a further proof, if that were needed, of the practical quality of their statesmanship.

There is a lesson in this method of negotiation which reaches far beyond the confines of diplomacy. We have not appreciated fully enough the extent to which the continuance of war as an instrument of national policy has falsified the economic situation of the whole world. It is only after we can be freed from the ominous threat of another world war that we can turn all our energy and devote all our resources to the one great aim of national and individual prosperity. In a world of credit the cost of war in destruction and displacement of productive forces is postponed and disguised so that only the thoughtful student realizes its full extent, as shown in depressions bringing economic hardship decades after the war is over. But everyone knows or should know the ruinous cost of maintaining armies and navies as an insurance against the violent outbreak of lawless governments or even against the chance and hazard of less criminal wars.

We have spoken above of the great reception accorded Mr. Hull by the Congress of the United States when he reported on his mission to Moscow. High tribute was also paid to him by Mr. Anthony Eden, the British Foreign Minister, speaking to a crowded House of Commons, not only for Mr. Hull's "very gallant venture in making the long flight" to Moscow but also for the "Hull declaration," a significant phrase which gave the chief credit for the Moscow success to the American Secretary of State.

Mr. Eden was careful to disarm the fears expressed by some Allied governments and the French National Committee that the Advisory Committee would impose the views of the three Great Powers on the other nations. He emphasized the fact that "this small body had been established solely for an exchange of information and ideas between us upon certain questions which will certainly arise as the war progresses." It was not an executive but was merely a helpful organ of those nations whose association was based upon the "firmest of foundations—common interests."

Not only was the Government of the United States a prime

mover in the framing of the Moscow Declaration, but apparently the American people were the most ready to respond to it and the most enthusiastic in its endorsement. We have referred above to the unparalleled scene in Congress when Secretary Hull made his report to it and through it to the nation. But all the measurements of the attitude of private citizens on public affairs showed that there was a tidal wave of opinion in support of the obligations taken at Moscow. Among these measurements perhaps the most significant was the referendum taken by the United States Chamber of Commerce. Two questions were submitted in the month of December, 1943, to the Chambers of Commerce of the entire country, the first of which referred not only to the Moscow Resolution but also to the Fulbright and Connally Resolutions of House and Senate. The vote on this question was 1931 in support of the Moscow Resolution and 9½ against. The second question was whether "this peace and security may best be safeguarded by the use of the armed forces of peace-loving nations acting through the combined chiefs of staff organization developed to meet further conditions." On this question the vote was 1829½ in favor and 71 against. Seldom in the history of American public opinion has there been such unanimity as that which is registered in this referendum of the United States Chamber of Commerce. The leaders of the business world in every town and city of the country have responded in no uncertain terms to the obligation to cooperate with other peace-loving nations in the maintenance of peace and security.

It was not long, however, before this brightening prospect was clouded over by problems arising in Moscow itself. Of these, the most important was the question of Russia's frontier on the west. The Polish Government-in-exile, resident in London, strongly anti-Bolshevist in tendency, looked upon the series of Russian victories with mixed feelings, and was by no means ready to regard the Russian advance as a war of liberation. On the contrary, they expected—and the event proved that they were right—that the Soviets would again claim all the territory east of the Curzon Line. The Soviets, on their part, were conscious not only of this opposition but of a deep-seated hostility to them on the part of some members of the Polish cabinet, who had even gone so far as to accept without question the German propaganda charge that Bolshevist leaders had massacred thousands of Polish patriots. So bitter was the Soviet resentment against these Polish leaders that Stalin's Government refused to recognize any Polish cabinet of which they were a part.

This created a situation of grave concern to the governments of Great Britain and the United States, both of which had recognized the Polish Government-in-exile. While it is true that Great Britain went to war not to maintain the independence of Poland, but to maintain the principles of international law and order among nations, it was over Poland that this issue finally flamed into war. Therefore it could not be indifferent if its great Ally on the east were to attempt similar active violence against Poland. Even if it were unable to thwart such a policy, it could not connive at it. This feeling is strongly shared in the United States. Moreover, by a strange and pernicious paradox, it is in the former isolationist press that the most ardent pro-Polish protests against the Soviet claims have appeared, interpreting Soviet policy in the worst possible light. It is not a very happy situation when those who have been opposed to or have been skeptical about the international organization of peace are the very ones who are most vociferous partisans in a territorial dispute in which this country has no direct interest except that of finding a peaceful solution. The very kind of question from which Americans should abstain is the kind which, incredible as it may seem, is used by those who adhere to the general principle that the United States should stay out of foreign disputes. It is doubtful if it will mean much to the villagers in the Pripet swamps whether they are to be under Soviet or Polish rule so long as they can have the local freedom to maintain their religion and their customs, for from all accounts, they are not politically minded. We have, of course, a right and a duty to express our opinions and to bring what influence we have to bear upon the just settlement of such disputes, but we must be sure in the first place, and we are not sure in this instance, that the opinions are based upon accurate information and that the facts are in violation of justice and morals. The method to achieve redress is by insistence upon institutions in which this information will be made available no matter under what government the territories may ultimately be left.

Here, then, was the first test of that clause of the Moscow Agreement which declared that the four Great Powers would "pending the re-establishment of law and order . . . consult with one another . . . with a view to joint action on behalf of the community of nations." Literally construed, it looked as though this test was being definitely ignored by the Soviet Government only a few weeks after it had signed it. But was the test a fair one? It apparently did not seem so to Stalin who was never left a moment in doubt as to the attitude of the British and American Governments toward the states along Russia's frontier. The guarantees of freedom and self-government in the Atlantic Charter had been reinforced by the British guarantee to Poland and by the statement of the American Undersecretary of State, Mr. Sumner Welles, in support of the independence of the Baltic states. The sympathy with Poland in the countries of freedom had apparently not been shared by Moscow, cherishing as it did the grievances against the Polish occupation of White Russia and part of Ukraine. Therefore the British and American proposed intervention between the reactionary Polish Government and that of the U.S.S.R., Stalin refused. The reason given for rejecting the overtures was that the Polish Government-in-exile contained personalities with which the Soviets could not treat because of their past record, but the rejection of the good offices of the British and American Governments was obviously due to the fact that Stalin regarded them as somewhat un-free agents, owing to the way in which they had previously committed themselves to the cause of Poland.

Stalin's refusal to allow his Allies, Britain and America, to intervene, was at once interpreted in anti-Soviet quarters in the worst possible light. But the best excuse for his action in rejecting American intervention was furnished by the threat of Polish-

American citizens to avenge themselves at the polls in the next election against the Administration if it did not champion the Polish case.

In a few days' time things went from bad to worse. The continued advance of the Russian armies made it necessary for the Soviets to begin definitely planning the administration of the occupied territories. The solution which they arrived at was characteristic of Stalin. He took action immediately, but it was action of a wholly unexpected kind. Refusing to negotiate with any external government, he proposed to meet the situation by a major political change in the structure of the U.S.S.R. But this proposed solution raised still more serious questions with which we shall deal in the following chapter.

VI

Soviet Russia Prepares for the Post-war World

ON FEBRUARY 1, 1944, the All Soviet Union Congress held an extraordinary session to consider a major change in the Constitution of the U.S.S.R., constituting it a confederacy of quasi-sovereign states instead of a federation under close central control. Each of the sixteen republics in the Union was granted the two symbols of sovereignty, control of its military forces and of its political relations with foreign states. The proposals were presented by Foreign Minister Molotoff whose address, with the accompanying decrees, had apparently been well prepared beforehand, because the full texts were made available for the foreign as well as the domestic press for immediate publication.

In the outside world, utterly unprepared for this dramatic move, the news came with the sudden impact of something like an international *coup d'état*. Following upon some minor incidents, like the newspaper attacks upon Wendell Willkie, scare news from Cairo of alleged British-German negotiations, and a denunciation of Vatican policy in Europe, the Molotoff decrees were at once interpreted in hostile circles as a sign that Stalin was taking this way to undermine the Four-Power Agreement for a post-war organization of sovereign states. Without stopping to study the text of Molotoff's speech or to compare the decrees with the Constitution of the U.S.S.R., these critics leaped to the conclusion that here we had a definite proof that Moscow had no intention to build upon the foundations laid by Secretary Hull only three months before.

In his address Mr. Molotoff showed a clear appreciation of the fact that other nations would have a vital interest in this change in the Constitution of the Soviet State. But his claim that the granting of local liberties was a recognition of the freedom of the peoples which was inherent in the Soviet system, in contrast with the centralized tyranny of the Nazi Government, did not convince the skeptics in other countries. It looked to them much more like a device for camouflaging the transfer of the disputed territories of eastern Poland and the Baltic States, who could thus be admitted as of their own free will, within a federation of nominally self-governing republics. If, however, the Soviet federation were really to become what Molotoff described, then the entry into it of the territories along the border would be less a conquest than a natural process of affiliation. The question as to how far the grant of autonomy would be carried out thus became a matter of international importance.

The clue to what really happened was soon found to lie in the history of the U.S.S.R. and above all in the ideas of Stalin. Although it was Molotoff who spoke, no one could doubt who was the real author of the decrees. With a fine sense of the dramatic contrast to the boastful, blatant manners of Hitler, Stalin on this occasion slipped quietly into a back seat in a shadowy corner of the platform from which his Foreign Minister was speaking. There are two ways to keep the loyalties of political followers: one is by imposing upon them the outward trappings of power and the other is by the assumption of a modesty which outwardly disguises the real strength of the leader's position. Stalin can play both roles, but on this occasion chose the latter. Molotoff was therefore able to present the decrees as the logical fulfillment of Stalin's long years of matured reflection as well as the fulfillment of Soviet history.

The question which confronts Soviet Russia is one which should be best understood in this country, for it is nothing less than the old question of States' Rights. It is also a question deeply rooted in Russian history. Under the Czars the policy of Russification advocated by the extreme centralists of St. Petersburg, met with opposition on the part of liberal movements, especially those connected with countries that had a history of their own like Poland, Finland, Ukraine on the north and west, and Georgia in the

Caucasus. Among the revolutionists there was, however, a division of opinion on this point. The Social Democrats believed that a strong central control would help to prepare the way for Communism while the Social Revolutionaries cherished the principle of federalism as an inherent element of the principle of freedom and self-determination. Both in those early years of the Revolution and throughout all subsequent history, Stalin has been the outstanding advocate of federation or confederacy, having preached that doctrine as long ago as 1913, four years before the Bolshevik Revolution. It must be remembered that, as a native of Georgia, he was brought up in an atmosphere of strong local and cultural aspirations of a border people who, in the breakup of imperial Russia, had a keen enough sense of nationality to declare their freedom. Among all his comrades, the most sympathetic to this point of view was Lenin. In contrast with the ideas of the majority of the party he saw the need for a compromise which, while retaining central control in the economic sphere through the unity of the Communist Party, would allow a degree of local political autonomy. At the Eighth Convention of the Communist Party, in 1919, Lenin went so far as to rebuke Bukharin, the Calvin of Communist orthodoxy, who inquired ironically whether autonomy should also be given to Bushmen and Hottentots. Lenin replied, "There are no Bushmen in Russia, and I never heard of any Hottentots . . . but there are Bashkirs, Kirghizes, Sarts, and a whole series of other nationalities, and we cannot refuse to recognize them. We cannot deny this to any one of the nationalities dwelling within the territories of the former Russian Empire." Lenin carried the day and in the new program of the Russian Communist Party adopted at that Convention, clauses were inserted in favor of "a Federative Union of States" organized on the Soviet model. Stalin, whose only speech in the Bolshevik Party Congress was in support of local autonomy, became Commissar of Nationalities, which in itself indicates his particular line of interest at that time. Studying the American and Swiss Federations, he pointed to them as proof that in the case of states made up of different elements, the path toward union lies through confederation and federalism. Although he did not force this thesis to the point of heretical disagreement, he seems to have held to it consistently, awaiting the time when it could be applied.

It is hard for us to realize how large a part is played in Soviet politics by ideology. Heresy is not confined to economics, for the form of government is almost as much a matter of orthodoxy as the belief in Communism. With this in mind, it is worth our while to read what Stalin wrote to Lenin on June 12, 1920, commenting on Lenin's Thesis on the Nationality Question which spoke only of federation, not of confederation. Stalin wrote to Lenin:

> For nations which were part of old Russia, our (soviet) type of federation can and should be considered expedient as a road toward international unity. The motives are known: these nationalities either had no statehood of their own in the past, or lost it long since, wherefore the soviet (centralized) type of federation is taken on by them without particular friction. But the same cannot be said about those nationalities which did not form part of old Russia, which existed as independent formations, developed their own statehood and which, were they to become soviet, would in the nature of things have to establish certain state relations (ties) with Soviet Russia. For example, the future Soviet Germany, Poland, Hungary, Finland. These peoples . . . becoming soviet, would hardly agree to establish immediately federative ties with Soviet Russia . . . because they would consider a federation of the soviet type as a form of lessening their state independence, as an attempt on the latter. There is no doubt in my mind, that for these nationalities confederation (a union of independent states) would be the most acceptable form of coming together. To say nothing of backward nationalities, *e.g.*, Persia, Turkey. . . . I think that the point in your thesis concerning transitional forms for bringing together the toilers of different nations should be amended to include (along with federation) *confederation*. Such an amendment would give the thesis greater elasticity. . . .

Through Lenin's and Stalin's insistence and against the opposition of their centralist comrades, this doctrine of local autonomy was carried to the final point of the acceptance of the right of secession in all three Constitutions, those of 1918, 1923 and 1936. The fact that it was accepted in 1936, almost twenty years after the final consolidation of the Soviet State, is a fact of great importance in interpreting the history of today. The question still remained, however, as to how far it was now a gesture in the realm of political theory and how far it would be applied in actual practice.

The test of this fundamental question in the Constitution of the U.S.S.R. came as a result of the second World War, and it is a tribute to the boldness of conception of Stalin's statesmanship, that he met it directly and unequivocally in the decrees of February 1, 1944.

To understand the purpose and scope of these decrees, it is necessary to consider first of all the three main problems confronting the Moscow Government at the time. These are the place of the Red Army in the State, the question of the western frontiers, and the participation of the U.S.S.R. in the "general international organization" foreshadowed at the Moscow Conference.

There is no doubt but that the chief political effect of the second World War upon Soviet Russia is the rise of the Red Army to a place of importance and power within the state. In the early days of the political state, the fear of militarism led to the socialization of the army under political, that is to say, Communist, Commissars. In the first phase of Bolshevist history, the army was the instrument of the Communist Party rather than of the political state. The military command was interfered with to ensure absolute loyalty to the established creed. Leveling tendencies prevailed which made everyone a comrade and prevented the rise of an officer class. Under the test of actual warfare this system broke down and in its place a new and efficient militarism began to show itself. Disciplined and rebuilt into a hierarchical system on the pattern of other armies, the Red Army became the victorious expression of Russian nationalism. The Stalin Government welcomed this strengthening of the morale which was shared in by civilian workers in the munitions as well as by the fighting forces.

But there is always a danger to the civilian government of a state if there grows up alongside it a military machine with a life of its own. Even Bismarck had to repress the ambitions of that very Prussian Army which was the instrument of his policy. Observers of Soviet Russia have long noted with interest the way in which Stalin's generals have been subordinated to him. On the average the length of command has been short and in some cases they have been moved about or replaced at the very height of achievement. No one can say whether Stalin has done this because of the apprehension of rivalry or whether it was merely the outcome of local military situations, but Stalin's policy with reference to the army is, at least, well designed to prevent it from becoming an unduly powerful instrument of a purely nationalist movement.

If this analysis of the trends in Soviet Russia holds, the division of army commands so as to divide them up under the sixteen Republics can be readily explained as the solution of a purely domestic problem. Moreover, it might well give added zest to the fighting forces by recalling to them the loyalties to their own countryside and their own people. While the process of unification under the Soviet Government has made marvelous strides with the rise of literacy and the missionary zeal of local as well as national leaders, there still remains the deep and lasting sentiment of attachment for the neighborhoods which speak their local tongue and treasure a common heritage. Far from obliterating this trend toward local loyalties, the second World War has apparently given it new life. The Molotoff reform, whatever its purpose, offers a chance for it to find new and more pronounced expression.

The second hypothesis, that the revision of the Constitution is for the purpose of solving the problems of the frontier peoples, seems also beyond question. It goes without saying that the Latvians, Estonians, Lithuanians, White Russians and Ukrainians would find it much easier to become partners in a federation which recognized their local patriotisms than to accept the single highly centralized sovereignty of Moscow. As we have seen above, this was Stalin's opinion a quarter of a century ago and he seems to have maintained it consistently throughout the years. But the problem is not so simple as this. For the Soviet system is not merely held together by a federal union, it is also held together by the unifying force of the Communist Party. It is this fact which makes the political structure seem somewhat unreal. From the standpoint of other nations, the U.S.S.R. still remains to a large degree on a revolutionary basis. Although in 1936 it accepted a revised constitutional regime like any other settled legal system, the Communist Party remained unreconstructed within the structure of the state, and continued largely to control its functions (*Cf.* Articles 126 and 141) or rather it should be said that the party gave unity to the whole and that through it Stalin ruled the state. If this remains the situation in 1944, the Molotoff decrees modifying the political constitution do not deal with the real government, that of the party. There were already signs, however, before the second World War, and more especially during it, of a nationalist movement strong enough to challenge on some points the all-pervading supremacy of the Communist Party. In other words the economic framework of the U.S.S.R. began to show signs of yielding to the political. The chief agency in this transformation was the Red Army, the steady advance of which we have just been tracing.

Even in this short survey it should be clear that the statesmen in the Kremlin have problems of their own. Happily for them, the solution for their major problems could be found in Stalin's own political philosophy, that of the development of the nation to unity through confederation and federalism. Beginning with the recognition of the realities of today, it seeks the evolution of the state by strengthening the vitality of every part. As seen from Moscow, the Molotoff reform was apparently in line with the evolution of the British system of self-governing states. Stalin's associates, therefore, began sometime ago to evince a strangely new interest in the study of the British Commonwealth of Nations. But if Moscow thought that the new regime would bring relief to the worried officials in the British and American Foreign Offices by offering them a way out of their dilemma in the boundary dispute, it could not have been more mistaken. On the contrary, the proposal to grant more self-government to the republics constituting the Soviet Union raised a wholly new set of problems in international relations. It was almost bewildering to have suddenly to face the prospect of having some sixteen Soviet Foreign Offices brought into the family of nations, especially when it was believed that they would still be largely, if not entirely, under the dominance of the central Soviet Government.

This brings us to the third surmise as to Stalin's motives. There is no need to assume that Stalin was scheming to undo the work of Secretary Hull by having sixteen votes instead of one in the international organization of the future.

Nothing could be further from Stalin's way of thinking than to have major international problems settled in an international body in which all states would have equal voting power. There would be no surer way of losing control of Soviet foreign policy than to permit the various republics of the Union to debate their political differences in a public forum of all the nations. Stalin's theory of political evolution, as we have already seen, looks toward a stronger ultimate unity than even that already achieved. The three steps toward this unity, as outlined by him, are confederation with its States' Rights doctrine yielding to federation and then to centralization. If the February decrees carried the political fortunes of the U.S.S.R. backward from the federalism of today to confederation instead of moving forward to unity, then it would seem as though the first victim of the decrees was Stalin's own political philosophy. Since this does not make sense, it is necessary to find another explanation.

It is possible that a clue to the solution of this paradox is to be found in Molotoff's address to the All Soviet Union Congress in which he introduced the decrees. He clearly indicated that it was not intended to have the republics of the Union deal with the major questions of international politics. Pointing to the "multifarious and growing requirements" of the republics, he stated that they "have quite a few specific economic and cultural requirements which cannot be covered in full measure by all-Union representation abroad and also by treaties and agreements of the Union with other states. These national requirements of the republics can be met better by means of direct relations of the republics with corresponding states."

Taken at face value, this text means that the republics of the Union are not granted foreign relations on major questions of national policy but have to deal with "specific economic and cultural requirements" which cannot be adequately dealt with by the diplomats of the U.S.S.R. It is to meet "these national requirements," and apparently only these, that direct relations with other states are to be established. In other words the central government still has set the limits for the foreign relations of the states within the Union, in a way which might well seem to Stalin to be both economically, practically, and politically safe.

The reach of the Soviet Union is now so vast and its potentialities in the post-war world are so great that a major change in its political structure is of interest to everyone everywhere and especially to every American citizen. It is worth while therefore to pause a moment to look at the exact way in which it is proposed to revise the Constitution of 1936. The first point deals with the all-important Article 14 of the Constitution which enumerates the powers of the central government. There is a list of some 21 major activities of state over which it has authority. This includes questions of war and peace, the organization of defense and the direction of the armed forces, control of financial and economic administration and the judicial system. The revised Constitution touches only the first paragraph of this long list of powers which places under the authority of the U.S.S.R. "representation of the Union in international relations, conclusion and ratification of treaties with other states." To this sentence is added the words "the establishment of the general character of the relations between the Union republics and foreign states." The additional phrase is apparently inserted to make sure that the revision does not lessen the control of the U.S.S.R. over the general policy in foreign affairs. In other words, all of the lesser representation referred to later on will have to fit into the plans of the Moscow Government. There is, for example, no thought of lessening the control of the U.S.S.R. over "questions of war and peace" or any of the other major fields of politics and economics referred to in Article 14.

The other major change in the Constitution is the addition of a sentence to Article 18 which stated that "the territory of a Union Republic may not be altered without its consent." To this is now added the sentence "Each Union Republic has the right to enter into direct relations with foreign States, to conclude agreements with them, and to exchange diplomatic and consular representatives with them." Taken alone and without the context of the rest of the Constitution, this sentence might well imply that the local governments could engage in all sorts of diplomatic negotiations with their neighbors. But the scope of these negotiations is already indicated by the first revision which retains major questions of policy for the central government. On the other hand, it is significant that this grant of diplomatic and consular representation to the various republics occurs in the article which deals with the boundaries of their territories. This may very well mean that the modifications of frontiers can now be made by the local republics which are directly concerned, if they can make terms with their neighbors, without the responsibility falling back upon the U.S.S.R. This interpretation would be quite in harmony with the statement of Stalin in 1920 quoted above.

The line of development which we have just been sketching is by no means parallel to that of the British Commonwealth of Nations. The British system takes for granted the steady growth of federalism toward real independence not only in domestic matters but in foreign affairs as well. The strength of this trend toward the complete sovereignty of the Dominions was shown recently in the reaction to Lord Halifax's suggestion that their foreign affairs ought to be more unified under the aegis of the Foreign Office. There was a nation-wide protest against this in Canada and a repudiation of the whole idea by the Canadian Prime Minister. Stalin is certainly not looking forward to that kind of political evolution for Ukraine or the other states of the Soviet Union. The recognition of the variety of local interests in culture and economic life is a different thing from the recognition of nationalism which is the expression which those interests have sought in nineteenth century political evolution. On that point we can only repeat what we have said above, that Stalin's ultimate aim is not the creation of a group of nations each intent upon its own political independence. The revised constitution of the U.S.S.R. safeguards the final sovereignty of the central government by providing that it retain control of "the general character of the relations between the Union Republic and foreign States," but within that framework each state works out its own destiny on the basis of its own inherent needs. One might call this scheme a cooperative commonwealth of states, and the description fits all the more aptly when one recalls that the politics of the central government are not intended to be divorced from the economics of the Communist Party. Under these conditions there is no further need to emphasize the continuing unity of Soviet foreign policy.

It is clear that the political philosophy of Soviet federalism is as distinct from that of the British or of the American type as its economic philosophy is distinct from capitalism. While refusing to recognize the political sovereignty of the republics in the Union like that which the British Dominions have achieved for themselves, it is contrary to the American tradition which reserves the conduct of all foreign affairs for the central government. As a matter of fact, in spite of all the studies of comparative government which have been carried on in Moscow, the new Russian system is rooted in Russian history as definitely as British federalism is rooted in the old colonial system or American federalism in the self-government of the colonies. Unlike the French Revolution, the Russian Revolution did not obliterate the old provincial and other internal boundaries which had been left by the government of the Czars. The result was to leave the Soviet Union with one vastly preponderating unity, Great Russia (Velikaya Rus), with almost 100 million inhabitants, one great province, the Ukraine (which means "The Border"), with some 38 million inhabitants, and one secondary province (White Russia) with ten million and some thirteen others averaging two to three million each. The dominance of Great Russia in the Union is therefore like that of Prussia in the German Reich, although this situation is somewhat disguised by the fact that Russia itself is a federation (R.S.F.S.R.). Obviously there can be no real political equality of states in a federal union which includes a state of 100 million inhabitants and one like the Karelo-Finnish Republic of half a million. Moreover, the new nationalism which now shows such vigorous signs of growth, is a nationalism which looks to Russian leadership. The new anthem of the U.S.S.R. which has replaced the call of the

"International" for workers of all countries to unite, begins by an appeal to history, that the "indestructible union of the free republics was welded together by Great Russia." The word used for Russia is not "Rossia," the modern word, but the poetic and almost archaic term "Rus," which has been avoided in all official Soviet usage until now. The creation of the Soviet Union, one of the most revolutionary facts in the history of politics, is thus linked with that sentiment which accumulates in the course of centuries around the evolution of a nation.

Obviously Soviet foreign policy will not be determined by the votes of the little republics in the Congress at Moscow any more than in their negotiations with foreign States. This fact was clearly brought out in the meeting of the Congress which passed the February decrees. The reporters describing that historic occasion noted that only a fraction of the delegates paid attention to the text of the decrees and that the Congress gave its unanimous approval without debate. But if the February decrees have not endowed the republics of the Union with power to deal with the major questions of foreign affairs, then what is left for them? This is not a problem to be solved by attempting to psychoanalyze Russian statesmanship. It is a problem the solution of which will not rest entirely in Soviet hands, for the other nations will act according to their own interests both in determining with whom as well as on what subjects they will be willing to negotiate. Upon the whole, however, we can readily see that the international dealings of the separate states will primarily be concerned with special problems in the livelihood of the local population, while the great problem of peace and war remains with the central government.

The question at once arises, just what are the "economic and cultural requirements" of the republics which are to be left in their own hands? While it would be futile to try to anticipate just what problems will arise in the future, the whole trend of twentieth-century world history shows that with the growth of an independent economic world, the peoples of different countries have many contacts which were never covered by the old diplomacy of foreign offices in the days when foreign affairs occupied a relatively minor part of a nation's political life. A whole new area of economic and social interests has developed in recent years and promises to keep on developing at an ever-increasing pace. The tendency in foreign offices has been to continue and extend their control over these new relationships. But this means that they remain in the setting of politics, from which they often ought to be divorced. Technical as well as special interests should find the way to direct or at least to offer weighty advice upon such matters. In the plan for international organization considered below, this point has been kept constantly in mind. Whatever the intent of the Soviet legislation may have been, it offers a constructive and helpful suggestion for the solution of the problems that lie alongside but are not inherently dominated by political considerations.

This brings us back to our starting point. The "general international organization" envisaged in the Moscow Agreement was "for the maintenance of international peace and security." The pledge of Moscow to go ahead with this organization therefore remains untouched by the first of the two Decrees of Moscow, that which recognized and delimited the foreign relations of the states. But there was a second Decree to organize military formations of the republics, which recognized that "each Union Republic has its Republican military formation [Art. 18-b]." It is unnecessary here to enter into a detailed analysis of this apparent federalization of the armed forces of the Soviet Union. We have spoken above of the possible reasons for it, but its political implications at the present time need not concern us, because the Constitution still leaves questions of peace and war in the hands of the central government. In passing, however, it should be noted that the final achievement of sovereignty by the British Dominions was due to their having maintained separate armed formations in the First World War, backed by an imperial war cabinet on which the Dominion Premiers were members. This brought the Dominions participation in the Paris Peace Conference, membership in the League of Nations, and finally the Statute of Westminster which recognized their national sovereignty, leaving the British Commonwealth of Nations little more than a mystical expression of spiritual affinities. History has shown that these spiritual affinities are a deep reality, but it is more than doubtful if Stalin intends to rely upon them. We can take it for granted that the second Moscow Decree was designed, not with reference to external politics, but with reference to the problems of military administration within the U.S.S.R.

The conclusion to be drawn from this short survey is that the revised Soviet Constitution, instead of rendering the post-war organization of nations more difficult, brings us face to face with realities which have long been obscured in international relations. It would be a genuine contribution to peace if the vague but potent sovereignty of national states were to be broken up into its constituent parts and peoples across frontiers deal with each other more directly in terms of their own interests. Just how that can best be done, however, falls within the second half of this study, on the possibilities of an effective international organization of nations.

To end our analysis at this point, however, would still leave untouched the most serious question of all. This is the long-range use which might be made of the Stalin policy of federation to enmesh or absorb not merely neighboring states but also those at a distance, such as the Danubian and Balkan states in Europe and the disturbed areas of Asia. In these cases the argument of security for Russia itself would no longer apply, but Communism would spread both west and east by the multiplication of governments of the Soviet type, all of which would naturally look to Moscow for at least spiritual leadership if not for more. This is apparently the new technique for the extension of Soviet Communist principles which, according to Stalin's theory, would replace the Comintern by a method to be followed if the capitalist states prove hostile to Soviet policies or inefficient in cooperation with them. If this method were to succeed it might therefore change the whole orientation of international affairs as well as of the domestic economy of the peoples concerned. This is a situation which must be faced in realistic terms. It will not yield to wishful thinking on our part. Neither will it yield to policies of force. It is not the kind of movement in human affairs which can be suppressed by armies and navies. Quite apart from the fact that the second World War has shown the military strength of Soviet Russia and that its prestige as victor over Germany outweighs all other elements in the politics of power, the defense of freedom must be by other means than those which enslave its defenders. The way to meet the spread of Communism is by the spread of prosperity both within each nation and among the nations so as to make the existing order of society and the whole body of the citizens the loyal defenders of a society in the prosperity of which they all share.

It is the creed of the Communist that this cannot be done, that capitalism by its very nature cannot rid itself of exploitation; that it lives and prospers by the exploitation of the economically weak and that it will not yield to anything but force. The answer to this challenge has hitherto been partial and incomplete, for the world of free enterprise not being revolutionary by nature has to take into account all the existing differences in human society and work out compromises as it goes along. Nevertheless in a situation as grave as this, when the issues which confront us reach to the very foundations of the civilized world, the time has come to meet it with something more than half measures half-heartedly applied by those with no faith in them. The British democracy seems ready to meet it, if one can judge by the nation-wide support given the Beveridge Report, that great document which deals with the problem of unemployment in the characteristic British way of thoroughgoing but not revolutionary reform. In the United States the situation is more confused, but by no means so dark as the pessimists would have us believe. True, there is nation-wide lassitude over the efforts of the New Deal, and the "forgotten man" is in danger of being again forgotten. The reaction is a healthy one so far as it is a protest against inefficient bureaucratic management and waste by an inadequate officialdom. But it would be a grave and perilous blunder for us to fall back upon a "do nothing" policy at a time when there is so much to do. Fortunately, in this case as nearly always throughout history, the pessimist is wrong. The conscience of the American people is not dead. What is lacking is not good will, but a program for the nation which all, or nearly all, can accept. Fortunately too, this is, next to the war, the chief interest of the American people at the present time. The three great economic interests of the nation, business, labor and agriculture, are all concentrating their best thought upon the economics of the post-war period. The problem is to provide employment for all who can work, not by bureaucratic devices but by combining increase of production with safeguards against exploitation.

In this program will be found the final answer to the challenge of Communism, for it brings the consumer into the picture along with the producer. Production always stops when there is no one to buy, and the only way to have a universal and permanent market for the goods produced by labor is to ensure it an ever-increasing standard of living which its own efforts will provide in proportion as excessive profits are denied to private ownership. American industrial leaders are now growingly aware that these principles of economics are not mere unreal promises of a golden future but sound business here and now. Moreover they know that the crushing burden of post-war debts and the needs of reconstruction cannot be met by any one nation for itself. Just as national security is now seen to be an international concern of world-wide scope, so national prosperity is now seen to be a world-wide problem. The wages of American workers will be paid in part by those who buy their goods in Asia, Africa, or Europe, as well as at home. Therefore, alongside the organization of defense against war, and indeed, as a basis for it, there must be a Magna Charta of freer trade to be applied throughout the whole world. In this great constructive measure lies the hope of mankind for a world that will combine freedom and social justice so that every day's work of the common man in every land adds its mite to the permanent structure of world peace.

The answer to Communism is not to be found in policies of hostile intrigue, but in the betterment of our own welfare.

PART II

FUNDAMENTALS OF THE ORGANIZATION OF LASTING PEACE

I

The Security of Nations

(a) *Definition*

THE problems of economics have long been brought within the scope of scientific analysis. As long ago as 1776 Adam Smith wrote his "Inquiry into the Nature and Causes of the Wealth of Nations." No such comprehensive survey of the problems of the Security of Nations has ever been written. Amid all the writing on war and peace, there is, even today, no scientific analysis of politics comparable with the body of economic thought that has developed from Adam Smith's pioneering study. The one parallel to such a treatise was written much too early to deal with the vital problems of contemporary international political relations. One has to go back to Hugo Grotius, the Dutch refugee in the France of Louis XIII, in the first half of the seventeenth century for the formulation of the principles of war and peace. His work was a monument of learning and sagacity, and laid the basis of modern International Law. But it was written at the very dawn of the state system which it was to serve. Grotius could draw only upon the history of the ancient world and the Middle Ages for its precepts. During the next two centuries, international law made little progress because the national states which were then taking shape insisted upon the right of warfare as the symbol of independence and sovereignty. This was a doctrine which, carried to its logical conclusions, made for anarchy rather than for law and order among nations. Fortunately, the growing interdependence of a world of commerce which Adam Smith depicted, and which the British in course of time made the basis of their economic system, checked this political trend and, instead of war becoming the normal expression of conflicting nationalities, it kept steadily getting less, both in frequency and in extent, throughout the nineteenth century.

The problem of security seemed therefore to nineteenth-century students of history and politics to be reaching a solution through the normal operation of natural laws. This was part of the theory of progress so familiar in nineteenth-century thinking. Optimists even held forth the hope that with the progress of intercourse and enlightenment war might be narrowing down to a vanishing point. Nineteenth-century liberalism thus furnished the link between economic freedom and international morals.

Meanwhile, however, sinister suspicions and rivalries kept darkening this bright picture of progress. With every nation insisting on the right to go to war in defense of "national honor and vital interests" the forces of militarism had a sound argument to insist upon adequate armament against surprise attack. It was not, however, until the Industrial Revolution had begun to change completely the weapons of war, that this rivalry revealed the full extent to which the security of each nation had been imperiled by the preparations of their neighbors for their own security. The way in which this vicious circle drew the civilized nations of the world into the vortex of two World Wars can best be seen by tracing the preparations for those wars in the growth of rival armaments. Each nation knew that the problem of security could not be solved by armaments but it had no other solution so long as policies of power dominated international relations. The problem of security had to be solved by a whole-hearted effort to eliminate war and the threat of war from international politics or by preparing with equally whole-hearted devotion for national defense. Temporizing and compromising on the edge of the vortex which militarism had created, the peoples of the world were swept into it. It was a major failure of statesmanship that it lacked either the courage or the foresight to come to grips with the whole problem of national security in its final terms after the first World War had shown the revolution which had taken place in the science of warfare, a revolution which made war or the threat of it anywhere a danger to all countries. Either the League of Nations had to be made efficient and peace safeguarded by cooperative action or the peace-loving nations had to match the armaments of those whom they suspected were secretly arming.

Future centuries will certainly find it hard to understand how a generation which was confronted with the problem of national security as the central problem of its time, could have been so careless about it. Even the term "national security" needs definition, because it has been used very commonly in recent years in another connection, that of the social and economic security of the individual within the state, and not of the nation itself with reference to war. This is especially the case in the English-speaking countries, all of which lie somewhat apart from the uneasy politics of continental Europe. The French word *sécurité* has a much more definite application to the problems of war and peace, which was one of the reasons why our delegates at disarmament conferences failed to appreciate the basis for the French insistence upon our dealing with the question of security before proceeding to disarm. The French were right; the second World War has, or should have, taught us that major lesson, for it is the beginning of wisdom in the effort to eliminate war.

The definition of security has been stated in its shortest possible form in the Atlantic Charter as "Freedom from Fear." This of course means freedom from the fear of war, for it was with the problems of War and Peace that the Atlantic Charter dealt. A nation that is secure is therefore one which has absolute confidence in the continuance of its peace, and not merely one which is free from war at any given time. This confidence may rest upon one of three foundations: geographic situation and natural means of defense, political and military preparations by the nation against the hostile acts of others, or cooperation with other nations to create a system of security by mutual insurance against the outbreak of war and the erection of substitutes for it.

It is well to pause a moment over this definition and its application to practical politics, for it should be clear at the outset that we are not dealing with a single large general truth that means the same to all peoples. The security of each nation has always been conditioned by its situation, its history and its relations with other nations. It means less to those nations which have most of it than to those which have little, just as good health means least to the healthiest man. The result has been that the nations which have enjoyed a large degree of natural security have felt no such urge to deal with the problem as those who have had to provide, by artificial means, obstacles on the pathway of the invader. Now, history shows that it is especially those peoples so happily situated behind barriers of mountains, deserts, swamp lands, or oceans, as to feel safe from attack, who have been able to develop the institutions of liberty more than those peoples not so protected. The results of this situation are two-fold: in the first place the nations that are the natural champions of freedom have been the least interested in the problem of security because it has not forced itself upon them. On the other hand, the nations which are at grips with war or the fear of war cannot escape a degree of militarization for the sake of their own defense, which is not needed by those countries which lie less exposed to external dangers.

It should be clear from this short summary of a vastly complicated problem that unless the problem of security is dealt with on an international and not on a purely national basis there is no escape from the conclusion that more and more armaments will be needed for security as the barriers of nature are overcome by military science. The heart of the whole problem lies in recognizing that the civilized nations have a common interest in the prevention of war or the threat of it. There is no other way by which nations of the world can henceforth achieve any sound measure of security. There must be general agreement upon the principle that war of aggression is a criminal act and that each individual case of it must be suppressed, not only for its own disastrous consequences and the danger of its spreading throughout the world, but also because the establishment of peaceful relations among nations as a basis for law and order cannot make headway if single crimes are tolerated or connived at by the governments of nations not directly affected by the act of violence. The cooperation of sovereign powers in the suppression of wars of aggression is the fundamental condition for the security of each.

(b) *Isolation*

Those who advocate policies of isolation as the best safeguard against involvement in war would be wholly justified if the nation's natural defenses were always adequate, if distance and difficulties of access could always be relied upon. Generally speaking, the isolationists are the conservatives in the field of security, for they look to the past as a guide to the future. If the history of their own country has relatively few foreign wars to record, it breeds a confident habit of mind which tends to minimize any apprehension of danger. In the past, natural barriers against invasion have been sufficient to afford security for even small peoples with relatively slight military organization, even when they are neighbors of a great power. It is essentially nations protected, like Great Britain in the past, by encircling seas, or like America, by oceans, which have most consistently felt the sense of safety from invasion. But however much these conditions may have justified policies of isolation in the past, they are now challenged by a novel set of material conditions, those created by modern science. The defenses which nature supplies are steadily being breached by the work of the engineer, not for the purposes of war, but for those of peace. The distances which divided nations are growing steadily less and are bound to be lessened more and more with the progress of invention. There are no mountains or deserts on the airways of the stratosphere. The geography of the world is being remade before our eyes, and although it will continue as a major problem for military strategy, it will never again furnish a full measure of defense against attack. This is true of large nations even more than of the small; for the great powers, when they fall out among themselves, have in their industrial mobilization for war a greater possibility of changing the conditions of the physical world.

Under such conditions, policies of isolation cannot be adhered to with the rigidity which is natural to conservative minds. But neither can they be rejected by equally rigid, unqualified opposition to them. The alternative to freedom from fear is not eternal preoccupation with imaginary dangers. Either extreme is equally to be avoided in the field of security. As everywhere else in politics, each problem has to be studied in its own terms, for the solutions will vary with time and circumstance. The best safeguard for a nation's security is open-minded but thoughtful consideration of how to adjust its defenses to the changing conditions of modern life. These conditions have changed fully as much in the science of war as in the arts of peace, and security in the world of today and tomorrow must take this fundamental fact into account.

This brings us from the problem of natural security to that of political security, by the man-made devices for suppressing, avoiding, or preventing war. In the larger sense, that includes the whole field of international relations, not only diplomacy, conference, arbitration and tribunals for the settlement of disputes, but every policy and institution which helps the nations to work together for their common good, in political matters as well as in those of economic, social and cultural relations. These constructive methods for the day-to-day conduct of international affairs are treated in subsequent sections of this survey. Here we shall concentrate upon the problem of security in the narrower sense of the word: measures of prevention against the outbreak of war and defense against it after it has begun, that is to say, diplomacy to preserve the peace and military action to restore it, both techniques operating under recognized rules of international law.

(c) *Nationalism*

Here again, in the field of political security, we come upon the same kind of conservatism as that of the isolationists in the field of economics. To most people, the old ways are the best unless the reasons for change are overwhelmingly convincing, and this applies especially to those techniques which are called into action only rarely or do not immediately concern the common affairs of daily life. The conservative in the field of political security is the nationalist, a new name in American political life, but one likely to be much heard of in the future. The nationalist falls back upon his nation's own defenses for its security and in that way resembles the isolationist, but unlike the isolationist, he is ready to embark upon adventures abroad, extending the bulwarks of military protection overseas or wherever the rapidly extending scope of modern war may threaten the world-wide interests of his country.

It is of course evident to any fair-minded student of national security that nationalism is compounded of the same elements as the imperialism against which it inveighs most vehemently. For the nationalism of one country is imperialism in the eyes of its neighbors if it goes the whole length of relying upon its military strength to secure what it calls its rights against those who were themselves wronged by such policies. There is little to be gained, however, by pointing out such inconsistencies in the doctrine or practice of nationalism because, like all the major creations of politics, it has no regard for logic, being the natural expression of a sentiment which all good citizens share, that of a supreme concern in the welfare of one's own country. Nationalism owes its strength, not to well-thought-out plans or policies, but to a much deeper core of action in us all, that of emotion. But this fact, which constitutes its strength, is also the source of its weakness, for the whole history of politics shows that the emotions offer no sure guide for times of crisis. Indeed, most political institutions have been created to restrain or direct the wayward impulses of men insisting upon getting what they want when they want it without due regard to the rights of others. This curbing of lawlessness within the state has given us the institutions which safeguard life and property and provide for the welfare of all against the arbitrary acts of any. Nationalism, with its roots deep in the soil of every land, operating by threat or act of violence in international affairs, offers a last, but a mighty, outlet for those activities which we have ruled out of our lives at home as immoral and illegal. Its most intelligent advocates, to be found in certain schools of international law, frankly state their belief that the morals which should guide the conduct of the individual do not apply to the conduct of nations. The supreme law for international dealings, in their eyes, is either expediency or magisterial cunning, masquerading under the guise of statesmanship.

It is well to pause a moment on this matter of nationalism because of the insidious dangers which attend its growth, dangers from which we have been shielded in the past by our isolation rather than by matured conviction based upon knowledge of where it leads, but dangers which confront us from now on because that isolation has almost certainly ceased to exist as a dominating force in American policy. The point to keep in mind is that nationalism of the conservative temper relies and must rely upon maintaining a war establishment of overwhelming might, even if it has no thought of using armaments except for defending its ancient inheritance or what it has more recently taken from others. For nationalism cannot exist in one country alone; it is a continual challenge to the security of other countries because of its reliance upon the war system. This is a matter for plain speaking. The demagogue who pretends that American nationalism in the world of the future would lessen the danger of war is either willfully or ignorantly disseminating one of the greatest lies in history. Nationalism of the kind that seeks to ensure a nation's safety by policies which, consciously or unconsciously, threaten the safety of others, is the very kind of danger to world peace from which the civilized world is now trying to escape.

That the time has come for a thorough-going reform in both of the techniques of safety, diplomacy, and military defense is clear to all thoughtful men everywhere. The lesson can be read in history by the light of the flames that have consumed one civilization after another; as country after country tried to win and to keep its place and its possessions by force of arms. This is as true of the civilizations of the Orient as it is of antiquity in the western world. Century after century, as cities and peoples grew more civilized and ceased to make the technique of warfare their chief concern, their security was menaced or overthrown by peoples less advanced than they or by those who remained devoted to the profession of arms. Their only hope of escape lay in devising a militarism as efficient as that of the enemy. But unless they then militarized themselves to use the instrument they had invented, it was the enemy which profited by it, as when the Greek-invented phalanx was taken over by the mountaineers of Macedonia. If, on the other hand, they attempted to make their defense adequate against every attack, as in the case of Rome, the result was that either the freedom of the citizen had to be surrendered for chain-gang marching under military leaders or safety had to be purchased by engaging mercenary soldiers who ultimately would destroy the state. It is an iron law of history that the nationalism which attempts to safeguard a peace-loving country by outbuilding or out-fighting the military establishments of potential enemies, imperils liberty at home and stimulates into action nations more military by instinct than its own. Nationalism of this adventurous type is more suited to the supreme high command of the German army or the warlords of Japan than to us, for they know better than we the way to security by force of arms, and they know also that a docile people will follow their commands.

(d) *Cooperative or Collective Security*

Two world wars have already shown that no one nation is any longer strong enough by itself to ensure its safety from attack. Nations which have every desire to remain neutral suffer so much from the all-enveloping industry of destruction that only the more fortunate of them can escape involvement. As long as there are nations in the world whose diplomacy is disguised blackmail backed by military threats, peace-loving nations must either yield to them or combine against them by arrangements designed first to avert the danger and if that fails, to meet it with equal or greater force. The only defense which will be adequate in any major threat to peace is by cooperative or collective action. This follows from the simple fact that countries devoted to the arts of peace do not maintain a strong enough military establishment to provide for their own defense when attacked by a militaristic nation. Their reason for this inadequacy in the preparations for war is that if they make it their chief preoccupation they will have to militarize their whole economic life to meet the many-headed dangers of modern war. Thus, in attempting to hold back war from their frontiers, they will find themselves its victims, losing their prosperity by the falsification of their economy and becoming tributary to those nations upon which their war industries depend for their raw materials. There is no security in the maintenance of a peace which is only an armistice between armed and uneasy partners. This kind of international anarchy tempered by alliance breeds war from the poison of suspicion.

It is or should be self-evident that the only way to rid the world of international anarchy is by providing for cooperative international action. Yet that great reform, the only one which can promise general security, will not be easy to bring about, no matter how necessary it may be. The problems of politics are those of sentiment rather than of logic, and the military might of a nation is to most people the visible symbol of its will. He is a poor patriot who does not thrill at the sight and sound of marching men enlisted in his country's service. The pageantry of peace has hitherto been weak compared with that of war with its reminder of great achievement and of sacrifice. Behind this military establishment, as behind the natural barriers of sea and mountain, there has grown up whatever sense of security nations have possessed, always recognizing that it has been inadequate. In the past its inadequacy was made good by out-rivaling one's neighbors, but with the advent of total war, armaments are no longer a specialized technique. They include every activity of the life of the nation, and military strength is no longer to be measured by the size of armies and navies. The increased capacity for destruction is now brought home not only to governments but to the people themselves by the development of air power, a last great step in the evolution of war which makes isolation no longer possible. Nowhere in any country, including the United States, can the individual be wholly safe from attack when militarist nations are permitted to plot against the peace of the world. Pearl Harbor has made this fact sufficiently clear.

The only real solution for the problem of security is to erect a quarantine against aggression by cooperative agreement between peace-loving nations; to create the machinery for the prevention of war and to make it work. We may pause a moment over that word quarantine, to note that its use by President Roosevelt in a speech some years ago created only apprehension in the minds of those who did not believe in the possibility of a second World War. So vocal was the reaction against this warning note of the President that the Administration came to the conclusion that isolationist sentiment was then so strong as to make any such preventive measures impossible or to allow only such as were too slight to be effective. The argument for the so-called neutrality legislation of 1937 was much the same as that which kept us out of the League of Nations, namely, that to join in measures of war prevention by anything resembling deterrent action against lawbreaking nations would merely imperil our safety by assuming unnecessary risks. This is not an argument to be lightly dismissed. Nevertheless, the whole history of politics has shown that law and order can be maintained only by having more force in support of them than can be brought against them. Fortunately, the application of this great truth to international affairs is now being clearly seen by the American people, but they are anxious, and properly so, not to be drawn into plans for war prevention which carry us too far afield. We have no desire to be policemen in the far corners of the world and will accept the obligation to enforce peace only under conditions which afford us a full opportunity to decide when, where and how much we should contribute along with other nations.

The problem which confronts us now is not whether we are willing to cooperate in war prevention but how we can do so without an undue surrender of national sovereignty. Just what this solution will ultimately be, as it develops in the long future, is not for any of us to know. We are dealing here with plans for the world as it now exists. The parallel with the way in which the national state established peace within its borders should not be pushed too far. The world is not yet ready for a super-state, with a world government speaking in terms of authority to nations of differing degrees of political development and widely varying cultures, each of which treasures its independence with equal zeal. Nevertheless, the history of the national state, especially our own, offers a definite clue to the solution of this fundamental problem of the preservation of national sovereignty in an international association of the nations. It is the provision for safeguarding the freedom of the individual even against the possible tyranny of the very government which provides law and order for his protection. The nations associated for the prevention of war could have their Magna Charta or their Bill of Rights, reserving a sphere of liberty for themselves, as did the barons who laid a foundation for limited monarchy in England and the champions of freedom against the Stuart kings. The Founding Fathers of the American Constitution, building upon these foundations, erected a federal system with provision against the undue prerogatives of every government local as well as central. In both nations the state was strengthened rather than weakened by providing for the liberty of the citizen. That liberty, however, was only freedom under the law. Similarly the freedom of nations within the framework of their political association would only be freedom to pursue such policies as do not conflict with the vital interest of other nations.

Thus the central problem of all, that of sovereignty, would find its solution along the lines of our own national history, which not only offers the negative safeguards of liberty against tyranny but also provides for it positively in the varying degrees of participation in government, so that every citizen in every community has a chance to express his opinion and to share in those institutions which most especially affect his own life. That fundamental principle of the American Constitution, the division of the powers of government, has a much wider application than is commonly realized. It is not just the balancing of legislative, executive and judicial powers, important as that device has proved. It includes as well the other devices by which communities preserve their liberties against the central power in a democratic federal system. Federalism is designed to adjust the responsibilities of citizenship in the way that most fully preserves the liberty of the citizen. It is essentially a democratic process. That is why its principle of graded responsibility should be made the basic principle for the organization of the United Nations, for, as Secretary Hull and many others have pointed out, it is in the democratic peoples that the spiritual safeguards of peace reside. It is a happy coincidence that the devices of government which they have evolved for their own protection furnish the best framework for that of the international community.

The American plans for the League of Nations, strangely enough, bore little if any resemblance to the structure of a federal union. The conception of Woodrow Wilson was fundamentally that of the nineteenth-century doctrine of the sovereignty of nations, with emphasis upon the equality in sovereignty of all nations, small and great. This emphasis upon equality had been especially developed in our relations with Latin American states, partly for their reassurance and partly because of their own history. No one in Europe questioned the American insistence on the equality of sovereignty, because that was what each European nation had been attempting to establish for itself as the symbol of its independence in the anarchic international world. Sovereignty thus had become a fetish in the political science of the nineteenth century, particularly in Germany. It was the absolute expression of nationalist terms, brooking no limitation by others, and insisting upon full and equal treatment in the councils of nations. Naturally, therefore, the League of Nations bore the traces of this absolute doctrine in the rule of unanimity in its voting which permitted small states to register an equal vote in the Assembly with the great powers. Compromise with reality had to be made in the Council of the League, where the great powers dominated because of their world-wide interests. But the theory of international relations remained that expressed by the Assembly. Under these conditions the League of Nations never came to final grips with its fundamental problem, that of dividing up the responsibility of its membership for emergency action to meet the threat of war. All through its history there was a long debate as to whether the League should be universal or regional, and the issue was never solved, because the theory of collective security was universal while in practice it was limited to the vital interests of nations and therefore local. The confusion of thought can best be seen in the fact that while France theoretically stood for the universal obligation of security, no Frenchman ever dreamed of sending *poilus* to Manchuria to preserve the peace of Asia. Evidently the problem of collective security has to be thought through again and in the practical terms furnished by the experience of this war.

The fact of the failure of the League of Nations is no argument against proceeding with the study of these plans, any more than the breakdown of the Articles of Confederation was an argument for the impossibility of a strong federal union of the United States.

Turning from these more general, if fundamental, issues to the detailed examination of the procedure to be followed by the United Nations, we come at once upon the need for international arrangements which can be relied upon in time of crisis. Because it is always dangerous to interfere between belligerents after war has started, provision should be made to arrange for the friendly acts of good neighbors while there is yet time to avert hostilities. The need for speedy action in case of any such threat to the peace is imperative. The only way to provide for this is to have a political body capable not only of offering the good offices of the community of nations but of taking immediate action against a nation which persists to the point of becoming a violator of the peace. The creation of such a body would provide against future crises in proportion as it succeeded in averting successive disputes and providing the basis for continuing peace.

The history of both world wars has shown that the strategy of peace must be as rapid as that of war. When the deadly time-table of the General Staff supplants the processes of diplomacy, the outbreak of war becomes almost inevitable; but if it is known that there is an immediate plan of action which will automatically be carried out against an aggressor, even a powerful nation will pause before using war as the instrument of its policy, because it could not achieve its end without incurring new dangers. The arrangements, however, must be definite enough and strong enough for nations to rely upon them. The provision for adequate police action, which this implies, will depend for its effectiveness upon that of the whole method of international cooperation provided by the United Nations and, more immediately, upon the degree of disarmament which all sovereign states should accept as the ultimate condition of membership.

While it is recognized that such preventive police action is a responsibility shared by all the United Nations, it is not shared by all equally. The responsibility should be varied according to the interest which each nation has in preventing any particular threat to the peace of nations and according to its power to meet the emergency. The application of this principle implies greater responsibility upon the part of the Great Powers than upon the small ones, whether the police action is exercised universally or regionally.

Political security is therefore a process which begins with the prevention of war by international action and lessens the temptation to resort to it by measures of disarmament. But it remains inadequate unless it provides alternatives for war designed to prevent disputes from becoming so embittered as to endanger the peace of nations. These range from fact-finding commissions, through mediation and arbitration tribunals to the Permanent Court of International Justice. Peace can be maintained only under a regime which safeguards justice and the respect for human rights in a changing world. There must be provision for peaceful change as well as for maintaining existing rights.

II

The Pacific Settlement of Disputes

(a) *The Test of Aggression*

Most disputes can be settled by the ordinary processes of diplomacy. But the members of the United Nations should accept the obligation to submit their disputes either to "political" methods, such as mediation, inquiry, conciliation and other methods of conference, or to "judicial" methods, by arbitration or judicial decision. Resort to force by any nation against another nation except for the maintenance of peace would thenceforth constitute the crime of aggressive war.

There is nothing new in the provision for methods other than war for settling disputes; they have been in existence throughout all history. But their use has for the most part been purely voluntary. The obligation to accept pacific means of settlement instead of war is the revolutionary fact of our own time. The approach to the statement of this obligation in the Covenant of the League of Nations was the phrase: that war or the threat of war anywhere in the world is a matter of concern to all nations, whether immediately affected by it or not. Nevertheless, the Covenant did not wholly close the door upon war because it provided that if the pacific means of settlement proved ineffective, the members of the League reserved to themselves the right to assert their claims by force of arms (Article 15, Paragraph 7). In 1924, the Assembly of the League sought to close this "gap in the Covenant" by the Protocol of Geneva which forbade nations to go to war in violation of a given pledge to use arbitration, judicial settlement or the good offices of the League itself. Resort to war in violation of this pledge was defined as aggression which all members of the League would be called upon to repress with means varying according to their geographical situation or special conditions. This Protocol registered a high water mark in the history of the League's effort to provide against aggression and its rejection was the first step in the progressive weakening of the League's authority of which Japan, Italy and Germany took advantage in the subsequent years.

The obligation to accept pacific settlement is, however, unreal unless the instruments of that settlement are adequate to the task. At first sight this may seem like a vicious circle; but the opposite is the case, for the surest way to perfect the methods of pacific settlement is to oblige nations to resort to them. History shows that this is true of all political institutions, but more especially of the institutions of justice where, so long as their use is purely voluntary, there is less reason for their development with the consequent result that they are less likely to be used.

Although the distinction does not always hold, it is customary to consider the provisions for the pacific settlement of disputes as falling into two separate categories, the political and the juridical, and for convenience this classification may be followed here. The chief political means are diplomatic negotiations between the disputing nations and the intervention of third parties by mediation, inquiry and conciliation. Without attempting any detailed analysis of these various measures, their relative setting in the international organization should be kept in mind.

(b) *Political Settlement of Disputes*

Political procedures are those which seek to adjust difficulties and disputes between nations, not by a verdict or decision as in the case of juridical procedures, but by reasoning with the parties or by bringing pressure to bear upon them so that they may be willing either to compromise or desist from their claims. Political procedures, therefore, do not necessarily deal directly with the rights involved in a dispute. Their chief concern is to find some satisfactory working basis for a peaceful settlement. Therefore they may fall back upon compromise rather than insist upon the full measure of a nation's claim. Political procedures are less rigid than juridical, for they take into account what a nation thinks about its case fully as much as the merits of the case itself.

Although provision for the juridical settlement of disputes is essential and a permanent court of international justice must be the final guardian of international law, nevertheless political procedures are far more important in the one great problem of the prevention of war. For the causes of war lie more in what a nation thinks another nation may do to it as a result of the quarrel than what the case itself really amounts to. This distinction is fundamental. There must be as definite provision for conciliation procedure in the realm of diplomacy as for that of a court in the realm of law.

Diplomacy has been blamed for its failures, but has never been given full credit for its successes. The reason is that the failures bring disaster into the lives of millions and are therefore known to all the world, while the successes are part of the normal conduct of international affairs. The substitution of pacific settlement for war will increase rather than lessen the importance of diplomacy, for it will continue to offer statesmanship the chance to deal with current problems in the relation of one nation with another. Its task will be the dual one of preventing resort to war and at the same time of preventing a possible overburdening of court or arbitration by excessive claims of litigant nations. It is largely in this way, by keeping disputes within the field of politics instead of allowing them to accumulate in undue measure before international tribunals, that the rigid character of compulsory jurisdiction finds a solvent through the give and take of negotiation under the changing conditions of economic and political life. It is of the utmost importance to realize that a world organization for the maintenance of peace does not lessen, but rather enhances, the activities and the place of government of each sovereign state in its relation with others.

The rules of the great game of diplomacy will be fundamentally changed when it can no longer fall back upon the implied threat of the use of power to carry out a nation's policies. But that will give it all the heavier task of ensuring a workable machinery of pacific settlement. Just what that machinery might be and how it might work is too large a subject to be covered here, but the following brief outline of its main divisions may clarify the problem.

First of all, there is mediation. It has its origin in diplomacy, but may develop a definite procedure of its own. It is the friendly offer of assistance by one state or power to help in settling the disputes of others with their consent. Its aim is the reconciliation of the conflicting parties, but until the middle of the nineteenth century mediation had very limited scope because of the theory of the absolute sovereignty which tended to regard it either as unwarranted intervention or as departing from that strict neutrality which professed indifference to the rights involved in the conflicts of other nations. A distinct step forward was taken, however, at the Conference of Paris in 1856, when the nations which had fought in the Crimean War issued a declaration that "states between which any misunderstanding might arise should, before appealing to arms, have recourse so far as circumstances permitted, to the good offices of a friendly power." In this tentative wording one can sense the delicacy with which the diplomats of the nineteenth century approached the problem. Nevertheless the Peace Conferences at the Hague in 1899 and 1907 built upon this slight beginning an impressive structure of agreements for giving effect to these "good offices" by arrangements for fact-finding, conciliation and arbitration. Resort to them was still voluntary, but both public opinion and practical statesmanship was moving ahead in the opening decade of the twentieth century, and a signal triumph was achieved in the use of mediation by Theodore Roosevelt to bring the Russo-Japanese War to an end by the Treaty of Portsmouth. Nevertheless as long as mediation remained the instrument of single nations or groups of nations, it was open to the suspicion of ulterior purposes. The Hague Conferences sought to meet this problem by provision for international panels which could be drawn upon for either fact-finding or judicial settlement. The voluntary character of the Hague Conference arrangements was finally dropped in the Covenant of the League of Nations which, in Article XI, boldly proclaimed the solidarity of all nations in the prevention and stoppage of war, and their duty to act upon it.

Inquiry or "fact-finding" is a procedure which grows out of mediation to acquire a technique of its own. The first formal provision for fact-finding bodies in international law was that of the Hague Conferences. A similar procedure, never tried out, however, in practice was that to be found in the Bryan Treaties for the Advancement of Peace, in which some thirty nations agreed with the United States to set up bilateral commissions, composed of their own nationals and neutrals, who should be ready in case of disputes to investigate the causes and in some instances, to recommend the settlements. These were not arbitration commissions, as many people seem to think, but provided a "cooling off period" or interval during which the commission would function and in which the disputing powers were not to go to war. Later on the disputants could "recover full liberty of action," which is the diplomatic phrase for the right to go to war. These Bryan Treaties were disparaged by so-called realists, but they embodied a basic if only an initial principle in the settlement of disputes.

They had, however, one great weakness which tended to destroy their usefulness. It proved impossible to maintain so many commissions in active service. The members chosen were necessarily experienced men of mature years, and as these died the governments either forgot or neglected to appoint their successors. Moreover, the method could not be applied universally because it would have called for some three thousand commissions to cover all nations. This difficulty could be met only by a multilateral body such as the Assembly of the League of Nations, representative of the whole community of nations.

It is doubtful if the statesmen at Geneva were conscious of having applied the method of the Bryan Treaties when they set up their commissions of inquiry, but it proved to be one of the most

THE PACIFIC SETTLEMENT OF DISPUTES 105

effective instruments at their disposal. In addition to the investigations carried on at Geneva itself, there were such important investigating commissions as that which visited the Balkans on the occasion of the threat of war between Greece and Bulgaria in 1925 and the Lytton Commission which even Japan finally asked for some months after the outbreak of hostilities in Manchuria in 1931. This forthright effort at the clarification of the causes of disputes with recommendations for future action has been justified by history outside of the League as well as within it, for it opens the door to other kinds of pacific settlement. Indeed it plays so large a part in the history of international relations that it may be regarded as the indispensable basis of the structure of war prevention. Its strength lies in the fact that it does not attempt too much; but that is at the same time its weakness, for the presentation of the facts in the case leads naturally to recommendations for settlement. At this stage, therefore, the technique of inquiry passes over into that of conciliation.

Conciliation is the effort to settle disputes without necessarily dealing with their content. It is best carried out in conference, when friendly powers sit around a common table and attempt to persuade the disputants not to resort to war even if they leave their dispute unsettled. Its strength lies partly in the incalculability of war and the great variety of issues which would be affected by it. It is particularly applicable to political disputes, which are those not essentially based upon the facts in the case but upon the fear of what another nation may do concerning those facts.

The causes of both world wars lay in this political field. In 1914 the ambiguous policy of Germany with reference to Austria's threats against Serbia led not only the Russians and the French, but the English also, to believe that punitive measures were only a pretext for imperialist designs upon Germany's neighbors, while Germany thought that Russia's determination to prevent an Austrian conquest of the Balkans was a dangerous expression of pan-Slavism. The tragedy of these major misunderstandings was bound to grow wherever the policies of a nation were dictated in time of crisis by the General Staff or by militarist adventurers. The second World War was not begun by Britain and France merely to defend a Polish frontier but to prevent a complete denial of international law, which endangered all future relationships.

Alongside these two examples of political disputes in which solution failed, it is encouraging to cite a case, not sufficiently well known, in which solution by the League of Nations prevented a European rupture of the first magnitude. In March, 1927, the Council had before it the revision of the Saar Valley administration at the end of the seven-year period of occupation. The Germans seized the occasion to demand that the French police in the Saar be reduced from eight hundred to five hundred men. The French Government answered that they could not accept this demand and still be responsible for law and order. But the issue was not presented to either the German or French people on the basis of practical needs. The German newspapers had flaring headlines that Germany must not permit France to maintain a disguised militarism over German citizens, now that Germany was a member of the League of Nations. The French newspapers replied with equal vehemence that France would not permit itself to be bluffed out of its responsibilities for the maintenance of peace. The issue thus had ceased to be three hundred policemen and had become one of the national honor of both great nations. The newspapers of all the continental countries fanned the flame of discord, and both Briand and Stresemann felt that if they yielded the jingo politicians back home would accuse them of having bartered their country's interests. The solution, however, was found by the Italian member of the Council, in a formula so simple and yet so pliable that no court of justice would have presented it as a verdict. France could maintain its right to eight hundred men but must never show that many at any one time! This was common sense in action and it saved Europe from a serious crisis. The hot passions subsided and the newspapers turned from the debate at Geneva to deal with other things. No one lost face!

Conciliation of this character is the "good neighbor" policy in practice. All through the long day's session in the Council Room at Geneva, Briand and Stresemann, although personal friends, never greeted each other or addressed each other directly. Both of them talked to the group of statesmen around the table and to the hundred journalists in the hall, whose telegraph messengers were keeping the wires hot for the European newspapers. The political issues were too near those of war and peace for anything resembling surrender, and the tense atmosphere of the room reflected the strained attitude of the chief actors in this, now forgotten, drama. But at the close of the day when the dispute between Germany and France had been reduced to its proper proportions by the subtle, realistic mind of Signor Scialoja, the two foreign ministers turned to each other with a smile, and then Stresemann said to Briand in a tone of solid conviction, "If we had had this instrument of peace-making in 1914, there would not have been a world war, would there?" The Foreign Minister of Germany to the Foreign Minister of France!

And yet what had been lacking in 1914 was not the device of conciliation, for that is but a natural development of diplomacy, but the opportunity for getting together to use it. When questions reach into the area of either "national honor" or "vital interests," —which have been the untouchables in diplomacy because of the latent danger of war—it has proved extremely difficult and sometimes impossible to improvise conferences to settle them; for both the questions at issue and persons appointed to deal with them are scrutinized with suspicious eye, and in these preliminaries negotiations may break down. It is therefore of the utmost importance to have a standing committee of the nations, such as the Council of the League of Nations, already in existence to which these disputes would come as a matter of course. In that way there is no ruffling of national susceptibilities, for diplomacy is following a normal course.

Once it is clearly seen that conciliation is the most important political device which diplomacy offers for preventing international quarrels from developing into war, it is nothing short of criminal negligence for the civilized nations to fail in providing a ready means for using it whenever the relations of one nation with another are embittered or empoisoned by accumulated animosities. The very existence of a permanent conference meeting at stated intervals for the transaction of routine business is an absolutely necessary part of the machinery of pacific settlement of international disputes. Its chief function will be the least dramatic, namely, dealing with serious questions before they accumulate the explosive power of popular emotions. The time to settle a dispute is before it has begun. That is why a league of nations—whatever name it bears—is indispensable; for the conference method provides the means for anticipating disputes as well as for settling them, because it brings the statesmen together in informal as well as formal meetings. The furthest step taken in bringing Germany and France together was taken by Briand and Stresemann in the dining-room of the little tavern at Thoiry, a few miles from Geneva. Such meetings are always a part of successful diplomacy, and the conferences of the League of Nations furnished more opportunities for holding them than foreign ministers or diplomats had ever known before.

The conference method of the League of Nations is therefore the best instrument which has yet been devised in all the history of politics for the international settlement of political disputes. And it is the political disputes which bring war. Against this case for the League, however, the fact remains that the trend of war proved stronger than all the hopeful forces of peace. Many people have therefore drawn the conclusion that the League itself was to blame for its own failure, and that the path to peace lies elsewhere. No one who has studied the antecedents of the second World War can accept this conclusion, in spite of the fact that the Geneva machinery failed to work and ultimately broke down. The reason for this failure lay not in the machinery which Geneva had supplied, but in the tragic fact that two Great Powers, Germany and Japan, were ready to risk everything to overthrow a system of international relations which did not satisfy their nationalist ambitions. The strangling of freedom in Spain and the bullying imperialism of Italy would never have carried Europe into the vortex had it not been for the raucous voice of Hitler, stirring all the latent animosities of Central Europe. It is true that the League was too slow and undecided in the face of the rising storm of demagoguery. But the conclusion to be drawn is not that the processes of peace cannot be made effective, for that would be surrendering everything to Fascist and Nazi ideology. Either we have to perfect the conference method as the outstanding instrument of peace, or we have to prepare for a third World War. Half-hearted fumbling for national security by isolation or nationalism is an invitation to the militarists to conspire again against the freedom of peace-loving nations, an invitation of which they will certainly avail themselves if it is offered them, because that is their way of life.

There is no escaping the responsibility for making a decision as to which side we are on in this momentous crisis between war and peace. There is no question but that the warlords and their dupes will do their best to weaken or ruin every effort to strengthen the instruments by which war can be prevented. In sheer self-defense, we must be on the side of those who are struggling to build up a system of international peace strong enough to be relied upon not only for the crises of threatened war but for the assurance of justice in times of peace. This, of course, does not mean yielding to every clamor of nationalist demagoguery. On the contrary, it calls for a growing recognition of the fact that justice between nations, as between individuals, is not what each one claims for itself but what the community as a whole regards as essential for the common welfare.

(c) *Justice and the Law*

Mention of the great word justice is a reminder of the fact that in discussing these political means for settling disputes we have covered only half of the field and have yet to deal with juridical methods and institutions. This is the very part of the problem which is uppermost in the minds of many because it deals with law and order, registering its conclusions in international law. What has been said about the greater importance of political disputes in questions of war and peace must not be taken as implying any slightest disparagement of the value of treaty engagements or of the procedures of judicial settlement; for if the international community is ever to have the kind of stable relationships which have been established within the state, there must be developed within it systems of law and order respected by governments and peoples alike. This development has long been under way but has been hindered and delayed by the doctrine of sovereignty which, in its absolute form, maintained the theory of complete freedom of action for a sovereign state. This doctrine, already known to the Founding Fathers, was developed in America by German-trained professors in the last quarter of the nineteenth century, and found a fertile soil in a continental state which had a history of isolation. While no longer taught in American colleges in the extreme form in which it was formerly presented, it has exerted an influence upon American thinking which is still strong enough to offer serious impediment to policies which represent the real interest of the nation. In the field of international politics it was frequently invoked as an excuse for stressing or asserting the voluntary character of international arrangements. Nevertheless, from the very necessities of the case, international law was recognized in theory, as the obligations of treaties were generally insisted upon. Indeed it may very well be argued that the practice of international relations was better than the theory. Until these last years, when the very basis of Christian morality was challenged by the Fascists and Nazis in the Axis countries, the theories of international law could hardly keep pace with the wide extension of international dealings.

This priority of action over theory is as it should be; it means that the actions of civilized nations are upon the whole better than might be expected when in theory they were free to go to war to enforce their claims at any time. The common sense of mankind deals with situations of this sort effectively. The recognition of the right of warfare by sovereign states has, of course, not meant its constant use or the constant threat of it in international dealings. Primitive societies take it for granted that foreigners are foes, and even among them there is a beginning of progress toward a more civilized state in the recognition of the religious status of envoys who come on missions of peace. From these crude beginnings developed the rules governing the relations of tribes and peoples with each other in both war and peace which, in the process of the centuries, furnished the principles of international law. A hurried glance back over this history is necessary for an understanding of the importance of international law in the world today.

The Greeks, to whom we owe the beginnings of politics, made only a small beginning in this field of inter-state relationships because, like modern states, they overemphasized the independence of each one, with the result that war was so constant between them as to prevent the growth of any solid body of collective action. The few federations they achieved were either too weak or too late. Though the Romans built up their empire by arrangements with their "allies and friends" as well as by war, they were the relations between conqueror and conquered, and ended in final fusion in one great state. The Law of Nations *(jus gentium)*, which was to play so great a part in the legal thought of the western world, was not international law, but a fusion of the laws of peoples within the universal Roman state, so as to provide for the varying experience of all the different cultures brought within the framework of the Empire. This principle of universality, moreover, found expression in the Stoic idea of a "law of nature" governing the lives of men and nations which it is the province of reason to discover and of statesmanship to apply. This principle was taken over by the early Church fathers and the great scholastics of the Middle Ages, as a secular counterpart to revealed truth. It was destined to become an argument for freedom against tyrants, especially in continental European countries where the Roman law had been revived, serving the cause of freedom in much the same way as did the Common Law in England. It is from this background that we come, in the opening paragraph of the Declaration of Independence, upon a phrase which was not intended as a flourish of rhetoric, but a statement of real fact. The United States began its career acknowledging that there are "laws of nature" as well as laws "of nature's God."

This historical background is necessary for an understanding of modern international law, for it is philosophy as well as practice. The law of nature which recognized the fundamental similarities in all mankind is the philosophic principle upon which it is based; but the practical questions with which it has to deal are rather those of the differences between nations than their common interests; for the greater part of the body of international law has had to do with the conduct of war. The title of Grotius' great work is *On the Law of War and Peace,* and it is evident from his biography that the second half of the title was an afterthought. The great service of international law lay in its insistence upon the maintenance of treaties, especially those humanizing war by lessening its scope and horror. In the course of the nineteenth century, international law was able to register such definite progress along this line that its masters looked to this process of the devolution of war as a method by which, as we have noted above, it might ultimately, at some distant date, be reduced to a vanishing point.

These aspirations were based, however, upon the old-time methods of warfare before the advent of the Industrial Revolution. With the rise of modern science, however, the daily life of soldiers changed fully as much as that of civilians, and war began to be fought by machinery with the result that in the middle of the first World War it became totalitarian. It seemed like a step backward to barbarism when whole nations mobilized, instead of merely armies, and grappled with each other in the mass production of death and disaster. When the first World War revealed this changed nature of war itself to a shocked world, there was reluctance to believe that such a denial of what has been called the laws of war was justified. Yet Germany, which was the initiator of this apparent retrogression to savagery, has been copied by other nations because it is now, and will henceforth remain, the nature of war itself.

So important is this conclusion that it is necessary to repeat it over and over again in every study of the organization of peace.

The last great effort of international law to set a barrier against the barbarism of war was at the Hague Conferences of 1899 and 1907, when an effort was made to codify the laws of war. When, however, these rules were tested in the first World War, none of the belligerents felt obliged to apply them whenever they stood in the path of victory. Instead, the scope of warfare widened and, although some international lawyers in the 1920's sought to restore what they continued to call the laws of war, the trend toward total war could not be checked, a fact only too clearly evident in the second World War.

The failures of international law should not lead us to discount it, for it is one of the necessary safeguards for the stabilization of peace. What is needed is a thorough-going reform of that law itself, denying the legitimacy of war as an instrument of national policy. This revolutionary denial has already been made and subscribed to in the Paris Peace Pact of 1928. The failure of that treaty to provide any means of enforcement other than public opinion, has led to such disillusionment that the very gesture has seemed to many sober observers a great mistake. That adverse judgment will not continue to be registered against the Peace Pact unless the peace settlement at the end of this war repeats the blunder of not providing for peace enforcement. For the declaration of the governments of practically all the nations in the world is now registered in support of a principle for which the second World War is being fought, that of the elimination of war itself as an instrument of national policy.

Unless international law is to remain a mere statement of rules of international anarchy, it must definitely pass into the new era in which its task will be the regulation of peaceful intercourse instead of war between nations. The conclusion in this field is the same as that in every other field of human relations: it is that the only way to secure a lasting peace is to accept the terms which science has prescribed. It was perhaps a mere chance that Adam Smith's *Wealth of Nations* should have appeared in the same year as the Declaration of Independence; but both of them were declarations of freedom from the restraints of the past which were hampering human freedom, the one in the economic sphere, the other in the political. The time has now come to join these two great declarations as the fundamental principles of a community of nations. Freedom and justice cannot survive in a world dominated by war or the threat of it, but war cannot be eliminated unless substitutes are found for it, not only in the recognition of the rights of others, but in the creation of institutions to maintain and strengthen the guarantee of those rights.

This is the task of international law in the future. It is one much closer to that of the Roman law of nations, for as we shall see in the course of the following analysis, it will some day have to deal with the rights of individuals as well as of nations. This development of international law cannot be left, however, to the mere chance of politics. There must be provision for bringing together for continued consultation the jurists and students of public affairs who can represent the thought and the mature statesmanship of nations divergent in culture and political experience. The condition of their success will be the denial of the legitimacy of war; for then and only then will international law be in a position to become an adequate embodiment of justice.

The fact that international law has been violated from time to time does not lessen its validity but rather calls attention to the need for providing a more effective safeguard for it than has hitherto existed. The procedures which it has developed—primarily those of arbitration and of court—are therefore fundamental in the structure of the post-war community of nations.

(d) *Arbitration*

Arbitration has a long history; it begins with semi-savage life when the cooler heads of tribes or peoples are called in to settle their disputes. Sometimes it is indistinguishable from the procedures of conciliation, but it tends to be more formal because it culminates in definite verdicts or judgments and not merely in finding a *modus vivendi* or stop-gap to be replaced by a more adequate solution when passions have calmed and the atmosphere is more favorable for workable adjustments. Arbitration, a stricter method than conciliation, narrows down to the heart of the issue itself. It is true that the word is used carelessly to cover all kinds of settlement, but it is a highly technical operation of law dealing with a subject which has been closely defined by the litigants in what is known as the *compromis*. This much of the procedure of settlement by arbitration it is necessary to know in order to understand the way in which the United States Senate exercises a decisive control over the whole operation so far as this country is concerned. For the Senate has always insisted upon recognition in every arbitration treaty of its right to decide whether the matters defined in the *compromis* were of the kind that we could arbitrate.

The insistence of the Senate on the right to pass upon the exact terms of reference for any arbitration has had a deadening effect upon the negotiation of arbitration treaties. It is not too much to say that owing to the Senate's insistence upon its rights, the United States has not a single arbitration treaty with any country which is more than a statement that the other country is one with which we are willing to arbitrate our differences if the question at issue is the kind of a question we think we should arbitrate when the time comes! A long line of great statesmen have criticized this right of the Senate as hampering the freedom of action of the government in its efforts to enlarge the scope of arbitration as a technique for international settlements. But the efforts of statesmen like Bayard, Hay, Root and Taft have always failed to overcome the Senate's maintenance of a prerogative lodged in it by the Constitution and defended as a means of checking the growth of executive power to invade the field of legislation by way of treaties.

The full discussion of this issue lies outside the scope of this study, but it must be admitted that the Senate has a case when it insists that arbitral judgments which become the law of the land should not cover too large a field without the legislative branch of the government having a chance to consider them. Constitutional law and international law overlap each other on this point. It is partly because of these difficulties in our own scheme of government that the less formal device of conciliation and conference is better suited for American participation than a wholesale series of engagements to arbitrate, for that would be impossible of fulfillment. Arbitration is no substitute for conciliation.

In spite of these limitations upon our action, it would be misleading in any general discussion of methods for preserving peace if the subject of arbitration were not kept to the fore. It was the most hopeful method of the nineteenth century, and the first world court, that of the Hague Conferences, was but a permanent court of arbitration. The movement for general arbitration treaties was strongest in the '80s and '90s. In 1887 no less than two hundred and fifty-four members of the British Parliament signed a memorial for all-in arbitration between Great Britain and the United States, and its presentation to President Cleveland was the occasion of great public meetings in this country. The movement for arbitration with Latin American countries was fostered in the conferences of American Governments and almost succeeded in overcoming the susceptibilities of the Senate just when President Roosevelt and Secretary Hull gave greatest impetus to the doctrine of the "good neighbor." But so far as the Senate is concerned, the practical political situation still remains but little changed. Under these conditions it is surely unwise to conceive of arbitration treaties as offering a substitute for the much more practical methods of pacific settlement which were worked out in the history of the League of Nations.

(e) *A World Court*

When the historians of the future look back through the long perspective of time to the troubled years of the first half of the twentieth century, it is quite likely that the two peace conferences held at the Hague in 1899 and 1907 will stand out much more prominently than many of the political events of the time which now engage our attention. For they were the first pioneering efforts to change the emphasis in international law from laws of war to those of peace, by bringing the movement for international peace from the field of theory and morals into that of practical politics. Had they been more revolutionary in temper or membership, they would have been better known today, but they were summoned by the Czar of all the Russias and their members were experienced statesmen and jurists who preferred to take a step at a time rather than to indulge in altruistic dreams. Moreover, the action of Russia in calling the conference had taken them by surprise and they were not wholly clear as to the real motives for it. Three freedom-loving nations, the United States, Great Britain and France, led in the advocacy of reform, while Prussian militarism showed its hand with its customary frankness and furnished a constant reminder of the kind of world they were living in.

While the declared purpose in the eloquent call of the first conference was disarmament, the American and British Governments, ably supported by the French, seized the occasion to draw up not only more civilized rules of war but also rules for systematizing arbitration as "the most efficacious and at the same time the more equitable method" of "settling disputes which diplomacy has failed to settle." [1] Thus both peace conferences relied upon arbitration as the best alternative for the age-old way of settling disputes by force of arms; but at the same time it was agreed that the proper scope of a court of arbitration was a very limited one, dealing with questions of "legal character" such as "questions of interpretation and application" of international conventions. In this carefully defined area the second conference went so far as to accept compulsory arbitration as an abstract principle. As we have seen above, however, and as the first World War was to make clear to everyone, it is not over such technical, juridical points that wars are fought, but over the political issues which lie behind them. The Hague Conferences went on to establish an institution at the Hague which bore the somewhat misleading title of "Permanent Court of Arbitration." In reality it was only an agreement for the appointment of a panel of distinguished jurists and statesmen from whom a board of arbitrators could be drawn by governments which wished to arbitrate. So little business came before this Court that some

[1] Convention for the Pacific Settlement of International Disputes, 1907, *Art.* 38.

governments, including our own, kept forgetting to keep their list of nominees complete. Ours is full at present.

At the second Hague Conference the attempt was made to take the further step and establish a Court of Arbitral Justice, as a permanent body meeting periodically and composed of a limited number of permanent judges. This effort failed, however, because the smaller states insisted upon equal representation which would make the Court absurdly large. No solution for this difficulty was found until 1920 when advantage was taken of the fact that the League of Nations offered two electoral bodies, the Council in which the Great Powers dominated, and the Assembly in which all nations had equal votes. By combining these two methods in the election of judges, it proved possible to satisfy both the small and the Great Powers and thus to replace the unratified draft convention for the Court of Arbitral Justice by the constitution of a new court to bear the lofty title, "Permanent Court of International Justice." As Mr. Root himself so clearly stated, the World Court, as it is known for short, could not have been founded but for the prior creation of the League of Nations. Nevertheless, although it is connected with the political organization of the League in this respect and in the provision for advisory opinions, it is an autonomous body planned to be as free from political influences as the Supreme Court of the United States.

It is important to recall the fact that in the thought of President Wilson the plans for a World Court were quite secondary to those of the political association of nations under the Covenant of the League. The only reference to it occurs in Article 14, which reads as follows:

> The Council shall formulate and submit to the Members of the League for adoption plans for the establishment of a Permanent Court of International Justice. The Court shall be competent to hear and determine any dispute of an international character which the parties thereto submit to it. The Court may also give an advisory opinion upon any dispute or question referred to it by the Council or by the Assembly.

This more or less left-handed way of ushering in the World Court has a page of history behind it which it is to be hoped will not be repeated this time.

When Mr. Wilson was elected President in 1912 he inherited the Hague Conference tradition which centered upon the Court as the fundamental instrument of achieving and maintaining peace. Its chief advocates were to be found in that galaxy of Republican statesmen who made such a deep impress upon the American mind in the first decade of the twentieth century—Hay, Root, Theodore Roosevelt and Taft. Theodore Roosevelt had been awarded the Nobel Peace Prize in May, 1910, not only for his success in stopping the Russo-Japanese War five years previously but also because of his advocacy of peaceful settlement by judicial procedure. On receiving that award, he went further than any American statesman had yet gone, in suggesting that there should be an international police force to enforce the "peace work of the Hague." The connection between this and the effort to secure American participation in arbitration treaties, which has been described above, was certainly in the mind of ex-President Taft when he led the movement during the first World War for "A League to Enforce Peace" which also was known as a movement for "A World Court League." President Wilson was not unsympathetic with the purposes of this organization, as was shown by his speech in Washington in May, 1916. But he had a deep-rooted distrust of lawyers and held back from full endorsement of the movement to make a court the center of world planning, because he feared that international law would furnish too conservative a basis for an association of nations, based primarily as the law was upon precedent and treaty. In a changing world and especially after the vast upheaval of the First World War he was fearful that a scheme of world government might be fastened upon the nations and especially upon the smaller nations which would tie them down to the rigid obligations of contracts which they had been forced to make in the past and from which there should be freedom of escape without disrupting the whole international order of things. He was also fearful of the pettifogging lawyer in politics, having in mind the fact that in some countries the lawyers have a monopoly of political office and that it would be natural for them to try to hale into court those governments which offered opposition to any of their countries' policies. In short, Mr. Wilson, while not refusing a proper place for the law and judicial procedure in international relations, definitely discounted them as the alternatives to war or the chief instruments of pacification.

It was not until 1920 that the Statute of the World Court was drafted by an "Advisory Committee" composed of ten distinguished jurists from different countries who, however, did not represent their governments but acted in their individual capacity. Mr. Elihu Root was the American member of this Commission. This Statute is relatively short and wholly clear in its wording. It falls into three main parts: organization, competence and procedure. We have already seen how the problem of organization or membership of the Court was solved by a compromise between the great and smaller powers which had already been worked out under the Constitution of the League of Nations. The second part of the Statute, dealing with the competence of the Court, raises an even graver issue than that of its membership—whether the Court should have voluntary or compulsory jurisdiction and, if compulsory, what limits should be set on it. The Advisory Committee of jurists recommended compulsory jurisdiction for disputes concerning the following matters: (1) the interpretation of a treaty; (2) any question of international law; (3) the acceptance of any fact which if established would constitute a breach of an international obligation; or (4) the nature and extent of the reparation to be made for such a breach. The Council and Assembly of the League refused to go this far, holding that the Covenant only intended to provide for a Court with voluntary jurisdiction. The matter was settled in a skillful compromise known as the "optional clause" of the Statute (Article 36) which left each nation free to accept or refuse the clause as it wished. Those accepting it would recognize the Court in advance as having compulsory jurisdiction with reference to the four kinds of disputes listed in the Statute, provided that the other party to the dispute had also accepted the "optional clause." Some fifty states have accepted this optional clause which thus by a paradox becomes compulsory for them within the limits indicated.

The Court was set up in 1922. Practically every state in the world has conferred jurisdiction upon it and some fifty-three states have become parties to the Statute. During the eighteen years of its history, prior to the outbreak of the second World War in 1939, some sixty cases had come before the Court and it had made substantial contributions to the development of international law. Its procedure has given general satisfaction and its rules, which are the result of long and careful elaboration, provide guarantees for the process of international adjudication which could not easily be replaced. More than five hundred international treaties have been concluded providing for the Court's jurisdiction, most of which are now in force. To preserve this vast structure of treaty law, there should be no break with the past, and under the system of international justice of the future the World Court should be given the place of honor which is due it.

Further problems are bound to arise in this field with reference to the adjustment of the Court to new and unforeseen situations and to the possible creation of other international tribunals of more limited scope for the settlement of technical and local issues, especially those arising out of the war. This is not the place, however, to analyze in detail the extension of the institutions designed to apply international law or to extend its scope by application. As we have repeatedly stated above, the legal development of the international community, important as it is for the guarantee of stable relationships among nations, is not a development which stands on the front line of defense against the outbreak of war. It is the political branch of international politics, not the legal or judicial, which must hold back the passions of belligerent nations by diplomacy, conciliation and mediation to give the opportunity for law and order to establish whatever claims of right are in dispute. Indeed, the World Court must, in self-defense, keep itself free from the distorting passions of the world of politics so as to bring to bear that impartiality of judgment which in course of time will make its place increasingly secure and bring all nations to accept its compulsory jurisdiction. The very fact, therefore, that the Court is not a prime instrument in the prevention of threatened war is the basis for its increasing importance in its own field of law. Standing in the background, and not in the forefront, of conflict, it is all the greater symbol of international justice.

III

The Enforcement of Peace

(a) *The Obligations of Enforcement*

IN ANY case of threatened war, the United Nations should first offer to the disputing nations any or all of the possible means of settlement—political, juridical, or both.

All nations should be obliged to accept the obligation not to resort to any other than peaceful means for the settlement of their disputes. For the enforcement of this obligation not to commit aggression, the United Nations should agree to carry out measures of prevention or redress against an offending state or against dictators who seize power and pretend to exercise the prerogatives of a sovereign state but fail to observe its obligations.

Whenever possible, the whole body of the United Nations should be given the opportunity to offer its good services for the prevention of war, much as in the case of the Assembly of the League of Nations. There should also be a small international body, similar to the Council of the League, charged with the duty of meeting emergencies by appropriate diplomatic and economic measures or by police action if necessary.

The member nations should accept the obligation to have in readiness plans for concerted economic action and supplies, and contingents of armed forces, for their mutual defense and to take whatever other steps are necessary for the maintenance of peace when it is menaced. Their military, naval or air establishments should ultimately be of a character which would limit them to the fulfillment of this obligation for cooperative defense, according to the specifications agreed to by the participating powers acting on the advice of experts, both military and civilian.

All of these measures would be lessened by the acceptance of two other obligations. In the first place, in addition to agreements for cooperative action if peace is threatened, the United Nations should also arrange to have available for emergency action an international air police force recruited by voluntary enlistment from various countries along with a sufficient number of international bases in different parts of the world. In the second place, there should be progressive reduction and limitation of armaments. This last problem, of disarmament, is discussed in detail in the next chapter. Here we limit ourselves to the positive measures of prevention.

The listing of the measures which should be taken against the outbreak of war should be carefully studied because it contains obligations which no nation should subscribe to unless it is prepared to carry them out. They are serious obligations reaching beyond those which the United States refused to assume in the League of Nations. But while they are more forceful than Article X or Article XVI of the Covenant of the League, upon which the chief debate was centered, they are at the same time more precise and therefore both more effective and less dangerous than the relatively vague commitments to "preserve as against external aggression the territorial integrity and existing political independence of all members of the League," leaving it to the Council to "advise upon the means by which this obligation shall be fulfilled." This was the famous Article X of the Covenant, and re-examined in the light of history, one can see how its opponents might very well read into the sweeping character of its commitments more than was intended or would have been followed out in practice. As a matter of fact, it was not invoked in all the history of the League, prior to the Manchurian episode.

While it is generally wise to keep the statement of political obligations from being too detailed, because one cannot foretell the circumstances in which they may be invoked, nevertheless in matters of war and peace it is important to be as clear as possible upon the arrangements which a nation makes or which are expected of it. There is a definite distinction to be drawn between the measures which would be taken by nations acting in cooperation and those taken by them jointly. In the former case their governments remain largely free to decide just how they shall fulfill the obligation of which they are reminded by the international body. In the latter case the international body itself acts in the name of the United Nations and on their behalf. In the plan outlined here, this joint police action of the United Nations is limited to air power, and the latter again is limited to use against only those nations that refuse to accept the pacific means of settlement to which they have subscribed and plan for war instead. And it would only be called upon by the unanimous consent of the executive committee, which would include the Great Powers.

Unless there are provisions for the enforcement of peace which are at the same time effective in checking militaristic nations or imperialist adventures, the whole plan for the erection of a system of lasting peace falls to the ground. For the supreme lesson of the second World War is that there are factions in the world which deny that a system of enduring peace between nations is possible or even desirable. The issue which the Axis powers thus force upon us is one which must be met either in their terms or our own, either by permitting the continuance of the present anarchy of nations with the inevitable threat of a third World War or by putting the preponderant forces of freedom-loving nations behind the maintenance of peace.

The issue is one which cannot be evaded, for the consequence of evasion is the victory of militarism, which, in another war, would carry with it destruction so great as to overthrow the entire structure of civilization. If there were to be no organization of peace, and each nation were therefore left to itself, it would be obliged to seek safety either by denaturing its industries in time of peace to make them wholly subservient to defense, in conjunction with equally dislocated military allies, or by compromising its independence at the behest of powerful neighbors. In a future so given over to the fear of a third World War, the frightful cost of the present war could not be recovered, for the economics of peace are the opposite of those of war. Prosperity would have to yield to the provision for safety or for conquest. "Guns instead of butter" was no figure of speech in the Germany which prepared for the present war. It will be the watchword of all national economics in the postwar period if arbitrary force is to determine human relations.

It is only against this alternative that the provision for an international organization of safety becomes practical and realizable. No compulsion less than the danger of ultimate destruction could force free, independent, peace-loving nations to assume the responsibilities of international policing. Even as it is, those responsibilities should be maintained only at the minimum, and the principle of voluntary association should be adopted as far as can be done without lessening confidence in the reliability of international action.

The proposals set forth here are based upon the foregoing principles and are entirely conditioned on the degree of disarmament which the United Nations will accept as a further guarantee of their pacific intentions. No provision for international policing can possibly work among nations so heavily armed as the leading nations will be at the close of this war. On the other hand, the provision for policing becomes progressively easier with each step taken in the limitation and reduction of armaments.

(b) *Land, Sea and Air Power*

The magnitude of the revolution in human affairs which would be caused by the elimination of war as an instrument of national policy becomes apparent when we realize that the only use of warlike force permitted to a nation would be in the prevention of war itself by cooperative action. The Covenant of the League recognized the need for peace enforcement but compromised with the military tradition of statecraft by permitting war as a last resort. The Briand-Kellogg Pact attempted to avoid the difficulties by omitting any reference to police action, leaving enforcement to the "public opinion of mankind." Realistic statesmen at the time registered their sense of the incompleteness of the gesture which was best expressed by Briand himself in his address to the assembled diplomats on the occasion of the signing of the Pact: "Peace has been proclaimed and that is well. That is much. But peace has yet to be organized. For settlement by force we must substitute settlement by law." That was in August, 1928. The warning words and the exhortation of Briand, although clothed in as solemn eloquence as the Gettysburg address, remained unheeded and the only "sanction" or peace enforcement which this country evolved was the so-called Stimson or Hoover Doctrine, that conquest of territory or terms imposed by force of arms would not be recognized. This seemed like a way of enforcing law without the use of force, a kind of legal boycott of a warring nation so far as its ill-gotten gains were concerned. It was a doctrine with a fairly long history in the relations of American countries, going back to the first Conference of American States which met in Washington, under Secretary Blaine, in 1889; but it was applied, in support of the Briand-Kellogg ideology, in the struggle over Manchuria, first as between Russia and China in 1929 and then as between Japan and China in 1932. On the second occasion it was taken over by the League of Nations in a resolution passed by the Assembly, the only action taken by the community of nations against that Japanese aggression which was the real beginning of the second World War. The futility of such temporizing methods has now been taught the world at the cost of millions of lives and the greatest crisis in all the history of nations. The only way to have law and order among nations is for the lawbreaking governments and peoples to know that the only use of force which can be permitted is that in the service of peace.

It is a sad truth, however, of which there is ample evidence in history, that power, even when devoted to the maintenance of good causes, is a dangerous instrument unless it is circumscribed and limited to prevent its falling into hands which may misuse it. The domestic history of national states is largely filled with instances of struggle against arbitrary power and safeguards to prevent its rise. The same or even greater precautions must be kept in mind in the upbuilding of the international community because it is not yet ready for anything resembling a super-government. That is sufficient reason why the time has not yet come for the community of nations to have under its own command vaster forces than any single nation or alliance can bring together.

Fortunately that is not the way in which the problem need be faced. It is wholly wrong to think of the contributions which nations may make in opposing a war already begun as constituting police action. The only provision for international policing which should be considered is that of war prevention. The suppression of war by force of arms must equally be provided for, but sovereign nations will not readily sign away to an international authority the right to command their own armies and navies in time of war. But that is not the question at issue. International police action is as different from the mobilization of a nation's armed forces for defensive war as the local policing of town or city is different from the military establishment of the nation. The purpose of the policeman is two-fold: to remind lawbreakers of the presence and vigilance of the law and to stop the crimes of individuals in a locality. For these purposes not much armament is needed, and in some instances none at all, as for example in the case of the London police not even armed with a club. The one thing that is essential is that the police should be on the spot as soon as possible whenever crime is planned or committed. If the disorders spread, they may result in the breakdown of organized society and even the danger of civil war. Then a wholly different situation arises, to provide against which the nation must maintain reserves of National Guard, Army or Navy.

This distinction between the action of police and that of the military establishment of nations is of the utmost importance in any planning for the international system of peace enforcement. There is no need to arm the international community with a sufficiently large military or naval force to meet all the emergencies of war. This is fortunate, for no one knows the arithmetical ratios of the armed forces of nations, which would have to be worked out beforehand; much less the combinations of power of neighboring or allied States. The plans must be drawn to make unnecessary any such resort to militarism in the name of peace. The way to do so is just as in home affairs, by having a police force that is adequate to protect the citizen from crime. Too large a police force would endanger personal liberty, too small a force would be insufficient against violence. Fortunately, modern science, by the invention of the airplane, has at last provided the nations of the civilized world with the means for having just such a limited but efficient police force. Before its advent as a military weapon, it was impossible for a policing expedition to reach many a scene of possible disorders without providing for the transit of armies across the territories of unwilling states. And governments conspiring against the peace could count upon these difficulties of access to achieve their purposes by quick and decisive action.

The airplane has changed all this, for there is now no spot anywhere on earth that cannot be reached within sixty hours from some central airport. But more important still is the fact that it is the airplane which has brought the fear of war into the daily lives of those nations which have resorted to it most as the instrument of their policy. Not since the days of the Thirty Years' War or the ravages of part of Germany in the days of Frederick the Great has Germany itself experienced the horrors of war like those of fire and sword until now. But this time they are immeasurably greater. The haunting fear of the fire bomb on the flimsy houses of Japan is the only terror that strikes home to that fanatic nation. Here then is the instrument ready at hand for the enforcement of peace in true police technique. For no government can hide away in a distant capital and escape the consequences of its acts.

This reminder of the effectiveness of the airplane in war is not adduced here to suggest that its peacetime service on international police duty would resemble this cumulative horror. On the contrary, as has been said above, the very efficiency of this instrument of destruction in war would render its actual employment unnecessary in most cases. The point to be borne in mind is that if a nation knows that the horrors of war can be brought home to it, it will be less likely to try to inflict those horrors on others. In order, however, to have sufficient swiftness of action, air police should be under the direct authority of the international organization, for only in that way will the organization be able to count upon anticipating the aggressor. It would not be necessary to have such an air force heavily armed or heavily manned to check any initial tendencies toward war if at the same time other precautions were taken, such as the general reduction of armaments and increased provision for economic and political adjustment in national policies. All of this, however, is a matter for technical study and the case must not be prejudiced, as we shall see when we come to discuss the reduction of armaments.

There is also an argument from history in support of the proposal to limit an international police force to the airplane and its necessary equipment and bases. There is no reason why the airplanes should have the bad effect which has been the case when armies or navies are used to establish or maintain peace. Both militarism and navalism interfere with a nation's prosperity and if carried to the extreme, destroy it. The outstanding examples of the militarization of the state are Rome and Germany. In both cases the civilian power lost its freedom of action, becoming bureaucratized in order to meet with efficient management the ever-growing needs of the military establishment. Thus the state became rigid and the citizens lost their liberty by the very process which impoverished them. Naval power has the advantage over land power, that its economic effects are less apparent, because the nations which it may exploit are those of other lands and while it may impose imperialism upon them, it does not destroy the liberties of the country using it. The best examples are ancient Athens and the Netherlands and Britain in modern times. The measure of the advantages enjoyed by naval power in comparison with land power can be seen in the readiness with which it can be lessened or given up by the commercially minded folk who take to the sea. The contrast between the development of the British Empire into a Commonwealth of Nations and the failure of Germany to throw off the yoke of Prussianism are examples which should occur to everyone. Nevertheless both sea power and land power involve a great expenditure of a nation's resources and finally require them all for total war.

Over against these vast and dangerous procedures, air power opens a different perspective, partly because so little of it can reach so far and partly because of its prodigious power of concentrated destruction, so that if used in time it may make unnecessary the extreme diversion of national economies. In short, if it can serve as an effective police force rather than as one of the arms in total war, it may well furnish the third step in the process of pacification, preserving the liberties of its users without imposing continuous subjection upon those against whom it is used. It reduces international policing to a minimum; and yet offers a safeguard against the dangers of international anarchy against which individual nations would have to arm more heavily than before. It would be therefore not only a relatively light burden in itself but would lessen the total burden of war preparation.

The fact that air police reduces the problem of peace enforcement to its lowest terms does not, however, mean that those terms are low. On the contrary, its acceptance by the United Nations raises many new questions, some of which we are by no means ready for. The relation of the policing airplanes to the problem of civil aviation is but one of many which will confront the planners of law and order in the post-war world. The regulation of international civil aviation will be difficult enough in itself but it will be very much increased if there is an international air force. On the other hand, it will be far more difficult if there is no joint effort to prevent civil aviation from developing military potentialities to threaten again the peace of the world. Agreements for the reduction of armaments, which are treated in the following section of this study, will be ineffective unless there is inspection, and inspection will be ineffective unless there is policing behind it.

When these principles are accepted, the problem passes from generalities to that of finding the practical terms for its solution. This is largely a technical matter involving such questions as the possibility of creating a type of airplane which will be especially fitted for police use, a problem to which airplane engineers have already given some thought. To the engineering problems will be added new problems in international law; but these are inescapable in any case and therefore do not constitute a special obstacle to aviation police.

The way in which an international air police could be established is also a question of practical politics, for it could most naturally grow out of the terms of surrender of the Axis powers which, stated in the Atlantic Charter, will call for their complete disarmament, including, of course, disarmament in the air. With the elimination of any immediate danger from this quarter, the adjustment of the air force by the United Nations presents less difficulty than would ever be the case again if this opportunity were neglected. Complicated as it is, the technical problem is by no means so far-reaching as that which the disarmament conferences have grappled with. But as in the case of disarmament, the final obstacle to be overcome will remain the political question of whether the United Nations are really willing to assume the responsibilities which are inescapable in the maintenance of a lasting peace; or whether they are willing to accept the far heavier responsibilities, with truly terrifying consequences, of a third World War.

(c) *Teachings of the Christian Churches*

So far we have been considering the provision for peace enforcement as a part of the development of law and order among nations in which the use of force by legitimate authorities is taken for granted. There remains, however, alongside of and underlying the field of law, the sphere of morals in which the problem of enforcement is not physical but mental and spiritual. It is in this latter field that the great systems of religion chiefly operate to determine the course of human events; and yet with only one great exception religion has supported the use of power by governments or those who could establish their claim to sovereignty. The great exception—there are others of less importance—is that of those Christian sects which have taken the Sermon on the Mount literally and apply its teachings of non-resistance without either qualification or reference to other texts in the Bible.

Although throughout history these "non-resisters" have always been a very small minority of the total population, they have exerted a great influence upon the attitude of Christian peoples toward war and peace, because they can cite in support of non-resistance some of the noblest passages in the utterances of the Christ. Nowhere in the world's literature has there been a greater challenge to political "realism" than that of Jesus when he asserted the supremacy of the moral law of love governing all mankind over against even such triumphs of law as the use of force to compel the recognition of one's rights. To turn the other cheek for the added blow of the aggressor is an apparent defiance of the very principle upon which justice has been established in every civilized land. For the aggressor must be restrained from his career of crime or there is no civilization left. As long as the early church was powerless and insignificant, these political issues raised by the Sermon on the Mount were of little importance. But the question came to the fore as Christianity grew in strength just prior to the time of its recognition as a state religion by Constantine at the opening of the fourth century, when the era of persecution, largely based upon the charge of anarchy and disloyalty to the state, gave way to that of an almost imperial power. Fortunately the theologians could cite a whole series of other texts from the New Testament which dealt with the question of the use of force in more practical terms, while leaving the fundamental principle of charity as basic for Christian conduct. There was above all the admonition to "render unto Caesar the things that are Caesar's." This would naturally apply to military service as well as to the payment of taxes, a fact emphasized by the readiness of Jesus himself to have dealings with a centurion. Therefore the church fathers held that war for a just cause was permissible and only war for an unjust cause should be renounced. This distinction became the basic doctrine of the Church from the days of Augustine who formulated it, just after Rome had been taken by Alaric and when the Vandals were already on their way.

But how was one to know which wars were just and which were unjust? No final answer to this question was ever given down to our own day. As long as the Roman Empire was a political unity, the presumption was that fighting for the emperor was fighting for law and order against violence, and that was about as far as the theologians carried the distinction. But when the modern state system broke up the unity of the political world, each sovereign claimed that his cause was just and generally succeeded in mobilizing the clergy of his country behind him.

The Established Church in England and the Lutheran in Protestant Germany proclaimed and applied the principle that the religion of the country should be that of the ruling prince (*cujus regio ejus religio*). Under such conditions it was but natural that among the Protestant dissenters there should develop sects which, looking back to the early Church, renounced all use of force and refused military service. Of this trend, the Quakers in England and the Mennonites in Germany have been the outstanding representatives, and their conscientious revolt against all war has not only remained a dominant principle in their lives, but also made its influence felt in varying degrees in other Protestant churches. Among the Baptists and the Methodists, especially, non-resistant pacifism was sufficiently strong to create political opposition to any plan for international organization which relied upon the use of force for the maintenance of law and order.

This uncompromising section of the peace movement registered its greatest triumphs in the so-called Neutrality Laws of the 1920's, which were designed to keep the United States out of any war by preventing it from offering help to a belligerent even if the victim of aggression. The immorality of this act, which made the United States a potential accomplice with aggressor nations by treating them in the same way as the law-abiding nations, was at last brought home to the American people when the Axis Powers showed clearly that the rigid policy of aloofness of the United States was an added incentive to them to proceed with their aggression against others. It is perhaps going too far to say that the neutrality legislation was unfair to the militarist governments that

THE ENFORCEMENT OF PEACE 135

were planning war because we misled them as to our ultimate purposes; but it was certainly no help to peace for the most powerful industrial nation in the world to place its resources at the disposal of lawless nations.

Non-resistance as a practical doctrine can find its realization only in a world in which there is an efficient organization of peace to take the place of war, with instruments for conciliation of political disputes and justice for those which can be settled in court. The only way to establish these conditions is by refusing to allow resort to war; and that refusal must be buttressed and supported by police. Thus the ultimate aim of Christian teaching is achieved, as in all human things, by the long and painful road of political evolution, similar to that which has established peace within the state.

IV

The Reduction and Control of Armaments

(a) *General Statement*

THE great word "disarmament" needs definition. It is not a simple and absolute fact but a continuous and varied process. No one in authority in any country believes that the time has come for total disarmament. In a world not yet quite civilized, governments and peoples must have the right to defend themselves against disorders within their territories as well as against dangers from without. When, therefore, we talk about "disarmament" we really mean "the reduction of national armaments to the lowest point consistent with national safety and the enforcement by common action of international obligations," to quote from the text of the Covenant of the League of Nations. The extent of this "reduction and limitation of armaments" must take into account the geographical situation and the circumstances of each state. But the fact that different countries have different problems of law and order at home and security from external dangers must not be used, as in the past, to permit rivalries like the race in armaments which preceded the first World War or the unilateral resort to armaments like that of the Axis Powers before the second World War. The lesson of history is clear on this point. The "reduction and limitation of armaments" must this time be general and thorough-going. It must mean substantial disarmament.

Not all of this will take place at once, but there should be provision for it by the United Nations. It is a continuous process because of the progress of scientific discovery and invention. No single international agreement can deal with more than a fraction of it at any one time, and that fraction may turn out to be of minor importance. Therefore a Commission on Disarmament will be necessary to study and recommend appropriate measures to the United Nations. This Commission should be composed of both civilian and military experts and should be charged with the duty of inspecting the condition of armaments in all countries and reporting to a central political body of the United Nations.

This is perhaps the most urgent single problem confronting the postwar world, because if it is not solved the whole structure of provisions for lasting peace will either fall to the ground or will become so weakened as to be unable to meet the shock of another aggression by a powerful nation. At first sight it may seem utterly beyond solution because of the vastness of the armaments of the second World War and because of the feeling of insecurity which may very well linger on in those parts of the world which have suffered most and which therefore will want to defend themselves in the old accustomed way of national armaments. Moreover, the advocacy of "disarmament" has been too closely associated in years following the First World War with non-resistant pacifism to be well received even in quarters which are not militarist at heart. It carries too much of the suggestion of helplessness in time of trouble, and the experience of the European nations which Germany so easily overran in 1939 and 1940 is cited as a warning against incautious idealism in dealing with such terribly realistic problems as those of war and peace.

These are but some of the political, that is to say, psychological obstacles to any thorough-going reduction of national armaments in the post-war period. Nevertheless the situation is not so hopeless as it may seem at first, because the nations which have been the chief producers and users of armaments, the Axis Powers, will be forced to surrender them and destroy the means for replacing them. This part of the process of disarmament, which in normal times would be the most difficult, therefore promises to be the easiest. The disarmament of the Axis powers is not, however, a proper subject for the post-war organization of peace with which we are dealing here. It will be carried out by the military authorities of the United Nations as one of the final acts of the war. Nevertheless, these military measures must be more than temporary to be effective, for the ex-enemy nations must not be permitted to begin again that sinister process of rearmament which made possible their early triumphs in the second World War. As time goes on they must come under the continuing oversight of the United Nations and its technical committees in order to ensure good faith in the performance of their obligations. This second phase of the disarmament of the Axis powers raises the question of the willingness of the United Nations to disarm themselves. While the terms of surrender are not likely to contain any such contractual phrase as that of the Treaty of Versailles, which was that German disarmament was "in order to render possible the initiation of a general limitation of the armaments of all nations," the implication just the same will be there. For it will be impossible to keep one half of the world disarmed and retain the armaments of the rest.

There is of course no reason for supposing that the United Nations will want to maintain a heavy burden of armaments or will be able to do so. There would be no surer way of keeping alive the animosities of the present war and of blocking the return of prosperity than by a continuation of the false economic structure of militarism. War, having become an engineering industry, the demobilization of its establishments and the reduction of armaments are to a very large degree technical matters. The creation of a Commission on the Reduction and Control of Armaments should therefore be one of the first acts of the United Nations, as soon as they shall have organized politically on a continuing basis. The final decisions on all armament questions are political, and must be made by the United Nations in conference, but the details will have to be worked out on technical as well as political grounds. Until that Commission is set up and its work gets under way, it is idle to speculate as to the armament program of the future. All that can be stated now is that it must measure up to the needs of the community of nations, which will be lessened in proportion as those powers which have a tendency to dangerous militarism are rendered helpless. There should be little trouble in getting rid of all the heavy armaments which are needed in a major war like the present. The real problems will be those of war potentials, especially in the chemical industrial fields, and of setting up provisions for peace enforcement which cannot be misused by nations conspiring against the peace.

Because disarmament is a symbol of peace and a symbol which everyone can understand, one might expect to find encouragement from its history, but the efforts to lessen armaments in the past are anything but encouraging. The first resounding challenge to a world in arms was issued in St. Petersburg in August, 1898, when the Czar of all the Russias, the ill-fated Nicholas II, speaking through his Foreign Minister, called for a conference to rid the world of the "crushing burden" of the cost of armaments. "Economic crises," he pointed out, "due in great part to the system of massing armaments to the point of exhaustion and the continual danger which lies in this accumulation of war material, are transforming the armed peace of our days into a crushing burden which the peoples have more and more difficulty in bearing. It appears evident then, that if this state of affairs be prolonged, it will inevitably lead to the very cataclysm which it is desired to avert, and the impending horrors of which are fearful to every human thought." The first Hague Conference, which met the following year in response to this call, failed utterly to reach agreement on even the matter of the limitation of military expenditure. All that it succeeded in doing was to pass the following meaningless Resolution:

> The Conference is of the opinion that the restriction of military charges which are at present a heavy burden on the world is extremely desirable for the increase of the material and moral welfare of mankind.

The Resolution did not even express the opinions of the countries taking part in it, for they were not named. It only expressed the opinion of the members present who thought it worth while to vote for it. The second Hague Conference in 1907 made no further progress, merely confirming the Resolution of 1899 and stating that "It is eminently desirable that the governments should resume the serious examination of this question." Seldom has there been a more complete fiasco in a major question in international relations.

After the first World War the movement for the reduction of armaments succeeded at least in clarifying the problem. It showed that, when viewed without prejudice, very definite steps could be taken to eliminate the menace of armament rivalries. The Disarmament Conferences at Geneva covered all the political and technical problems and, in spite of popular misconceptions arising from their ultimate failure, they contributed much upon which future action will be based. The long, wearisome and discouraging effort finally ended in proposals which, had they been carried out, would have reduced the military establishments of the world by over 70 per cent. Even Germany agreed to the proposal to abolish the submarine, which the smaller powers and France were reluctant to give up in the mistaken belief that it afforded defense against navalism. This incident shows the complicated nature of the problem of arms reduction. But it also shows the urgent need for universal agreement, for Germany used the technical disagreements at Geneva as one of its excuses for withdrawing from the Conferences and openly beginning its rearmament. While Germany's withdrawal was resented, the other Powers were not in a strong position to protest, because they had reached no settled policy upon some of the major questions. There was no longer confidence in collective security through the League of Nations, but the peace-loving nations were unwilling to face the consequences of this fact, while the Axis Powers went ahead to make the most of it. The event showed that there was no security outside the League; but that was to be the lesson of the tragic years ahead.

While armament does not create wars, they cannot be fought without it. Had Germany not rearmed, it could not have overrun Europe, but the other nations furnished it with a pretext by their partial measures, and awoke too late to the consequences of a policy of compromise which played directly into the hands of the militarists. The lesson from this history was obscured by the fact that when Germany got ready to use its armaments the other nations were not so well prepared. There will, therefore, be strong demands that the freedom-loving nations keep their powder dry for the next possible conspiracy against their freedom. The flaw in that reasoning is that this is just what they were trying to do when Germany took advantage of their indecision. For non-militaristic people will never be willing to make sufficient sacrifice to have enough dry powder to guarantee their safety. The advantage in such policies of partial disarmament will always lie with those nations which are willing to give up their butter for guns; because the preparation for war today calls for a complete surrender of accustomed ways of living which no free people is willing to accept before the actual outbreak of war itself.

The peace-loving nations must, therefore, in their own interest be willing to engage in a progressive scheme of arms reduction which will be thorough-going and universal. It is recognized that such a policy cannot be fully realized in the period immediately following upon the war, for the problems of police will be greater than ever before. The more serious of these problems will, it is true, solve themselves in the days immediately following upon surrender; but some of them, as we shall see below, will remain as a continual challenge to the maintenance of peace. Therefore the United Nations will need to retain some military force for international policing. But in proportion as the military establishments are liquidated, the armaments required for policing will also become less and less. How fast or how far this process will go in our time, no one can tell.

Finally, armaments are not only a potential danger in themselves; they constitute a symbol of a nation's strength and a reminder of its history, of the sacrifice of patriots, and of its unity of purpose in the face of danger. Any major reduction of armaments will fail in any country if it involves the renunciation of these age-old symbols for an unreal internationalism that takes no account of history. On the other hand, the cooperation of free nations in their own interests as well as that of other peoples is a process which has been slowly developing throughout the whole history of civilization, for it is nothing less than the recognition of the moral law as a supreme guide to the conduct of nations as well as of individuals.

(b) *Disarmament Conferences Between the Two World Wars* [1]

Only once in history has the peace movement supplied a drama equal to that of war. This was at the Washington Conference on the Limitation of Armaments in 1921-22, when Secretary Charles Evans Hughes, taking most, if not all, of the delegates completely by surprise, proposed in the name of the United States that the great sea Powers should not only halt the building of battleships but should actually destroy a percentage of those already built, and that they should henceforth keep to an agreed ratio. The race in armaments was to give way to cooperation in limiting and lessening the chief instrument of sea power. Never before had any government taken so bold a step. The Hague Conferences had failed to secure the adoption of any such plan for practical measures of disarmament. The League had only just begun to explore the intricacies of the field. And here, suddenly, from the nation that held aloof from Geneva, came leadership.

The challenge to the imagination of the world which lay in the act of Secretary Hughes was destined to influence the whole direction of the peace movement for the next twelve years. The spectacle that it offered—in anticipation of the fact—of nations towing battleships out to sea and sinking them in the cause of international good will, was much more absorbing than the dull routine of discussion in the bodies of the League or of argument in courts or arbitration tribunals. It was then that success or failure in disarmament became, for most people, including most statesmen, the acid test of the peace movement itself. The authority of men like Lord Grey of Fallodon was invoked to prove that the race in armaments had been the prime cause of the World War itself—a theory widely shared in a grossly exaggerated form. The more cautious students of politics, who could not wholly share

[1] The text of this section is an abridgment and revision of Chapter X of my volume *The Rim of the Abyss* (New York, Macmillan, 1937).

the conviction that peace was dependent upon disarmament, found themselves classed among the "militarists" and "navalists" who were frankly out to save armaments for the free exercise of their old-time uses.

As a matter of fact, the solution at the Washington Conference of the problem of naval disarmament was much too simple. A ratio was set for capital ships allowing three to Japan for every five allowed each to Great Britain and the United States. The ratios of the other Powers were so much lower that they hardly came into the picture. The basis of this arithmetic was that Japan would need fewer ships because they would only be needed in the far eastern seas, while Great Britain and the United States have world-wide interests. Japan accepted the ratio at the time, in spite of its apparent recognition of a slightly inferior status in naval power, because it left the Japanese navy supreme in the Far East. This was bound to be the case because of the lack of an international police force, which was a proposal utterly remote from the ideas dominant at the Conference. Nevertheless, in spite of the temporary advantage which it had gained by the tacit recognition of a Japanese sphere of influence in Asiatic waters, Japan grew restive under what seemed a failure to recognize the importance of prestige or, as the Japanese call it, "face" in the unequal ratio.

Indeed misunderstandings began at once, even in the Washington Conference itself. The impression which had been created, that Secretary Hughes' dramatic act was planned without reference to its political implications, was a mistake that beclouded most subsequent negotiations. Although the formula 5:5:3 became a popular slogan in the United States, it soon became evident that no single measuring rod could calculate sea power. Naval engineers devised other craft and other instruments of war to fill the gap created by the Conference limitations. The result was that year by year throughout the twelve years following the Conference, armaments grew by leaps and bounds. It was clear that the problem could not be solved by any simple mathematical equation. But if one studies the diplomacy which made possible Mr.

Hughes' success, one finds that the arithmetical solution was only reached after long and involved negotiations with reference to the political problems involved in the then existing alliance of Japan with Great Britain. It was a statesman who was not present at the Washington Conference, Arthur Meighen, the Prime Minister of Canada, who made the settlement possible by inducing the British Government to denounce its alliance with Japan. This important service of Canada to the United States took place at the Imperial Conference in London in 1920, and was largely due to the influence of one of the most powerful molders of public opinion in Canada, John W. Dafoe, the editor of the *Winnipeg Free Press*. Although the Japanese alliance was defensive and had included a clause releasing Great Britain in case of war between the United States and Japan, the alignment of naval rivalries was such that the United States, standing alone, could hardly have risked curtailing her building policy so long as the alliance stood.

All this means that disarmament is a fact of politics, the expression of political relationships, and that the resultant mathematical formulae tell only part of the story. Political relationships are the most uncertain elements in history, and it is rare indeed that they can be adequately expressed in terms of arithmetic. Nothing is more misleading than statistics in the hands of those who do not appreciate the variables in the character and outlook of peoples. The strength of nations depends upon imponderable, incalculable factors fully as much as upon the material elements that can be stated in terms of an equation. The outstanding illustration of this fact is the contrast between China and Japan.

But mathematical formulae have this advantage, that in their simplest forms they impose themselves upon the mind with the force of a conclusion that seems final and inescapable. The diplomatic side of the Washington Conference, although it was registered in the Four-Power Pact and the Nine-Power Treaty, providing for the use of pacific procedure in the settlement of disputes affecting the area of the Pacific and China, did not seem to lend itself to future development as did the ratios of naval disarmament. Here was a key that seemed to fit or to be adjustable to fit other doors that were closed along the pathway of international peace. Small wonder, then, that in succeeding years the movement for disarmament should concentrate upon finding arithmetical ratios for armies as well as navies.

Spurred on by the British, the League of Nations tried to work out a system of comparative strengths for the standing armies of Europe. There was, for instance, the plan of Lord Esher, according to which the unit in man-power should be 30,000 men for the military and air forces. France could have 6 units, or 180,000 men; Italy and Poland each 4 units, or 120,000 men; Belgium 3 units, or 90,000 men; and others proportionately in a definitely established ratio. This scheme was examined by the technical experts, and while they hesitated to reject a method which had the high sanction of the Washington Conference, they found the practical difficulties insurmountable in view both of the changing situation in Europe and of the almost insoluble problem of determining what should be the unit of measurement as well as the ratio to be employed. In short, this scheme, the chief merit of which was its definiteness, failed of adoption largely for that very reason. But, although the calculations made by experts proved of value in the plans of the Geneva Disarmament Conference, the total result demonstrated the unreality of any parallel systems of measurement, in view of the different geographic, historical and economic positions of the nations concerned. Moreover, the warfare of the future is bound to be more and more conditioned by these other factors, especially by the increasing rapidity with which industrial and chemical mobilization can be carried out.

There is no 5:5:3 or any other single formula that can measure the potentialities in the ever-shifting field of science. The arts of peace are more and more of direct service to war. There is no more striking fact in the history of international relations than that so serious a question should have been treated with such amateurish simplicity as it was in the plans for armament reduction after the first World War. The French were right when they insisted throughout the long controversy upon the theory which was summed up in the phrase: "Security first; disarmament in proportion to security." But the British and Americans were also right in pointing out that, while this statement is sound in logic, it may lend itself—and did lend itself—to a mistaken policy by putting the accent so strongly upon the one kind of security with which Europe was most familiar, the security that lies in a nation's armed strength. Yet the aim of all the effort was to secure and maintain a condition of peace; and, just as guns are a substitute for nature's obstacles on the possible pathway of attack, so arbitration and pacific settlement are the peacetime substitutes for guns themselves. The fundamental basis of security lies in provision for the development of pacific policies and the furtherance of an international community, breeding confidence on both sides of the frontier and making foreign policy genuinely pacific.

Unfortunately, these two elements of security—armaments and pacific policies—are not always easy to reconcile with each other. The resort to pacific means for settling disputes can operate well only in an atmosphere of international confidence, and the surest way to destroy confidence is to point guns at one's neighbors. On the other hand, the revision of treaties, the willingness to compromise with those who feel equally strongly on the other side of a question, creates the kind of understanding which tends to make guns relatively less necessary. It is true that the revision of treaties can sometimes be secured by threatening war unless revision is granted, but such measures do not secure a permanent lightening of international tension. They tend to make the weaker nations seek through alliances to balance the power that has been directed against them, and once embarked upon this policy of measuring force with force, the nations that become involved in it tend to concentrate more and more upon the possession of the weapons which may be called into action, and less and less upon the devices for pacific settlement. The progress of science makes this trend all the more disastrous, for the apprehensions created by the development of chemical and industrial warfare reach through the whole body of the nation. Thus this vicious circle ends with the search for security making nations still more insecure.

A further difficulty in dealing with the problem of security is that when a nation undertakes to strengthen both elements at once—armaments and the instruments for pacific settlement of international disputes—the increase in armaments goes on steadily, while recourse to the pacific settlement of disputes may perhaps not occur except at long intervals. This is perhaps one of the reasons why a nation like France has been charged with militarism by the liberals of other nations who have not been aware of the extent to which the French Government accepted the obligation to settle its disputes by pacific means.

Now the French, in the Disarmament Conference, properly called attention to their record in this regard and built upon it their program for armament limitation and reduction. However, the failure to move rapidly along these lines so as to recognize the equality of Germany and to call for its cooperation fed the mounting fires of national resentment across the Rhine, and the sensible measures of disarmament advocated by the French, still more strengthened by those of the British, did not come into operation while there was yet time.

The program of France was set forth in its memorandum of November, 1932. This stated in the clearest possible terms that France was ready to lessen its armaments in proportion as nations organized themselves for peace. Never was the collective system of security better described than in this document, which put in the foreground the obligation which a nation owes to the community of nations to ensure peace. It was not merely peace for itself but peace among other nations as well which created that condition of security necessary for any major steps in the reduction of armaments. The paramount issue in the eyes of France was the upbuilding of that "organization of peace" which, as M. Briand pointed out on the occasion of the signing of the Pact of Paris, was called for by that Pact, although not definitely provided for in its terms. The primary obligation is a universal one, that all signatories of the Pact of Paris engage themselves never to be a party to any breach of it, even by financial or commercial support of the aggressor. Nothing was said about military measures for international policing. The "Stimson Doctrine" that conquest does not constitute title, was accepted by all. Thus upon the background of a universal concept of security the French memorandum proceeded to grade the responsibilities of nations for the maintenance of peace. It then proposed a scaling down to armaments which would be measured by the increased security brought about by this realistic plan.

This practical policy was accepted by the British Government when, after some months of deliberation, it produced its plan for disarmament in March, 1933. As it was this British draft convention which became the basis of negotiations at the Disarmament Conference in the ensuing months, we have thus come at last to the belated but effective participation of the United States in the organization of peace which grew out of the disarmament discussions.

It was on the twenty-second of May, 1933, that Mr. Norman Davis stated, with the full approval of the Administration, the extent to which the United States was prepared to cooperate in the international peace system. Both ex-Secretary Kellogg and Secretary Stimson had stated that consultation with other interested nations was implied in the Pact of Paris. Building upon this and having in mind as well the proposals for placing an embargo upon trade with nations that had violated the Pact, Mr. Davis summed up the policy of the American Government in the following words:

> I wish to make clear that we are ready not only to do our part toward the substantive reduction of armaments but, if this is effected by general international agreement, we are also prepared to contribute in other ways to the organization of peace. In particular, we are willing to consult the other states in case of a threat to peace, with a view to averting conflict. Further than that, in the event that the states, in conference, determine that a state has been guilty of a breach of the peace in violation of its international obligations and take measures against the violator, then, if we concur in the judgment rendered as to the responsible and guilty party, we will refrain from any action tending to defeat such collective effort which these states may thus make to restore peace.[1]

[1] Department of State, Press Releases, May 27, 1933, p. 390.

This is as far as the United States ever went in its commitment for applying the Kellogg Pact to secure a reduction of armaments. The fact that it was finally given in order to save the Disarmament Conference from failure was an indication that the United States itself had at last become the proponent of the principle that the limitation of armaments by ratios in the various categories of armaments depends less upon finding the correct ratios, important and difficult as that is, than upon finding how far nations will participate in that kind of procedure which is designed to prevent war from breaking out at all. The more the instruments of peace are strengthened, the less the need for armaments.

(c) *The Inspection of Armaments*

In dealing with the history of the Disarmament Conferences we have concentrated upon the one central problem of the relation of armaments to other means for safeguarding national security; but, as we have indicated in an earlier section, very real progress was made in the technical problems of armament reduction and control. While complete agreement was not reached on such matters as the distinction between offensive and defensive weapons, the pioneering effort to survey that field was an encouraging example of forward-looking collaboration on the part of most governments. But it was recognized that the nature of armaments would be changing with the advance of science so that no one conference could anticipate the nature of future warfare and codify its instruments. This was what the London Conference of 1908 had attempted to do in fulfillment of a request from the second Hague Conference. By 1914 it was already evident that the specialists, working only six years before the outbreak of the first World War, had completely misjudged the military value of many things as set forth in their list of contraband articles. The conclusion to be drawn from the fact of the dynamic character of warfare under the regime of science was that the best provision for the reduction and control of armaments is the creation of an international body meeting at regular intervals and provided with a permanent staff to study the shifting possibilities in the light of policies agreed upon by political bodies.

Major political decisions would probably not fall within the program of the Disarmament Conference, although it would be a mistake to prevent it from ever availing itself of the chance to contribute to such decisions. The work of the Conference would normally be taken up with two activities, both of them definite and technical: the preparation of proposals for armament reduction and the international inspection of armaments and armament potentials.

The provision for inspection is fully as important as the actual provisions for armament reduction. Both Germany and Japan have shown the sinister nature of secrecy in preparation for war. The race in armament is largely due to what one country thinks another may be plotting secretly in its munitions plants and on its trial grounds. The spy system which is maintained by all military authorities to keep themselves informed concerning this military rivalry in peacetime, is much more likely to be efficient in the service of militarist nations than in those which, in the confidence of peace, are careless about their precautions for war. An international system of inspection, distasteful as it is to submit to it, is therefore almost wholly to the advantage of the democratic countries. Without it there will be no lasting sense of security anywhere, because military experts know only too well that half the value of the preparations for war lies in preventing a prospective enemy from knowing their nature and extent.

The proposal for international inspection of armaments was accepted by the members of the League of Nations in the Assembly at Geneva as long ago as 1924, in the famous protocol which has been referred to above. In the discussions which took place at that time, it became evident that more opposition to international inspection was to be found among the politicians than the soldiers of a country. Those civilians who had given least thought to the problem were often the most outspoken opponents of the one most practical measure to prevent the secret growth of armaments. This is not reassuring, because democracies, jealous of their freedom of speech, offer a chance for discussion of vital matters of which demagogues are sure to avail themselves. Nevertheless, provision for security in this regard fortunately lies in the further use of this method of discussion, with its appeal to that sense of reality which is the justification of democracy itself.

V

Livelihood and Welfare

(a) General Statement

UNLIKE the problems of national security and international justice, those of a nation's welfare are primarily domestic. They have to do with the day's work and the conditions of life of millions of people so busily engaged in earning a livelihood that the problems of international relations seem like an unreal intrusion, and foreign commerce a matter of little importance. This way of looking at things seems at first sight justified by the trade statistics of even a great power like the United States, for some 90 per cent of its products are consumed at home. The economic situation is reflected in politics, not only in the United States but in every country which has developed constitutional government. For the determination of economic policy has everywhere been taken over by the legislative branch of the government in order to ensure the fullest measure of responsibility to the electorate. The jealousy with which Congress has held to its traditional prerogatives in tariff legislation, is part of a long historical process, closely interwoven with the fundamental right of free peoples to tax themselves.

It is well to have all of these negative aspects of the problem of international trade clearly in mind in the planning for a post-war world, because there can be no permanent progress in the building up of better international economic relations if they are not based upon sound domestic economy, or if they lessen these safeguards of freedom within the state. These cautions must be kept constantly in mind; but we must be equally upon our guard against allowing them to hold us back from taking well-considered steps by well-considered means for the furtherance of trade and commerce. The cautions are not for the purpose of lessening trade but for securing the best of conditions under which we may prosper. The welfare of a nation cannot be fully realized by economic isolation any more than its security can be fully realized by political isolation. In both cases the fundamental problem is the same: to discover and develop the best way by which national interests can be served. In both cases the solution lies in finding the proper adjustment with other nations. Common sense leads to but one conclusion, namely, that to secure prosperity at home we must enlarge the market for our goods, for prosperity depends not only on our capacity for production, but also on the capacity of others as well as ourselves for consumption. The old saying, that trade is a two-way street, is also true of prosperity. The classic principle laid down by Adam Smith for the English people as a nation of traders, holds true of world economics as a whole: the limits of our prosperity are set by the prosperity of others, provided that the conditions are such that we can have a fair share in the increased economic activity of all.

We must not repeat the blunder of the 1920's in which we blocked the imports of other nations while lending them money to produce goods which they could not sell. Fortunately this experience is sufficiently fresh in our memory so that no argument is needed to drive it home. The magnitude of the Great Depression of 1930 was due to two things: the economic cost of the first World War and the acceptance of disastrous economic policies after it, especially the erection of tariff and other barriers against a revival of trade. We were left to ourselves to recover from a situation which could only be cured by a healthy world economy. Not having prepared beforehand to meet the crisis, we stumbled through the dark years of the early 30's, while Germany led in the creation of a hostile economic alignment the ultimate aim of which was war. The one notable effort made on our behalf was Secretary Hull's great battle to solve as much of the problem as could be solved through reciprocal trade agreements dealing with one nation at a time, but offering the benefits to all nations which do not discriminate against American products. The point should not be overlooked, however, that when Congress was asked in the spring of 1943 to renew the permission which it had given the President and Secretary of State to make these tariff agreements, there was opposition to the method of making them by executive action and the authority for making reciprocal trade agreements was extended, for only two years. Indeed, the extension was due more to personal confidence in Secretary Hull than to a desire to have more and better agreements, for during wartime conditions everyone knew that the possibilities were definitely limited.

We are thus brought back to the point mentioned above, that the way for making trade agreements with other countries is fully as important as the content. The legislative branch of our government is unwilling to surrender its ultimate control of the making of such agreements because of their profound effect on our domestic economy and also upon our methods of taxation. But, on the other hand, the executive branch of the government can make very little headway by way of treaties if questions like the tariff are debated solely upon the basis of the local and vested interests which so largely determine the votes in Congress. Moreover, there is the added danger in this regard, that the laws affecting foreign trade might become the plaything of partisan politics, and that with successive changes of administration foreign policy would change or be so unstable as to make impossible the calculations of businessmen upon which long-term investments can be made. This reaches out to affect foreign business fully as much as our own, if not more so. For example, Canadian economists have stated that Canada's trade with the United States suffers more from the uncertainty of what the future conditions may be, than from any single tariff at a given time. Business can accommodate itself to known and established situations, but not to the sudden swing of policy from one extreme to the other as may happen under the party system of government.

The development of pressure groups, representing special interests, only complicates this problem by insisting upon a one-sided settlement. And yet, with all its faults, the political machinery for democratic legislation is the best safeguard of a nation's freedom; therefore we must not curtail its operation in the largest of all fields of government, that of economic welfare.

All this leads us to the one inevitable conclusion, that the only clear pathway to that ever-increasing prosperity which the material wealth of the world provides is by a major reform if not a revolution, in world economics. The twentieth century has been building up fully as dangerous a system in the field of economics as in that of security. In both cases we have been developing the practice and psychology of conflict. Barriers to trade, higher than the great wall of China, have closed around all nations, great and small. Secretary Hull's efforts to pierce these barriers, while successful as far as they have gone, remind us at the same time of their strength and of the embattled hosts of vested interests and special privilege which lie behind them. The mercantilism of the seventeenth century, against which this nation revolted, has been so far outdone in our own time that a great industrial nation like Germany could pass from the economics of peace to those influenced and then dominated by war considerations, without any one being able to tell just when it had crossed the frontier. If we are to have total peace after this total war, we must demobilize our economy as definitely as we demobilize our fighting forces. Unless we do this, there can be no guarantee of a lasting peace.

But no one nation, not even the United States with all its power, can take this great step of economic emancipation alone. It can lead the world, as no other nation can, but it can no more take down its barriers by itself in a world where other nations maintain them than it can reduce its army and navy while other nations keep theirs at maximum strength. Moreover, we are not talking of total free trade any more than of total disarmament, but only of the reduction and limitation of trade barriers so as to strengthen instead of check the healthy flow of commodities and services where they are most needed in a world which will need them badly.

Happily, the present situation is one which offers a rare chance —perhaps the only chance in all our history—for instituting this policy of economic liberation. From now on and at the close of the war, we shall be an exporting nation to an extent undreamed of in the past. There are a few imports, chiefly raw materials, which we cannot get along without, but they are a relatively small fraction of the nation's whole balance of trade. This is not the place to introduce a full discussion of so large a problem. But even here we must not pass by the fact that competition in the international field raises domestic difficulties which have to be met and solved on their own terms. What is needed is not a transference of control of policy from legislative to executive, as some have argued, but more education of the nation as a whole so that it may escape from the tyranny of economic militarism, which is what we have had in recent years, into a world of ordered freedom, based upon the principle of mutual advantage in increased trade. There must be safeguards for the worker in industry as well as on the farm, but these are to be found in the erection of a world community rather than in the narrow localism of the past. In the international field this means that we must have consultative bodies composed of representatives of government and of each nation's business, to which technical experts should be added, capable of analyzing the complex problems of international trade and industry in the light of the interest of each nation. Such bodies would have an educative influence on public opinion generally, quite apart from the solution of special problems at any one time.

So far we have been dealing mainly with trade and commerce, but the same arguments are equally applicable to other matters in the economic field, such as monetary questions, communications, food and agriculture, social security and the other problems affecting the interests of labor. Alongside these and other economic organizations there should be similar bodies to deal with such matters as public health, protection against the drug traffic, and other anti-social evils. In all these bodies representation should be given to private associations as well as to government, following the precedent set by the International Labor Organization and, to a less degree, in the technical organization of the League of Nations.

As these fields cover, or may cover, practically the whole range of normal peacetime activities, provision should be made for each of them according to its own special function. In view of the great variety and changing nature of economic and social problems and their inherent interdependence, the international organizations necessary to deal with them should not be thought of in the same terms as those which deal with the problems of security and justice. They must be more adjustable to circumstance, for the conditions of economic life are continually changing. It would only hamper economic progress in international relations to have a whole system of bureaucracies develop, making for rigidity instead of increased freedom of relationships. Each of the technical organizations should be entrusted with those direct responsibilities which experience proves to be best discharged in international agencies. If this trend were carried too far, however, it might result in confusion because of the number of organizations working independently of each other. That would discredit the whole method of dealing through international bodies of this kind. They must be coordinated in order to avoid confusion and delay and the limits of their operation must be defined as far as possible.

Fortunately experience also shows that in general such organizations tend to fall into a common mold, providing for consultation, discussion, technical study, and either a recommendation to governments, or final settlement, according to the nature of the subject and the organization dealing with it. This machinery, however, will not work unless the material for it has been well prepared beforehand. Therefore, in addition to public conferences there must be provision for research and for the clarification of problems, either by the international body or by the governments using it. This is a field in which we are still frankly in the period of pioneering and experiment, both with reference to subject and method, a fact which causes conservatives in all countries to hesitate before accepting membership in any organization for which the need is not fully apparent. The path of wisdom seems to lie somewhere between such negative policies as would block progress, and the opposite extreme of attempting to force progress upon reluctant nations by an international bureaucracy. It was the appreciation of this fact in the Paris Peace Conference which led to the creation of the one most successful international economic organization in the world, the International Labor Organization. It has therefore been suggested above that the constitution of that body should be studied as a model for the constitution of each of the autonomous bodies which are necessary for the proper functioning of economic international life. This model has not been followed in detail, however, in the organizations which have already been formed to deal with the economic problems at the close of the second World War, as will be seen from the outlines of the organizations created to deal with food and agriculture and with relief and rehabilitation.

The subjects with which these institutions deal are for the most part technical, and the general reader may be tempted to turn these pages over without reading them. But the problems with which they deal are vital, for they are the substitutes for war in the strategy of peace. There can be no lasting peace among nations without provision for the shifting impact of economic pressures, and the only provision which reaches into the unknown future is that which is the creation of continuing institutions designed to keep pace with a changing world. None of us know what the problems of tomorrow will be, or at least under what conditions we shall have to meet them. No one economic settlement can last for more than a term of years when the field is that of the whole economic life of nations. Viewed in this light, the institutions described below form but the beginning of a whole series of international technical organs which will be created sooner or later if we are seriously to set about the great task of applying knowledge instead of force in the adjustment of nations with each other.

The three most important international bodies which already exist are the International Labor Organization, the United Nations Relief and Rehabilitation Administration and the United Nations Conference on Food and Agriculture. The need for an international Communications Organization also has become increasingly evident in the light of the controversy already developing in the field of commercial aviation. Indeed it is doubtful if there is any other problem more pressing for solution at the present time than that which has arisen from the conquest of the air. The progress of invention calls for continuing study of adjustments in this new technique of travel and shipment. It must be articulated with all the other methods of intercourse. Separate *ad hoc* conferences, held under the stress of emergencies, are wholly inadequate to deal with so large a problem. More fundamental still, because more far-reaching, is the need for stable international monetary policy, which in turn calls for the creation of an international Fund and a Bank for the reconstruction and development of the United and Associated Nations, to use the term already proposed by the United States Treasury. The problems of money and credit are perhaps the most difficult and illusive in all human relationships. In order to help clarify these issues, a summary is appended here of the plans at present under negotiation. The reader need not feel discouraged, however, if he finds this description opening still other problems which lie beyond the reach of this survey. One of the wisest of economists has well said that the mystery of money is but another term for the mystery of the universe itself.

Before turning to look at each of the international economic organizations described below, we should pause a moment over the question of their setting in the whole scheme of things. Otherwise we may be lost in the details and unable to see the woods for the trees. And not we alone, for governments can become confused as easily as individuals. The war government of the United States is itself an example of how bureaus and departments need constant oversight by a central authority in order to prevent overlapping of functions and confusion of policies. Any listing of international organizations in the field of economics and welfare should therefore be prefaced by a reminder of the need of a general body at the center of the whole system, such as that to which reference has been made above. It is not clear whether this body should be the central political body described in the following section or whether there should be a general international advisory body for the whole field of economics, drawn from and representative of the various special organizations. The argument against the creation of a central international economic organization is that it would tend to a multiplication of offices. The argument for it is that it would clarify the problems and coordinate action with regard to the removal of trade barriers, encourage international investment, advise in the stabilization of commodity prices, and the registering and publishing of cartel agreements. Its committees could continue and extend the valuable work of the Financial, Fiscal and Economic Committees of the League of Nations and the statistical and research studies of the League's Economic Intelligence Service. It could organize machinery through which national governments would be able to conduct their economic, financial and monetary policies in agreement instead of at cross purposes. Among its most important functions would probably be the operation of an International Development Authority designed to stimulate the steady and productive development of countries which now lack modern equipment. It could also register and advise on private international investment and maintain a continuous economic audit so as to forestall strains on the balances of international payments.

Finally, alongside the economic organizations and in some cases overlapping them, there is a more pressing need for some of the organizations for health and social welfare, especially at the close of this war. The operations of U.N.R.R.A. are only partly economic. They lie more in the humanitarian field. In the nature of the case there is no hard and fast line to be drawn between furtherance of normal economic life and the removal of disabilities and obstacles. There should be an adequate provision through international organizations, to deal with such matters as public health and contagious diseases, migration and settlement, child welfare, the spread of the drug traffic and of immoral practices. Unfortunately, the conscience of mankind has been dulled to the extent of these evils in the world, because they have been with us since the beginning of time. Reform, however, is bound to develop with the progress of civilization, of which it is an index; for history shows that the dictates of humanity are also those of self-interest.

It was in this field of social welfare that the League of Nations achieved some of its most striking successes. The need for further developments in the postwar world will be recognized, however, on all sides and needs no argument. It is a field which calls for a greater degree of technical competence than do the more general fields of international relations; and therefore it is essential that the program should be prepared by semi-autonomous boards composed of competent specialists, and that it be carried out with as little interference as possible from politicians in the various countries concerned who might be influenced by other motives. As examples of the possibilities already envisaged by the Health Sections of the League of Nations, mention should be made of epidemic control and the safeguarding of public health in backward areas which will be a very important task after the war. A vast new field is opening up in the study of nutrition and provision for improvement of nutrition. The work of the Central Opium Board has not only been important in itself, but offers suggestions for similar controls elsewhere. The international control of the traffic in narcotics should be extended and developed with renewed vigor. Conferences on rural life, such as those organized by the League of Nations in the Balkans and southeastern Asia, should be built upon. Problems of housing, which will be especially pressing after the war, can be helped along by comparative study of developments in different countries. Finally, the good work of the League of Nations for social hygiene to maintain the decencies of life, its efforts to suppress traffic in women and children and the like, are reforms which could be brought about only by international action pillorying corrupt societies in the light of investigations which cover problems that extend beyond national frontiers. In this area, the League has nobly pioneered.

(b) *The International Labor Organization, a Model for Others*

The greatest challenge to the conscience of the world at the Paris Peace Conference is not to be found in the pioneering document of the Covenant of the League of Nations; it is to be found in a relatively obscure sentence in the preamble to the Constitution of the International Labor Organization which forms Part XIII of the Treaty of Versailles. This is the statement that "Universal peace can be established only if it is based upon social justice." In other words, peace is the expression of the moral order of the world. It is more than a truce between peoples nursing grievances or dealing with each other in sullen enmity. War having now become total war, peace must be total peace, a phrase which means much more than diplomatic relationships or the readjustment of armed forces to provide police against disturbances. These externals of peace, which are being widely discussed and which are dealt with in the earlier part of this study, form only a single chapter, though an essential one, in the plans for total peace. The mere repression of violence is not enough; only a just world can be free and safe from the menace of war.

Social justice is nothing more or less than the application of the Golden Rule to the affairs of daily life. In economic relationships it means the elimination of exploitation in human affairs, a reform that goes far beyond the elimination of war. Indeed, from one point of view it can never be achieved, because with each advance new horizons open before us, and the conscience of mankind becomes more alert the more it is exercised. So far, however, we have hardly more than begun to build a society in which the common man will be safe from exploitation. The intimate daily things, like wages and the conditions of work, are still to a large extent matters of conflict between stubborn, unyielding interests, and the whole social fabric suffers from the threat of violence which rises to the surface from time to time when the maladjustments seem intolerable.

The problem which this situation presents is more a domestic one, to be settled by each people for itself, than an international concern of world affairs. So at least it had appeared to the nineteenth century and so it appears to most people still. Already, however, in the middle of the nineteenth century, Karl Marx and Frederick Engels called attention in *The Communist Manifesto* to a "spectre haunting Europe," that of international socialism. It is doubtful if the specter began to haunt the statesmen of that time until the Manifesto declared that it was there; but from 1848 on, the revolutionary protest against intolerable conditions in mine and factory and in the slums of the cities grew steadily, in spite of all efforts at repression. The final, militant form of this underground revolt against capitalist exploitation took shape in the Bolshevist movement when Lenin became the militant caliph of a Marxian crusade. At the close of the first World War this crusading movement not only conquered the greatest land empire in the world, Russia, but had its embattled hosts in the cities of central Europe. For a few months' time, while the Paris Peace Conference was drawing together the text of the Treaty of Versailles, the threat of a complete economic and social overturn lay heavy on the minds of the statesmen and peoples of the western world.

Under these conditions—which may recur if the peace settlement pays no attention to the problems of social justice—the Paris Peace Conference set up a commission to create the International Labor Organization which should substitute reform for revolution, working through governments and by the process of law instead of by force and violence. This body, established at Geneva alongside and integrally connected with the League of Nations, was finally adhered to by the United States Government on June 16, 1934, as the result of a joint resolution passed unanimously in the Senate and by over a two-thirds majority in the House of Representatives.

By that time it had justified itself in history as an indispensable instrument for the advancement of social welfare through the stimulation of national safeguards against undue exploitation of labor. Prior to 1914 there had been almost no effort at securing uniform standards of social legislation among European countries, although lower standards in neighboring countries were a constant argument against bettering conditions in the more advanced. With the creation of the I.L.O., as the International Labor Organization is known for short, this situation has greatly changed. Prior to its creation there were only three international agreements on labor legislation, prohibiting night work for women and in bakeries, and the use of white phosphorus in matches. The I.L.O. has now secured sixty-seven international conventions signed by over fifty countries, covering a wide variety of labor and social conditions, in the negotiation of which it has registered over eight hundred ratifications. This remarkable development continued until Germany withdrew its membership on the eve of the second World War. Even throughout the war, the offices of the I.L.O. in Geneva have not closed although most of its working staff has moved to Montreal, Canada. From there, however, it has maintained its organization and continued active and important work especially in the field of social security in Latin America. There can be no doubt but that the United States will continue to find this instrument of social betterment of real value to itself; not only in the stabilization of peace but also in the increased prosperity which accompanies social tranquillity—a prosperity in which all nations have a chance to share in varying degrees.

The structure of the International Labor Organization is unique. Its central body, known as the General Conference, is composed of four delegates from each country of whom two are government delegates and two represent respectively "the employers and the work people of each of the Members." This tripartite representation in which capital and labor share with governments so as to give an equal voice to the non-official representation, has been a real source of strength enabling the I.L.O. to prepare recommendations and draft conventions for the governments of the countries represented in it for which there is already support in the public opinion of the interested citizens. Without attempting to override or by-pass the governments, the I.L.O. proposals for legislation have a vitality greater than would normally be the case with diplomatic negotiations between foreign offices.

The conferences alone, meeting usually only once a year and composed of a changing body of delegates without a full sense of continuity in legislation, are by no means adequate to deal with world-wide economic problems. Therefore, there is a permanent organization known as the International Labor Office with a large secretariat, mostly research workers, acting under the control of the Governing Body. This Governing Body consists of 24 persons, 12 representing the governments, 6 elected by the delegates representing the employers, and 6 by the delegates representing the workers. No project is permitted to come before the Conference without having previously been studied by the secretariat and discussed by the Governing Body. This preparation is so thorough that it has taken an average of from one to two years before the Conference takes action.

It is doubtful if any other legislative process in the world has developed as adequate safeguards against ill-conceived projects as those supplied by this machinery of the I.L.O. It would, therefore, be reasonable to hope that the method employed by the I.L.O. will be applied in other organizations in the international field especially in the general economic conference referred to above. The world of business has long felt the need of an international organization in which commerce and finance would have adequate representation. The International Chamber of Commerce, for example, has developed a representation of business in which governments have been interested while disclaiming responsibility. This is an inadequate form of organization, and a more consistently developed plan with greater provision for the study of specific projects would seem to be among the essential needs of the postwar period. In the formative stages of an organization of this sort, the governments would naturally insist upon their right to determine the scope of action of the international body. But if the effort is made to secure a forum for the development of general economic policies for which the material is carefully prepared by competent specialists, the exact way in which government and business cooperate can be left to be determined by the event itself. There is, however, one fundamental principle in the plan as outlined here; it is that free enterprise of private economic interests should be safeguarded alongside the development of the government activities. The method will vary in different countries.

In any case, the economic history of the last quarter of a century has clearly shown that the only way in which private business can achieve permanent security or ultimate prosperity is through the strengthening of an orderly society of nations as well as an orderly society within each nation, with liberty under the law and with appropriate governmental organs to ensure economic justice for the whole community. No one can any longer doubt that this holds true in international relations. The business world would commit suicide if at the close of this war it were to fall back into the anarchy of unrestricted private capitalism protected by policies of *laissez faire* which, under the guise of economic freedom, would repeat the calamity of the 1920's by re-establishing the system of economic warfare, using the weapons of tariff and other trade restrictions. The danger to civilization in such a reversion to the past is fully as great as in the field of armaments. The machinery of international economic organization, such as that indicated in this section, is therefore of fundamental importance in the post-war settlement.

(c) *The United Nations Conference on Food and Agriculture*

The first international body to be set up under the United Nations was the Conference on Food and Agriculture which met at Hot Springs, Virginia, in June, 1943. Although its chief purpose was to draft a long-term program to be carried out in the post-war years and not to deal with the immediate wartime emergency, there was much anxiety in official circles for fear disagreements might arise between the different nations which would be seized upon by Axis propaganda to weaken morale and united effort in the war. This was the main reason why the Conference was not held in public, to the great dissatisfaction of journalists, especially

American journalists. Bitter charges were made that the United Nations were using the technique of the old diplomacy with all that that implied. As a matter of fact, the only reason for hesitancy in opening the meetings to the press was a fear that the Conference might fail and even break up in disagreement. Events showed that this was a mistake in judgment, for seldom has an international conference been more successful than was this first conference of the United Nations.

One of the reasons for its success was the high quality of its membership which was composed for the most part of competent specialists in the fields of agriculture and food supply. These specialists could make up for any deficiency in the technical preparation for the Conference so that its discussions were direct and to the point. The Final Act of the Conference, published in the *Bulletin* of the Department of State for June, 1943 [1] is an inspiring document covering the whole field of food supply in all its ramifications, reaching even as far as the conservation of land and water resources for food production.

The Declaration at the opening of the Final Act states the problem with which it deals in such challenging terms that it should be quoted here. It is to be hoped that the challenge will be met.

This Conference, meeting in the midst of the greatest war ever waged, and in full confidence of victory, has considered the world problems of food and agriculture and declares its belief that the goal of freedom from want of food, suitable and adequate for the health and strength of all peoples, can be achieved.

1. The first task is to complete the winning of the war and to deliver millions of people from tyranny and from hunger. During the period of critical shortage in the aftermath of war, freedom from hunger can be achieved only by urgent and concerted efforts to economize consumption, to increase supplies and distribute them to the best advantage.

2. Thereafter we must equally concert our efforts to win and maintain freedom from fear and freedom from want. The one cannot be achieved without the other.

3. There has never been enough food for the health of all people. This is justified neither by ignorance nor by the harshness of nature. Production of food must be greatly expanded; we now have knowledge of the means by

[1] Reprinted in *International Conciliation*, September, 1943. No. 392.

which this can be done. It requires imagination and firm will on the part of each government and people to make use of that knowledge.

4. The first cause of hunger and malnutrition is poverty. It is useless to produce more food unless men and nations provide the markets to absorb it. There must be an expansion of the whole world economy to provide the purchasing power sufficient to maintain an adequate diet for all. With full employment in all countries, enlarged industrial production, the absence of exploitation, an increasing flow of trade within and between countries, an orderly management of domestic and international investment and currencies, and sustained internal and international economic equilibrium, the food which is produced can be made available to all people.

5. The primary responsibility lies with each nation for seeing that its own people have the food needed for life and health; steps to this end are for national determination. But each nation can fully achieve its goal only if all work together.

6. We commend to our respective governments and authorities the study and adoption of the findings and recommendations of this Conference and urge the early concerted discussion of the related problems falling outside the scope of this Conference.

7. The first steps toward freedom from want of food must not await the final solution of all other problems. Each advance made in one field will strengthen and quicken advance in all others. Work already begun must be continued. Once the war has been won decisive steps can be taken. We must make ready now.

For carrying out the vast and splendid program outlined here, the Conference proposed the erection of an Interim Commission which should finally give way to a permanent organization at some undetermined future date. It is important to note that this Conference concentrated on getting things done rather than upon setting up an elaborate machinery for international management. No constitution was drafted but only a series of recommendations for doing this and that. It is one of the most practical documents ever to come from a conference and at the same time one of the most far-reaching.

Through the good offices of the Government of the United States, the Interim Commission held its inaugural session on July 15 at which it took up its two-fold task of negotiations with governments represented on it and the drafting of the constitution of the permanent international body. In the opening address at the inaugural session of the Commission, Assistant Secretary of State

Acheson stated that this task of creating a permanent body consisted of two parts: first, what form it should have and, second, what it should *do*. He went on to emphasize that the second question was the heart of the problem for, "if the activities of the proposed body are clearly indicated and agreed upon it is far easier to decide upon a satisfactory organization for that body than if the organization is approached first, without references to specific functions." In this connection he asked the Commission "to study carefully the work of the various war bodies functioning in this and similar international fields, for they may offer valuable clues as to the operations and possible organization of the permanent body on food and agriculture." This statement of the policy of the American government was unanimously agreed to by the members of the Commission. It is highly significant that this first step toward the goal of a United Nations organization should have been so practical and so far-sighted. It is a good augury for the future.

The structure of the proposed United Nations Organization for Food and Agriculture has still to be worked out in detail, but the following outline indicates the way in which those responsible for its creation have viewed the problem. It will be seen that it resembles the constitution of the I.L.O. in the provision for expert and technical advice and administration, but that its central body lacks non-governmental representation. The supreme body will be a Council consisting of representatives of the member governments. This Council should meet at least once each year and formulate the general policies of the organization. It should elect an Executive Committee with special delegated powers to facilitate action when the Council is not in session. It should act in support of the Director General against political or other pressure. The Council should further appoint standing committees which would have continuing responsibility to advise the Council on the various aspects of the organization work. An advisory council committee should be appointed, consisting of persons selected on the basis of their personal classification as scientists, technical experts, or economists, or because of great administrative experience. The members should be appointed for a term of years. It may ultimately be found necessary to establish a number of standing advisory committees, corresponding to each main division of the organization.

The staff of the organization is to be headed by the Director General. The staff of the organization should include persons competent in all of the branches of knowledge required to give a solid foundation to the work of the organization. They should be drawn from different regions and from as many different countries as possible. The Council might appoint a special committee of experts for dealing with some particular problems in certain instances. Such a temporary committee would be sent on field missions.

To facilitate much of the work, it would be desirable for the Organization to have attachés in convenient centers throughout the world to keep in touch with conditions in a single country or a region including several countries. In such a case, it may decide to establish regional offices. In order to have machinery which would enable the Organization to be in close touch with public opinion and to receive various suggestions and to obtain the support of representative bodies, it is suggested that the Food and Agriculture Organization should convene a general conference every two or three years for the purpose of bringing together representatives of responsible groups to consult together on the outstanding problems in this field. This general conference would be in the nature of a forum. Governments would see that their delegates were fully representative of their interests involved. Furthermore, the Administration should convene technical, regional or other special conferences organized in a similar way.

The permanent Organization should establish relations with other international authorities, especially with the United Nations Relief and Rehabilitation Administration, and the International Labor Office. It has been suggested that the International Institute of Agriculture be taken over by the new organization and appropriate action should be taken in due course with a view to the transfer of the functions, records, and property of the Institute to the Organization.

(d) *The United Nations Relief and Rehabilitation Administration*

On November 9 the representatives of forty-four nations met in the East Room of the White House and signed a pact creating a world organization unique in history, the United Nations Relief and Rehabilitation Administration (known henceforth as U.N.R.R.A.). There was a consciousness upon the part of all that history was being made. The Conference on Food and Agriculture had begun in the subdued light of an uncertain dawn, but the doubts which had enveloped its early meetings had been completely dissipated in the course of the summer and autumn, and U.N.R.R.A. began on a note of confidence. When the President signed for the United States he summarized in a word his method to be followed in the creation of the United Nations Organizations, when he said, "Nations will learn to work together only by actually working together." In order to drive the thought home he added, looking around the table, "Why not?" The conference which followed this opening ceremony fully justified the confident note of the President's speech. In three short weeks, from the tenth of November to the first of December, this full dress rehearsal of the parliament of nations agreed upon its program and the machinery for carrying it out.

Never before has there been so great an effort by so many nations to cooperate in the relief of suffering and the re-establishment of normal life. The Red Cross, splendid as is its record, has never dealt with more than a small fraction of the problems confronting U.N.R.R.A. There was no such organization as U.N.R.R.A. at the end of the first World War, for the American organizations for relief, the greatest of which was under Mr. Hoover's direction, were never officially coordinated and the organizations of other nations, especially the Dutch and the Scandinavian, ran independent courses. This was inevitable so long as the governments, as well as the private organizations, still thought in terms of charity.

By contrast, U.N.R.R.A. is conceived as a cooperative enterprise in which the stricken nations would share as far as possible. While the emphasis of U.N.R.R.A. is on relief and it is expressly stated that the task of rehabilitation must not be carried over into reconstruction, no hard and fast line could be drawn at which the work should stop. This is wisely left to the organization itself. The devastated areas are to receive not only food, fuel, clothing, shelter and medical supplies, but the seeds and fertilizers, raw materials and machinery necessary for reviving farming and industry; and the public utilities of towns and villages are to be restored to meet immediate needs such as light, water power, transportation, sanitation, communications, and at least the bare essentials for restarting education. The administration of U.N.R.R.A. cannot be called upon to help restore continuous employment, and no new construction is contemplated except for urgently needed agriculture and industry. The contributing nations are not called upon to do more than assist the stricken peoples to start once more the routine of daily life. The organization of U.N.R.R.A. follows the same general model of the other organizations with which we have been dealing. Anything resembling bureaucratic control of economics on an international scale is distinctly rejected. The policy-making body is the Council composed of one representative from each member government, with provision for alternates when necessary. In a general way this parallels the Assembly of the League of Nations. It is to meet twice as often, however, not less than twice a year, and it may be convened in special session if necessary either upon a request of one third of its members or by the Central Committee which also, in a general way, parallels the Council of the League or the Governing Body of the I.L.O. The Central Committee not only convenes the Council when necessary, but deals with emergencies between Council sessions. It consists of representatives of China, the Union of Soviet Socialist Republics, the United Kingdom and the United States of America. Meetings of the Committee may be called by any member and must be held within ten days after the request. The Director General also may convene the Committee, over which he presides without vote.

The Director General is appointed by the Council on the nomination by unanimous vote of the Central Committee. He has full authority to carry on relief operations within the limits of available resources and the broad outlines of policy determined by the Council or the Central Committee. He is to consult military and other appropriate authorities of the U.N.R.R.A. both with reference to the procurement, transportation and distribution of all supplies. He appoints his staff of Deputy Director Generals, official and expert personnel, who are to be regarded as truly international civil servants.

There are four important committees working under the Council, the Committee of Supplies, the Committee on Financial Control, the Committee for Europe and the Committee for the Far East. The Committee of Supplies is, in a sense, the heart of the whole organization because without supplies the work of the U.N.R.R.A. ceases. It advises the Council, the Central Committee and the Director General concerning the provision, the financing and the transportation of supplies, and cooperates with the Director General and other necessary agencies in efforts to secure increased production and availability of supplies. The Council appointed to this important committee comprises the members of the following countries: Australia, Belgium, Brazil, Canada, China, the Netherlands, New Zealand, U.S.S.R., the United Kingdom, the United States, and for France, the French Committee on National Liberation.

The Committee on Financial Control has to supervise the financial administration of U.N.R.R.A. and to advise the Council on all problems of financial as well as of a monetary nature.

The Committees for Europe and the Far East are primarily concerned with the distribution of supplies but they also consider and recommend to the Council and to the Central Committee any matters relating to relief and rehabilitation within their respective areas.

It was originally intended that U.N.R.R.A. would procure supplies and services for all the countries needing relief, but this was changed at the Atlantic City Conference. There are to be two groups of countries, those which are able to pay for relief supplies in foreign exchange, and those able only to pay in local currencies. The former group includes France, Belgium, Holland and Norway, while the other group is composed of the countries of Central and East Europe and China. This distinction between wealthier and poorer countries has been challenged by some critics who fear that the countries paying in foreign exchange may get relief supplies more quickly than the poorer countries, although their need may be less. The solution was a compromise between the West European countries and the three Powers controlling the combined boards. If the solution should work out to the disadvantage of the poorer countries, it makes the task of the Director General more complicated. He can proceed only in the allocation of supplies when in agreement with the governments concerned. The final decision on what quantity of goods the U.N.R.R.A. should obtain, and for what countries, will rest eventually for the greater part with the inter-government agencies controlled by the United States, Great Britain and, part of the time, by Canada. It seems likely that these two or three countries will have practically the final decision as to where the relief supplies will go.

It is impossible to pursue this problem further here, although it is of great importance in connection with the relative places of different countries in an international cooperative organization which deals with such vital problems as those of U.N.R.R.A.

It remains to point out that it will be necessary to interrelate the activities of U.N.R.R.A. with the general economic and financial policies of the post-war period. In spite of the fact that U.N.R.R.A. laid greatest emphasis upon the immediate task of relief, it cannot escape and should not try to escape laying the foundations of economic reconstruction. For that reason it is essential that the United Nations or the leading powers among them begin immediately the preparations for working out policies which will complement the work of U.N.R.R.A. It should have a European council as a center for all of the vast activities in war-torn countries. This body, or one like it, would fail in the fundamentals of its task if it did not, while dealing with the immediate problems of the day, also keep in mind a long-term economic program for the future.

(e) *International Monetary and Financial Organization*

We now come to a major problem, one which should not be treated in any subordinate way in an analysis of the processes of civilized life. For civilization is a conquest not only of a special and material world but of time. It began its advance in the primeval world when men began to calculate upon a future which as yet did not lie within the range of their experience. The cyclic calendar of the stars and of the seasons gave a conception of repetition to the processes of life. It is a long step from the origins of the calendar to the bookkeeping of modern business, but without the measurement of time there could be no conquest of the future. In the economic world this conquest of the future took on a wholly new character at the close of the Middle Ages when banking and credit began to play their part in the business of kings as well as of merchants. Down to that time money was hoarded as treasure rather than set to work in what we now term capital.

Now, after some four or five centuries of money economy we have come to a world crisis in which the orthodox ideas about money are being widely questioned, not merely on the national basis upon which it has so long rested, but on a new basis of world affairs. The organization which is designed to deal with this vast and difficult problem cannot be described in simpler terms, nor indeed, is there full agreement as yet as to how it should be set up, or what should be its terms of reference. But somehow or other the world of credit must be both strengthened and controlled so as to ensure more business within nations and among nations, and also to lessen the chance, if that can be done, of the disastrous recurring cycles of good and bad times which have periodically brought ruin when credit has been overstrained or rendered unhealthy by speculative practices.

The power of credit in the modern world is prodigious. Without it the processes of industry and the vast movements of goods which sustain the world's population would be impossible. If all domestic business were carried out on a day-to-day basis the purchases of the individual businessman would be limited by the amount of dollars he possessed in the form of bills or coin. Since he could acquire dollars only by selling the goods he produced, his capacity to buy would in fact be limited by his current sales.

When we pass from domestic to international transactions an additional complication arises. Each nation possesses its own currency system, and unless these national currencies are freely convertible at some stable ratio, trade cannot flow smoothly. No American importer would buy goods abroad, valued in a foreign currency, unless he knew to within a very small margin the value of that currency in dollars at the time of the purchase. If that value were subject to sudden and unpredictable changes he would be unwilling to enter into any purchase contract which provided for delivery at some future time.

In industry today the production process is often very long. Huge plants must be built; raw materials must be bought and transported over great distances; wages must be paid to the men who build the plant, the seamen and railroad operatives who transport the raw materials, as well as the workers who finally manufacture the finished product. Clearly such an intricate system of production and trade could never have developed if all payments had had to be settled immediately and in cash, often long before the final product reached the market.

Any workable international monetary mechanism must fulfill two major needs. It must make available a volume of international short-term credit sufficient to allow a large volume of trade to flow smoothly, and it must exercise a stabilizing influence on the values of national currencies in terms of one another, or, in other words, on the foreign exchange rates.

For a century after the Napoleonic wars these functions were discharged by the London money market and the international gold standard. The role of gold in that mechanism of international payments was, however, far less important than the ability and readiness of nations to observe the rules of the game and adapt their domestic production in response to external influences. Changes in the technique and organization of production and trade, together with the economic consequences of two major wars have now destroyed that system beyond hope of repair. If international trade is again to flow freely, new mechanisms must be devised to take its place.

Considerable progress has already been made in this direction. Within the past year separate plans for international monetary reorganization have been drawn up by American, British and Canadian officials, and conferences have been held to discuss them among representatives of the United Nations. Indeed, the widespread recognition by governments that such a system is essential to world order seems to be one of the consequences of the second World War.

The main objectives of all four currency plans are precisely those stated above. In much of the current discussion about them, far too much emphasis has been placed upon differences between the proposals, and too little upon their essential similarity. All aim at setting up a mechanism which will determine exchange rates by consultation and joint action among the member countries of the proposed monetary organization, and will make available adequate supplies of short-term credit to those countries in need of it.

Power to fix the gold parity, or gold content of the national currency was long a jealously guarded attribute of each national sovereignty, but governments have now explicitly recognized what economists have long known, that no nation ever did in fact possess full power to fix the value of its currency in terms of other currencies. For a rate of exchange is simply a ratio, whether one currency be expressed directly in terms of another or whether both are expressed in terms of a common medium such as gold. The American, British, and Canadian plans provide for the establishment by the United Nations of a new international monetary institution within the framework of which negotiations concerning exchange rates are to take place.

In all the plans these credits would be provided not by bilateral arrangements between pairs of countries, but multilaterally through the new institution. The plans differ both in method of operation, and in the amounts of credit to be made available.

The United States Treasury document proposed to establish an International Stabilization Fund of "at least five billion dollars" to be made up of contributions from each member country of gold, national currency, and government securities. Quotas and subscriptions are to be determined by agreement and are to give due consideration to "a country's holdings of gold and free foreign exchange, the magnitude and the fluctuations of its balance of international payments, its national income, etc." Management of the Fund is to be entrusted to a board of directors, one appointed by each member government. The distribution of votes is to be related to the quotas of member countries but, as the plan now stands, no country, regardless of its quotas, is entitled to more than one fifth of the aggregate basic votes.[1] No single member country would possess the power of veto over important matters of policy.[2]

The Fund, which would operate on the basis of an accounting unit, consisting of 137 1/7 grains of fine gold (equivalent to ten dollars), would make credits available to its members by selling foreign exchange to them against their local currency. These credits could be increased, subject to certain limitations, to enable the purchaser to overcome short-term disequilibria in its balance of payments.[3]

The British plan differs from the American in that it proposes

[1] In the first draft of the Treasury plan voting power was to correspond to the quotas of member countries. The quota of the United States would have been the largest, about 28%, and since important decisions such as changes in the exchange value of the currency of a member country required the approval of three fourths of the member votes, this formula would have given the United States the power of veto over such decisions. This caused considerable comment and in the revised text the clause was modified.

[2] With the exception of a change in the gold value of all member currencies, which would require the approval of all countries possessing more than 10 per cent of the votes.

[3] If the Fund's holdings of the currency and securities of a member country grew excessively small relative to the prospective demand for that currency the Fund would propose methods of rationing the scarce currency and would make recommendations to the country concerned, designed to increase the Fund's holdings of the currency in question.

to create an International Clearing Union without a fund or system of contributions. Instead of making deposits, the members would accumulate overdrafts with the Union. The new institution would use an international unit of account originally called *bancor*, which would be "fixed (but not unalterably) to gold and accepted as the equivalent of gold by ... all the members of the Union for the purpose of settling international balances." It is suggested that the borrowing power—and the voting power—might be fixed initially by reference to the average value of its foreign trade. The formula for assessing quotas may, however, take account of other factors. The British idea, as developed by Lord Keynes, is a bold departure from the orthodox policy of Great Britain, the traditional citadel of Sterling; for *bancor* would "supplant gold as a governing factor." In both cases the nations would have to adjust their national credit policies in accordance with their international possessions. If, for example, the United States were to continue importing few products other than gold and burying its hoards at Fort Knox, any system of international monetary organization in which gold plays an important part would quickly fail.

The principle in the British plan of making credit available according to the trading needs of the country concerned is theoretically unexceptionable. There are, however, certain practical difficulties in the way of its adoption. The British Commonwealth, with its large share in world trade, would have a very powerful voice in the management of the fund, a fact which was looked upon with some disquiet in the United States. It would also be difficult to distinguish an overdraft needed for short-term purposes from one serving a long-term need. In addition, the needs of impoverished Europe for imported goods at the close of the war will be so much greater than the need of the United States for foreign products that the Clearing Union would be likely to get into the position of holding substantial overdraft claims on a large number of countries, the bulk of which could be liquidated only by sales against American dollars. At this point the credit expansion would come to an end, unless the United States increased its imports, or decreased its exports, or made foreign loans. To use a gambling illustration, if one player accumulates most of the chips in the game and refuses to bet heavily, the game cannot go on.

Such pressure on creditor countries to put these balances to work is entirely justifiable and since these countries retain the right and the power to choose a solution suitable to them, they have little reason to complain. But, as is emphasized in the Canadian plan which is in many ways a practical compromise between the American and British proposals, the disparity of needs will be so great in the immediate post-war period that it would be wiser to place some definite limit, at least for a time, upon the borrowing power of member countries. Such a provision would make the plan more acceptable to creditor countries and, if the limit were not set too low, it would not hamper debtors unduly.

In the long run, however, if debtors overborrow or creditors refuse to recognize their position, no international monetary organization can long survive. As all the plans for international monetary reorganization will recognize, no monetary manipulation can solve the economic problems of the post-war world. If, for example, the United States were to follow the disastrous policy of the years after Versailles, and accept foreign promises to pay while at the same time making it increasingly difficult, by raising tariffs on imported goods, for foreigners to honor these promises, no international monetary institution, however intelligently conceived and capably managed, can be of avail. By the same token the success of any scheme of monetary organization will depend in great part on the degree of international cooperation in the fields of commercial policy and foreign investment.[1]

It is in the latter that the greatest changes in organization are needed. Long-term loans will be required for two purposes, the

[1] On April 22, 1944, a joint statement was issued by the technical experts of the United States, Great Britain, and the Soviet Union and approved by experts of thirty-one other nations. The plan presented follows the Canadian and American plans more closely than the British, but also includes some important features of the latter. The amount of the Fund is fixed at eight billion dollars. Twenty-five per cent of contributions is to be made in gold, but not more than 10 per cent of the country's reserves of gold and free foreign exchange. Provision is made for devaluation up to 10 per cent after consultation with the Fund; beyond that the approval of the Fund is required. Exchange control is foreseen at least in the transition period, but a program for the successive relaxation of restrictions impeding multilateral clearing is to be worked out.

rebuilding of devastated areas, and the modernization of countries hitherto industrially undeveloped. The post-war world is not likely, at least in the beginning, to offer much encouragement to risk-taking capital. Remembering their unhappy experience with international loans after the last war, investors are likely to be timorous and unwilling to risk their capital abroad even at high prospective rates of return. Besides, national resistance to the inflow of foreign capital has increased in the potential borrowing countries.

The United States Treasury has recently proposed that a Bank for Reconstruction and Development of the United and Associated Nations be established to facilitate such long-term international investment. The main function of the Bank would be to guarantee and participate in loans made by private investors and also to lend directly from its own resources what additional capital might be needed. The bank would not compete with private investors but would itself make loans or investments only when these could not be secured on reasonable terms from private sources. The repayment of principal and interest would be guaranteed by national governments.

The Bank would have a capital of ten billion dollars consisting of shares having a par value of $100,000 subscribed by the member governments of the International Stabilization Fund. Subscriptions would be determined by a formula mutually agreed upon and based upon data such as the national income and the international trade of member countries.[1] Only 20 per cent of the authorized capital would be paid in initially, part in gold and part in national currency.

Management of the Bank would be vested in a Board of Directors. Each member government would select one Director and would be entitled to cast one thousand votes plus one vote for each share of stock. No government, however, could cast more than 25 per cent of the aggregate votes.

Such an international body would not replace but would supplement traditional mechanisms for the placing of private inter-

[1] The subscription of the United States would be about one third of the total.

national loans and investments. The capital assistance provided through these channels in the past was sometimes wasteful and often spasmodic. Lack of care in the granting of foreign loans after the last war, for example, and lack of control over their expenditure played an important part in the collapse of 1931. Even when each individual loan transaction looks perfectly safe, the aggregate volume may make them all unsound and harmful. It may therefore be suggested that the new institution should register all international loan and investment transactions, both public and private, so that it would be in a position to advise both borrowers and lenders as to the desirability of prospective transactions.

The Bank could fulfill some of the functions of the Financial Committee of the League of Nations, but in a better organized manner. It would examine the situation of countries demanding credit similarly to the way in which this was done by the League of Nations. The confidence of private investors would increase greatly and the Bank would be able to mobilize international loans without lending from its own reserves.

These two monetary and financial institutions, one to stabilize exchange rates and provide short-term credit, the other to facilitate long-term international investment, are the main necessary instruments of international financial reorganization. As has already been made clear, no financial instruments are of themselves sufficient. For unless national governments do their utmost to correct domestic economic maladjustments, and unless the activities of the suggested international agencies are coordinated with international action in other fields, notably commercial policy, economic reconstruction after the war will not succeed.

VI

Human Relations

(a) *International Cultural Relations*

IN THE preceding chapter in the section dealing with labor, it was pointed out that the day's work and the wages for it depend in part upon the conditions under which workers live in other countries, as well as upon the capacity of the world market to absorb the goods which production turns over to trade. We have begun to learn, some of us at least, that this most intimate thing in our lives to which, indeed, most of our lives are devoted—work—has become a matter of world concern.

But alongside this world of the worker lies that of the thinker, the world of thought. Of the two, it is the more important. Work by brawn and muscle alone could never have built our civilization without the directing mind of the creative thinker. All through the ages, from the Ice Age down, every day there has been work to do for those who fed the tribe or built the huts that grew into towns and cities; but the thing that marked off mankind from the rest of creation was the power to think and reason. Slowly at first, and then with incredible rapidity in our own time, this capacity to think and plan and understand has become a mounting triumph, transforming the very conditions of life itself. Now, suddenly this world of thought is in deadly peril. The first triumph of the dictator is not over neighboring countries but over the mind and spirit of his own people. All the world shares in the loss of intellectual liberty when a nation surrenders to its demagogues, but after all, that is something for it itself to work out. Its destiny is in its own hands. When the process of intellectual blackout threatens to engulf the world, however, there is no ivory tower to which any nation can resort in safety and confidence. If the shots at Lexington were heard round the world, we should be hearing today the bombs which are defending the liberties of nations which have cherished their freedom and given the world the inspiration of their example; and just as we prepare material defense against physical invasion, we must look as well to our spiritual and intellectual defense against the invasion of those rights of freedom to think for ourselves which are the very bases of the American way of life.

Now, there are two ways of doing this. One is to declare an embargo on foreign ideas, to erect obstacles against their importation in some form of censorship, and even to penalize those intellectual leaders who insist upon the right to bring these ideas in. The other is to strengthen ourselves by a better understanding of both our own ways of thinking and those of other people, so as not to be taken unaware by the forces of reaction and anarchy.

Of these two ways the first is the most natural because it directs our attention against others. But for that very reason it is the least effective when it seems to be working best; for the repression of ideas breeds the habit of intolerance which in the name of liberty may end in persecution. It is not the purpose to discuss this method further than to point to the fact that the danger of its use is chiefly in times of crises, especially if we are confused and uncertain in our own minds as to what course we should follow. Then, if we are not on our guard we may find ourselves imitating the persecutors. It is clear that to maintain our intellectual liberty we need to do something more than to denounce its enemies or invoke the strong arm of the law against them.

It is the second way of defense, the development of international understanding, which offers the only sure hope of safeguarding our inheritance of culture and of preparing us to meet an uncertain future which seems to be shaping itself now in ominous and threatening forms. The only sure way to meet propaganda is to know what lies behind it and to have an independent judgment on the problems with which it deals. The present fear of it which has swept across the nation, while rooted in a sound instinct of distrust of the methods of molding public opinion in the United States, seems almost to have reached a point of not wanting to learn anything except what fits in with our previous prejudices. A forward-looking people must have a better way of sheltering itself against insidious ideas than by keeping its citizens ignorant. Even Mussolini and Hitler could do that.

Fortunately, the democratic countries of the world have already embarked upon a much safer course. In spite of the fact that in the years since the World War the religion of self-centered nationalism has gained fanatic hold in many countries, presenting new barriers to enlightenment, nevertheless, in this same period of history there has been a vast new wave of interest in what other people are doing and thinking and how their lives may affect ours. This new interest in the international world is to be found in every country, even those ruled by dictators, but in the democracies—by which is meant the countries that still treasure the institutions of freedom—this new interest in the world at large has become so important as almost to dominate both literature and discussion. We who are living in the midst of it can hardly estimate the importance of this change in outlook, from purely local things to world affairs. To find its parallel in history we have to go back to the close of the Middle Ages when the humanists rediscovered ancient Greece, and thrilled, as the poet Keats did three centuries later, at the widening horizon of knowledge. Just as they left the narrow confines of medieval thinking behind, so we have turned the corner on the provincialism and localism of the nineteenth century. Our windows are now open to all the world. It would be interesting, if we had time, to turn aside at this point and see ourselves in the looking-glass of history, to trace the change in the programs of social organizations in the last thirty years, from papers on Browning or Longfellow to discussion of disarmament, the rise of Nazi Germany, or the meaning of American solidarity; to compare the school textbooks of today with those of a generation ago.

We no longer think of Asia as merely the home of heathen peoples, nor of Europe as an old world of distance and romance. But the more we know about the world the harder we find it to understand. The things that seem most important to us are discarded by nations of equal intelligence and experience. For us, life, liberty, and the pursuit of happiness is more than a national ideal; it is the heart of the human problem. But half the civilized world today rejects these fundamental axioms of American history.

It is clear that if we are to make any permanent progress in international understanding we must go deeper than the day's news or even the study of history. We need international interpreters not only in politics and business but in the other ways in which nations express themselves, their arts, sciences, and literature.

Now, while it is true that specialists in different fields had kept track of what their colleagues in the arts and sciences were doing in different countries, there had never been a central clearing house to coordinate these efforts in the interest of a common civilization until the League of Nations set about the task of founding one. The story of this endeavor is little known in this country. It parallels to some extent the origins of the International Labor Organization. While that was being negotiated at the Paris Peace Conference, two Belgians, Professor Otlet and Senator La Fontaine, came to Paris to propose that the world of thought be recognized in the League of Nations as well as the world of labor. No one paid much attention to the idea at the time, although the French with their logical way of thinking saw something in it. The British and American delegations said that the League of Nations had a heavy enough task already without taking on the vast fields of thought and culture, and asked in their practical way what could be done about it anyhow. Nevertheless, the idea prevailed that "without a spirit of mutual understanding between nations the League cannot live" (M. Léon Bourgeois) and a section of the League later known as the International Intellectual Cooperation Organization was created.

In 1922 the first Committee on Intellectual Cooperation [1] was

[1] Henri Bergson was its chairman, and of the twelve original members the names best known to us are Marie Curie, Albert Einstein, and Gilbert A. Murray. G. E. Hale, of the Wilson Observatory, was the member for the United States; he was followed first by Robert A. Millikan, then by James T. Shotwell.

appointed by the Council to act in an advisory capacity to the Assembly. The Secretariat of the League carried out the recommendations of the Committee on Intellectual Cooperation until 1926, when the French Government offered it a special secretariat in Paris, known as the International Institute of Intellectual Cooperation.[1] Although Intellectual Cooperation has seemed to be an unfortunate title for this phase of international collaboration, at least for the English-speaking world, where people rather object to being classed as intellectuals, yet this Organization has had a remarkable history, and future organizations of the world will build upon its pioneering work if nations are to promote mutual understanding in the things worth while—art, literature, music, science, and in education generally.

This story of the activities of the Intellectual Cooperation Organization must be brief; yet even a partial enumeration of publications, of committees and of cooperating bodies will suggest policies and projects essential to the enlightenment of free peoples.

In the beginning, the disorganization of post-war Europe led the Committee to inquire into the conditions in the universities, the unemployment of professors, the plight of the students and the resources available in books, foreign publications, and instruments. In consequence, and in order to assist the rehabilitation especially of the universities of the new and smaller countries of Europe, where exchange was low and intellectual isolation and material poverty prevailed, National Committees on Intellectual Cooperation were set up in various countries. As soon as the usefulness of these Committees was apparent the Committee on Intellectual Cooperation, with the approval of the Council and Assembly, encouraged the organization of National Committees in all countries, authorizing such Committees to act as intermediaries with the International Committee. The National Committee of

[1] Although situated in Paris and supported largely by the French Government, the conduct of the Institute has been independent of control by that Government; its Director, M. Henri Bonnet, and the heads of departments have been appointed by the governing body, which is the Committee on Intellectual Cooperation; officials have included nationals of some fifteen countries. An International Act, passed by the Assembly in 1938 and designed to make this Organization into an autonomous body, resting upon the National Committees and financed by cooperating governments, was in effect in January, 1940, because ratified by ten countries.

the United States of America, financed by private funds, has acted in a liaison capacity for the United States with the Committee on Intellectual Cooperation and the Institute of Intellectual Cooperation, since 1926, even though the United States Government has not been a member of the League of Nations. The Chairman of this Committee has always been the United States member of the Committee on Intellectual Cooperation.

It is one of the strangest paradoxes of our times that when the Nazi infantry reached Paris, instead of destroying at once the International Institute of Intellectual Cooperation, they tried to take it over and to make it an instrument for propaganda in the French and Spanish-speaking countries, especially in Latin America. Thus the only part of the League of Nations which Hitler annexed was that which had been established to combat ignorance and prejudice among nations.

Fortunately this effort of the Nazis did not succeed. The National Committees set up in Latin America coordinated their work instead with that in the United States and held a conference at Havana in November 1941 at which a committee was appointed to reorganize Intellectual Cooperation in the Americas with the idea of keeping alive the spirit of the Geneva organization and to work out the basis of freedom. This committee met in November, 1943, under the chairmanship of the distinguished Brazilian scientist, Ozorio de Almeida, and accepted the invitation of the Government of Cuba to establish a provisional center in Havana until the time should come for the creation of a new and much more effective world-wide system of international cultural relations.

In the meantime many other efforts have been made to come to grips with the problems involved in the recovery of the world's heritage of intellectual freedom. This is especially true in the field of education. No other subject is discussed so often and with such differences of opinion as that of the need for the re-education of the Nazi mind. In London, ministers of education from the occupied countries meet with the British and American scholars to prepare workable post-war programs. In the United States, the newly established Division of Cultural Relations in the State Department has enlarged the sphere of its interest from Latin America to Asia and Europe and has added an expert in education to plan the program in that field which so long has been kept out of the purview of the Federal Government.

These miscellaneous activities of both government and private bodies need to be coordinated in an international cultural organization similar to that which existed in the League of Nations. This does not mean the creation of a vast bureaucratic system attempting international control in the world of thought and culture. On the contrary, it should be so planned as to strengthen each special movement for international understanding, both by bringing them a great degree of recognition throughout the world and by rendering more efficient their contacts with each other. Bilateral cultural relations will not be lessened by the widening of the horizons but will take their proper place in the perspective. The greatest stimulus to thought is the increased knowledge of what other people are thinking. And what holds true of the sciences holds true of the arts as well. Never in modern history was there so great a need for this combined effort to restore and strengthen the spiritual, intellectual, and cultural values which have become the proud heritage of civilized man in the long procession of the centuries. The terrible destruction and degradation wrought by the second World War in these higher realms of the mind is worse, if anything, than the destruction of life and property. Moreover, as we have seen in the opening chapter of this volume, total war begins years before the actual fighting—and this was equally true in the war against the Christian virtues and human kindliness.

Never was there a faster descent to the Dark Ages than that of the Axis Powers under Fascist and Nazi leadership, and the contagion of their malignant outlook was felt beyond the frontiers of their countries. There is no harder problem in the post-war world than the recovery of the lost decencies wherever the defiling touch of Nazi philosophy has reached. Well-meant efforts of a missionary character to reclaim a perverted generation may do more harm than good. It is a problem for careful and continued study by national as well as international organizations, designed to maintain and strengthen cultural intercourse between nations. These bodies should be representative of the spirit of man and not merely of the distinctive achievements of any one nation. They should not interfere with the process of education in any one country so long as the education was not directed against the interest of others; the first requisite in all this planning is the recognition that reform in education must rest upon a sound historical basis and accept a large degree of domestic control. Otherwise there is a danger of the same kind of regimentation as that to which the Axis nations have yielded. But unless the blind fanatic nationalism which has been prevalent in certain nations can be overcome, the institutions of international cooperation and all the efforts to create good neighborhoods will fail. The interchange of international cultures, which mutually enrich those undertaking it, should not be left wholly to private organizations, nor to individual nations distorting it into a medium of propaganda.

Government support for what has been termed the export of culture has long been practiced by the nations of Continental Europe, partly for the sake of the interchange with other countries which the practice invited, and partly for political prestige. This official recognition of national culture as an asset for diplomacy furnished the precedent for the corruption of the whole process by Fascist and Nazi propaganda, which, during a period of the impoverishment of culture, attempted to make it subservient to the religion of nationalism. The United States and the British Commonwealth of Nations have always been reluctant to use government agencies for this purpose, partly because of their inherent individualism and the fact that their educational systems are under local rather than national control, and partly because of a well-grounded fear of such use of the intellectual life of the nation as that of which Germany has been the chief exponent. Recently, however, both the British and the Americans have awakened to the need of explaining their method of government and way of life to the nations which have never known or appreciated what freedom means to us or the contribution of our intellectual life to the sum of things. This effort to explain ourselves to other nations has secured government support during the second World War. This is an unfortunate, if necessary, starting point, because it is difficult in wartime to keep the exchange of cultures free from political propaganda. A nation at war, fighting not merely for the preservation of its culture but for its very life, cannot keep a wholly unprejudiced view of the importance of its cultural heritage. Nevertheless, it is under these circumstances that it most feels the need for contact with the outside world. In any case, both Great Britain and the United States have now given official recognition to the need of international cultural cooperation. In the State Department, the Division of Cultural Relations was established before we entered the second World War, but its activities were limited at first to Latin American contacts and only this year has it finally been planned to enlarge it to cover the whole field. The British Government has not gone quite so far as this in the formal recognition of its interest in cultural relations, but the Foreign Office has recourse to a newly created body called the British Council and other more or less official bodies each composed of distinguished leaders in science, education, literature and the arts.

Thus the two nations are moving, if reluctantly, toward the recognition of the importance of cultural relations as an essential of a world-wide good neighbor policy. This trend toward government recognition of international cultural relations has possibilities beyond the range of our imagination today. When war no longer poisons the mind and warps the judgment, every nation will gain as it widens its horizons to include the experience and appreciate the achievements of other peoples. There is no better way to rid nationalism of the false conception of a superior people destined to rule the world than to open the windows to the winds of freedom and to the light of intelligence.

The structural problem of the International Cultural Relations Organization of the future will not be difficult if the need for it is clearly seen. It should, however, be planned with due regard to the differences just noted between the Continental European and the Anglo-American points of view. It should not be wholly governmental nor wholly unofficial. Its membership should be representative of national cultural associations or academies as well as of the governments. The precedent established by the International Labor Organization in having non-governmental representation, is especially important in this field in which freedom of thought and expression is of so great importance. In the United States, electoral bodies already exist in the Council of Learned Societies, the American Association for the Advancement of Science, the National Research Council, and the Social Science Research Council. Under the auspices of the National Committee of the United States of America on International Intellectual Cooperation, these and similar bodies could furnish a truly national representation in the international organization.

The relation of the central organ for International Cultural Cooperation to the national bodies presents less difficulty than its relation to certain regional groupings, such as the Americas and special international interests such as those of the United States in the Far East. Attractive and necessary as such limited areas of intercourse are, they need to be brought within the orbit of a world organization both for the sake of culture itself and in order to prevent the growth of antagonistic rivalries. International Peace has no solid ground to rest upon if nations are capable of accepting poisonous doctrines of racial or national denunciations against other people. The only adequate remedy lies in the schooling of intelligence to appreciate the variant achievements of peoples who have to work out their destiny under diverse conditions of history and physical environment. The greatest asset of a nation is not its material wealth but its intelligence, and the future of civilization depends upon the way in which that intelligence will be used.

(b) *The Safeguards of Freedom*

The closing words of the last section opens illimitable horizons. As we have said on more than one occasion, the greatest event which is taking place in the world today is not the World War nor a series of world wars, but the rise of science. More potent than all the armies of all the nations, thought is grappling with human destiny. As Marshal Jan Smuts has so eloquently put it, mankind has struck its tents and is on the march in a vast unending trek of pioneers into a new civilization of which only the distant outlines lie before us indistinct but shining far away.

We are leaving history behind as we make it. In the prehistoric past, the human pack and horde merged into the tribe and the tribe into the city-state or the military structure of empire and then, in the centuries of our own history, the national state became the sovereign political unit. Each of these social groupings cherished its own way of living and maintained it in the unending repetition and rhythm of the seasons through untold generations. The enemy to this sacredness of custom was the foreigner who had other habits and other gods. In the realm of taboo his very presence might be sacrilege. Therefore, the magician and the priest, with the support of the warrior class, guarded against the dangers from without. But war brought slaves as well as booty and as the artisans hammered out their tools or trinkets, shy but persistent merchants spread their wares outside the sacred city walls or in the bazaars of the Orient. Then culture traveled with the exchange of goods and the intermingling of the peoples. With the growth of property came the growth of law, a process older than Hammurabi which in the ancient world finally broke through the old taboos into the noble expression of human rights in Roman law. The only fitting law for a world empire was the Law of Nations (*jus gentium*) instead of the municipal law of Rome, for, in the creation of the universal code, the Roman jurists could call upon the experience of all mankind. Thus the Roman law in its final form was not purely Roman in origin; it was also the embodiment of Stoic philosophy and Christian morals. Because it drew from so many diverse sources and was applied to the citizenship of a universal empire, it proved to be the one contribution of ancient Rome which lives on in the world today.

Now the time has come for a new law of nations. The mingling of the peoples and the interplay not only of their cultures but of their rights in society are fully as great as was the case in those far-off days when the Roman jurists began their work. For they began it while Rome was still a Republic and the process of world conquest was in its early stages. Today the forces of science, stronger than all of Caesar's legions, are welding the world into a new formation which has no parallel in all the past. There have been two main patterns offered us to follow and our choice is being made in tragic but irrevocable decisions of the second World War. On the one hand, we have the German Peace (*pax Germanica*), a crude or rather a superficial imitation of the *pax Romana* based upon power but not implemented by justice; on the other hand, we have the cooperation of the freedom-loving nations. The German peace, military in conception, has no tolerance for variant forms of society and regards opposition to its political will as treason. This is the inevitable outcome of military control as Rome itself was to learn when the iron clamp of the dictator crushed out not only the liberties of Roman citizens but their very means of livelihood. The Roman Empire fell to the barbarians not as a powerful state pulsating with vitality but as a hollow shell decked in the outworn trappings of Byzantium. The same fate would ultimately befall any modern imitation of Roman militarism. The *pax Germanica* might have conquered the world in our time but it could not have furnished a fitting political embodiment for the dynamic forces of the world of science, the first condition of which is freedom.

The accent upon freedom, therefore, in our war aims is not mere rhetoric. In fighting for freedom, we are fighting for the only possible basis for the future—that which guarantees to each individual the open pathways of the mind and the free choice of a career. There is no hope for a society which revives the penalties of the taboo against the independent thinker; nor can justice develop under military regimentation. There must be freedom for the individual to experiment and to explore, to think and to express his thoughts, and that freedom must be safeguarded by both law and custom so long as it is not anti-social. This is what most people mean by democracy, not the rule of the many but rather the safeguarding of their freedom, a freedom that justifies itself by providing disciplined intelligence in its leadership and a critical, open-minded citizenship. It is worse than useless to create a vast system of international diplomacy and government if its control is to rest in the hands of those who are unfit for such high responsibilities, and that will be the case if the citizens are not alertly aware of their own interests and free to insist upon them. Civilization is not a mechanism but a vital principle, or rather an embodiment of many varied principles of life, which have their roots in diverse soils and their expression in divers cultures. It cannot flourish, it cannot even survive, if those in the seats of power deny it the fundamental freedoms of life itself. Therefore, tyranny, which denies these freedoms, is not merely a method of government, it is a crime against society.

This fact has long been recognized in the development of law and justice within the state, but never until our own time has it become a major question of international relations. It is true that throughout the centuries prophets and leaders of the great religions have denounced oppression and appealed for justice between man and man on a universal basis. But these general precepts have only been incorporated into law within the confines of each nation. While international law drew its inspiration from the universal principles of Christian, Greek and Roman ethics, its field was limited to the relation of one government to another. Each state, jealous of its sovereignty, has regarded any expression of foreign interest in the welfare of its citizens at home, as an interference in its own affairs. Now, as a result of the second World War, it has become clear that a regime of violence and oppression within any nation of the civilized world is a matter of concern for all the rest. It is a disease in the body politic which is contagious because the government that rests upon violence will, by its very nature, be even more ready to do violence to foreigners than to its own fellow citizens, especially if it can thus escape the consequences of its acts at home. The foreign policy of despots is inherently one which carries with it a constant risk to the peace and security of others. In short, if aggression is the keynote of domestic policy, it will also be the clue to foreign relations.

There is, however, a more fundamental reason for regarding

despotic governments as dangerous to the peace and prosperity of other nations than their own. No people can remain indifferent to the sufferings of innocent victims without losing something of their own spiritual life. We can no longer plead ignorance when these things happen in other parts of the world, for when oppression becomes a policy of state, the cries of the victims reach our ears from even the dungeons of the Gestapo. To ignore this suffering as having no part in our own lives is contrary to the dictates of Christian teaching. To offer only useless sympathy, attempting no measure of redress, is the kind of hypocrisy which lessens the moral fiber of those who attempt to satisfy their consciences with mere emotional appeals. Something must be done about it. But what?

The first step to be taken to safeguard freedom in the postwar world seems to most people too obvious to admit of argument. It is the proposal that there should be an international Bill of Rights to which all nations should subscribe, safeguarding the rights of citizens within the state against the encroachments of their own governments. This proposal is based upon the Bill of Rights in the Constitution of the United States and subsequent amendments to the Constitution and upon the still more basic institution of courts of justice provided with such implements as the writ of *habeas corpus*. The problem, however, is not so simple as that. Students of comparative law point out the fundamental differences in procedure between court systems based upon the English model and those of the continental countries which treasure the heritage of Rome. Moreover, the Oriental systems of jurisprudence offer another whole field of varied experience through longer centuries than ours. It has not taken long for the jurists to discover that this problem of finding a single formula for the safeguarding of human rights throughout the world is baffling and elusive.

Equally difficult is the matter of enforcement of the provisions safeguarding human rights after they are accepted by the country concerned. Wherever such measures are imposed from without, there will be difficulty in ensuring their fulfillment. The cases to be tried will ultimately come before their own tribunals, for the occupation of Nazi or Japanese territory will be purely temporary, and when the nation is left to itself there will be a tendency to view with hostile eye every innovation insisted upon by the conqueror.

It is easy, however, to exaggerate the difficulties in the pathway of this great reform. It must be remembered that the relatively short occupation of central Europe by the forces of the French Revolution and Napoleon profoundly modified the legal system of some parts of Germany, and even the jurists who sought a more Teutonic basis for jurisprudence were influenced by the Napoleonic episode to build a counterpart worthy of the German nation. There are those who fear that the occupation of France and other free countries by the Nazis may similarly affect, but adversely, the outlook of some of those who have witnessed at first hand the ruthless efficiency of the Nazi system of government. These apprehensions are probably unfounded because the Nazi, unlike the Jacobin, has violated the intimate relationships of domestic life. The fact remains, however, that both in the Axis countries and in those they have overrun, freedom can only be maintained in the postwar world to the extent that there is cooperation on the part of the nation to whom the boon is offered. Throughout all modern history, the safeguards of the rights of the citizen have been national. Anything resembling interference from without has been resented. International law as well as the practices of diplomacy have recognized the right of sovereign states to deal with their own citizens with only mild protests from other governments in cases of persecution and tyranny. There were, for example, protests over the Belgian atrocities in the Congo region, the pogroms of the Jews in Czarist Russia, or the conditions in Cuba where we took the risks of war. But it was not until the rise of the Fascist-Nazi doctrine of force and violence that the existence of systems of persecutions on a national scale began to be recognized as a danger to other countries and not merely a disturbance to the uneasy conscience of the onlookers. It became evident that governments which treated their own citizens with ruthless disregard of human rights were cherishing equal disregard for the rights of foreigners and were only held in check by fear of the consequences. When that fear gave way to confidence through the perfection of their military preparations, it was natural, if not inevitable, that they should turn from law to violence on the pathway to the second World War.

There can be no doubt that the disregard of human rights within the Axis powers was a psychological if not a real preparation for war itself. It therefore stands to reason that the structure of enduring peace must also include some provision for the maintenance of justice within states as well as between them, and that the time has come for agreement upon the fundamental principles of the Law of Nations. This cannot be achieved, however, all at once, nor by a simple formula, for there is no world government to enforce it. Having to rely upon the cooperative action of governments for enforcement, it must win the consent of each and all and be maintained by popular support. This does not mean, however, that nothing can be done about it. Indeed it would be more than absurd to rest with any such conclusions; for it would be equivalent to a connivance with despotism. The conditions which produced the second World War would soon be brought back, conditions of anarchy and violence and the denial of all the fundamental rights of men and citizens. We should therefore most certainly make a beginning now to bring these problems within the scope of a new League of Nations.

It has been suggested that the starting point should be a universal Bill of Rights, like those provisions which lie at the basis of the English and American systems of government. But a moment's reflection will remind us that the mere insertion of a formula in a constitution is not enough, because the enforcement of the provision is the all-important thing. It is a sobering fact that some of the countries in which human rights have been most violated have the best provisions in their constitutions against that violation. But it is also a universal fact that violent deeds are oftenest committed in the dark and that freedom of the press and public utterance are the best safeguards against injustice. In any case, this freedom of expression and of the newly-formulated right to listen should be the starting point, as indeed it has been in the past, for the development of institutions designed to build a Law of Nations for the world of today. Those institutions cannot of themselves be sovereign bodies. They can only study and recommend to governments the principles of a new jurisprudence which will deal, through governments, with the fundamental rights of human beings everywhere.

There should be a central institution, an Institute of Jurisprudence composed of the most highly qualified experts in law and government. It should be more than a conference of international lawyers such as the academy which the Carnegie Endowment for International Peace has supported. The outlines of it will have to be prepared in a constitutional convention called by the Political Organization of the United Nations, described below.

Attached to this Institute there should be an Office or Bureau constantly at work preparing the projects for discussion at the Institute and ensuring continuity and consistency of program. This too should be composed of an international Civil Service, drawn mainly but not wholly from the profession of the law, international as well as domestic.

Summing up, the project suggested here is not unlike that of the other technical organizations outlined above, all of which have as an initial model the **Constitution of the International Labor Office**.

VII

The Political Organization of the United Nations

(a) *General Statement*

THERE are two fundamental differences between the method described here for setting up the machinery of peace after the Second World War and the creation of the League of Nations at Paris in 1919.

In the first place, we are beginning earlier. The Fourteen Points of Woodrow Wilson came in January, 1918, almost ten months after the entrance of the United States into the first World War, whereas the Atlantic Charter was formulated four months before the United States entered the present war. There was no effort made by governments to create the post-war League of Nations machinery until the statesmen met at Paris. This time, with the end of the war scarcely in sight, we have already begun the creation of a United Nations post-war machinery.

In the second place, the method of creating this machinery is different. The League of Nations was created by a committee of the Paris Conference which met in hardly more than a dozen secret sessions, after which the Covenant was reported to the plenary session of the Peace Conference. The International Labor Organization was the result of a similar series of meetings of the Labor Committee, of which Samuel Gompers was the chairman and at which I had the privilege to assist. The League, then, was created in one piece by the Paris Conference. This time we are not beginning with the world organization as a whole, but we are following a more practical method, setting up special organs for specific purposes in a whole series of operations.

President Wilson's simpler plan had certain advantages. The League was a compact body, highly centralized, with the Secretariat, Assembly, and Council meeting in one place for efficient operation. Its scope was narrower than is now seen to be necessary. The task envisaged in 1919 was a pioneering one and could not go into all the details.

Today we begin with the details. The pattern is now unfolding for the creation of the United Nations of the World, which I presume will be the name of the world organization in place of the League of Nations. It would seem to be the holding of a series of conferences on various phases of world activity to create appropriate machinery, each one a room, so to speak, of the United Nations office. The architects of the new organization of international life will have to make sure not only that the rooms are provided, but that they fit with each other and that there are corridors connecting them without forcing the tenants to go out of doors when they wish to get together.

So far the contemplated United Nations conferences have had to do with economic and social reconstruction and not with major political decisions, which the four Great Powers have kept for themselves. The practical justification for this is that during the war all other considerations are secondary to securing victory and, in the nature of the case, military decisions cannot be shared by more than a very few persons who are responsible for carrying them out. But the present method of creating special organs for international action as they are needed, wise and necessary as it is, will eventually call for a coordinating center in the field of politics. For politics is, or should be, the general testing ground of all varied interests of economic, social and cultural life. This central body, in which the various international activities would be represented and weighed against each other, should be created before the end of the war because the necessary compromises between nations in disagreement can be reached much more easily while they are all engaged upon the common purpose of the war than after the war is over when their only concern is to get the fullest possible satisfaction by diplomatic and political pressures. The post-war world at best will not be a happy family of nations, and the more agreements we can make now as to the fundamental lines to be followed later, the better for the future peace of the world.

It is therefore time to think about the edifice of world peace as a whole and not merely the separate parts of it which are being created to deal with the most pressing problems such as relief and rehabilitation. All of these activities overlap and call for political judgments. The field of welfare cannot be organized without regard to that of security. Machinery to guarantee freedom from hunger or to stimulate sound economic practices will be worthless if we emerge from the second World War only to go into a state of preparedness for the third World War. The international organization will be an incomplete and unbalanced scheme unless we keep in mind the interplay of one subject with another, and above all, the necessity of working out a political cooperation to preserve the peace.

Before turning to examine this machinery, a word about the membership of the United Nations. Two questions at once confront us. First of all, how about the ex-enemy States, and second, how far is the "sovereignty" of a State limited by becoming a member. The question of membership of the enemy States need not bother us at the present time because no one could conceive of their acceptance in the United Nations so long as there was any slightest doubt of their sincerity in seeking to enter the new order. Nations which have risked their very existence in support of a theory of world organization, based on war and on the suppression of liberty, cannot overnight join in an organization devoted to the very purposes which they have so desperately attacked. Nevertheless, it is surely an axiom beyond debate that ultimately the United Nations must include the whole world. In no other way can it be a permanent safeguard of peace.

Now let us be quite clear about the question of sovereignty. Absolute, unqualified and unchecked sovereignty is a conception of anarchy. No civilized nation is free to do whatever it wants to without regard to the rights of other nations, committing acts of cruelty against their citizens, stealing their property, or otherwise conducting itself as a lawless state. International law is more than a philosophy to be taught in the schools. Every government knows that it is a member of a community of nations with well recognized rules of conduct, and is subject to the obligations in order to be entitled to the advantages of this membership. These advantages cover the whole range of international contacts, and every time a nation oversteps the mark by attempting to assert its absolute sovereignty without regard to the interests of other nations, it not only endangers its place among them, but it lessens its economic opportunities because other people no longer rely upon its word. It is time that the politicians understood this fundamental fact and stopped talking about national sovereignty as though there were no limits to it. Its limits are real and advantageous because all other nations live under the same conditions.

Summing up this discussion we have drawn a distinction between membership of the universal community of nations and active participation in administering its common affairs. Active participation should devolve at first, as we have said above, upon the United Nations which have been organized to win the war for freedom, but later it should be extended to all States which are willing and able to accept responsibility for maintaining the organization of peace and for supporting its program. The United Nations should aim to get rid of this distinction as soon as possible by the rapid liquidation of war. The international community cannot continue to exist, any more than the national State, half free. Nevertheless, if we move too fast, we may, as after the first World War, play into the hands of the militarist elements in both Germany and Japan. The timing and the planning of future cooperation with these nations will be a test of statesmanship. And statesmanship is good judgment when the time comes for exercising it.

Although the principle of universality cannot be achieved until the present war is liquidated, the plans for it do not have to wait for that event. On the contrary, they should be hastened to completion, for three reasons. In the first place, the organization of relief and rehabilitation must follow in the track of the invading armies, and preparation for such measures must therefore precede the final battles. This need has already been foreseen and is being met as the war progresses. In the second place, before martial law can be replaced by civil government, there will be need of cooperation with those elements in the enemy States with whom we can work, especially in the field of economics and finance. These arrangements should not be made in disregard of more general plans. It is quite possible for economic agreements by separate nations to block the path of the general settlement fully as much as was alleged to be the case of the secret treaties of the last World War. In the third place, agreement upon the general character of a constitution for the United Nations should be reached as soon as possible. No other act would have such a profound moral effect upon a world which demands that the challenge of the warlords shall be squarely met by an adequate organization of peace.

Once established on a universal basis, the organization of the United Nations should insist upon the loyal and active membership of every State. The principle should ultimately be accepted that nations cannot withdraw from the fundamental obligation of the maintenance of peace, however much they may lessen the scope of their cooperation in other ways. Withdrawal under such conditions would imply recourse to other methods than those of the peaceful settlement of disputes. Moreover, in view of the fact that the constitution of the United Nations would provide the preventive or remedial measures to be applied in case of war or the threat of it, a nation attempting to escape from those obligations would lose access to the cooperative procedures of the international organization. No nation would freely take this choice if the organization of peace were adequate, and it can only be adequate if it strongly holds to these principles and applies them for all. Expulsion from active membership under these conditions would be a futile gesture of the organized nations if it meant merely freeing an aggressor State from the disciplinary procedure applicable to members. Ultimately membership should be compulsory, as inevitable as international law itself.

The first of the tests for membership would be the acceptance of the Atlantic Charter, not only because it has been the basis of the initial organization of the United Nations, but because in itself it sets forth the principles of their future association, and does so in such general terms as to be applicable to all kinds of problems in an uncertain future. To those principles, already accepted in the Declaration of the United Nations, will be added further clarification from time to time; and insofar as the plans and principles here set forth, or any part of them, are accepted and applied, they would give concrete form and expression to them.

Alongside this principle of universality, however, as the final goal of the organization of the United Nations, provisions should be made for varying degrees of participation in its activities. In the field of security the distinction to be drawn will be mainly that between those powers most directly involved in any international dispute and those only secondarily affected by it. In this regard the great powers will inevitably have a more constant share in determining what should be done to preserve the peace, because no disturbance of it can take place without affecting them. Moreover, as the second World War has clearly shown, they must bear the chief burden in the maintenance of peace. They will, therefore, decide for themselves, and not upon the insistence of smaller nations, whether on any occasion they will take on that burden. This fact is unwelcome to those who dream of a superstate, but it is one of the firmest facts in all international relations. The great powers must have a recognized and special place in the organization of security of the United Nations. Happily, however, this situation creates its own counter-weight in obliging the smaller powers to draw together among themselves and the most effective way they can do this is to accentuate, both for themselves and the Great Powers, the procedures of collective security.

The same principle of varying degrees of participation applies to the other functions of the international organization. Economic relationships never fit a common pattern for all nations. They should be allowed to grow and develop freely so long as they are not directed against the welfare of other states in a disguised form of economic warfare. It is in this connection that the Molotoff reform of the U.S.S.R. constitution comes into the picture. As we have suggested above, that reform can be helpful in strengthening peaceful relations between nations by enlarging the economic and cultural contacts of the neighboring peoples whose autonomy is recognized in the constitutions of federal states. On the other hand, if those contacts are not under central control the responsibility for them is more difficult to trace. As we have seen in the case of our relations with Mexico and Canada, frontier problems are sometimes less easy to solve between adjacent local governments than between the national governments which must take into account more fundamental interests than those of the people along the border. On the other hand, international agreements which deal with the daily life of the common man will not work unless those citizens who are most concerned are willing to coöperate to help make them succeed. The issue upon which the Soviet statesmen have put their finger is one of the most real issues in the planning of an ordered world, but it is by no means a new issue in American history, for it has underlain the most serious of all obstacles that have confronted us in the policy of the good neighbor.

At last, however, we seem to be within reach of a solution. There is no insuperable difficulty in planning an international organization capable of dealing with the varied interests of economic life. The program and the solution have been well stated by the Prime Minister of Canada, Mr. Mackenzie King, in one of the most important pronouncements yet made by any responsible statesman:

"The time is approaching, however, when even before victory is won the concept of the United Nations will have to be embodied in some form of international organization. On the one hand, authority in international affairs must not be concentrated exclusively in the largest powers. On the other, authority cannot be divided equally among the thirty or more sovereign states that comprise the United Nations, or all effective authority will disappear.

"A number of new international institutions are likely to be set up as a result of the war. In the view of the Government [of Canada] effective representation on these bodies should neither be restricted to the largest states nor necessarily extended to all states. Representation should be determined on a functional basis which will admit to full membership those countries, large or small, which have the greatest contribution to make to the particular object in question. In the world there are over sixty sovereign states. If they all have a nominally equal voice in international decisions, no effective decisions are likely to be taken. Some compromise must be found between the theoretical equality of states and the practical necessity of limiting representation on international bodies to a workable number. That compromise can be discovered, especially in economic matters, by the adoption of the functional principle of representation. That principle, in turn, is likely to find many new expressions in the gigantic task of liberation, restoration and reconstruction."

(b) *Central Political Organization*

The general principles of world organization are now becoming clear. Each of the three great fields of human interest, security, justice and livelihood, must be provided with the instruments which will work best, and these will not follow any single model, but will differ according to the tasks which they must perform. In the field of security the great powers will dominate, no matter what the structure of international relations. Therefore this fact must be recognized and built upon, but the building will have to include the smaller nations as well. The inescapable conclusion is therefore that the organization of the United Nations will take shape—either now or at some future time—in a form very similar to that of the League of Nations. Two objections will be raised to this conclusion. First, that it awakens memories of a bitter political debate in the United States and, second, that the League of Nations has not succeeded in its major task and therefore something else should be tried in place of it. With reference to the first objection, the answer is that the sacrifices of this second World

War make it the solemn duty of every citizen to cast aside as far as possible the prejudices of the past and, looking only to the strengthening of the safeguards of peace for our country and for others in the future, clear our minds of everything that stands in the way of the best possible solution of so grave a problem. This is just what the American people have been doing in recent months and it seems not too much to hope that the same trend will continue in the future. As for the failure of the League of Nations, that is a history in which we can profit from mistakes as well as from successes. It is no argument against an institution that it is not always successful. No government of any State has a record that is free from failure. It took six hundred years for the British people to evolve their form of government. The Constitution of the United States, like all other constitutions, is a living organism capable of adjusting itself to changing circumstance and not a dry shell for dead issues. Similarly the world organization, starting with the institutions which are necessary for it in its early days, will develop under changing circumstances into forms beyond the reach of our imagination today. The evolution of the future is not, however, a matter for our concern. The practical needs of the present are definite and compelling. Fortunately the beginnings of the United Nations which have already been made are eminently practical; we have begun with first things first, but we need now to make sure that the machinery of international intercourse will fit together properly and will not break down through failure to support it.

All roads lead back to the political organization of the League of Nations as the starting point for that of the United Nations. It will need to have some central organization in which the work of the technical agencies can be brought into focus; but that organization cannot be a single body in which all nations will be represented on equal footing. It must also provide for the graded responsibilities of great powers and small and that means the creation of a smaller body in which the great powers dominate because of their relative size and importance in the world. In short, we have before us bodies resembling the Council and Assembly of the

League of Nations, but in addition, as we have seen when dealing with the Molotoff reform, there should be a plan for coordinating the technical international bodies so as to prevent their overlapping and yet keep them representative of their special interests in each country.

A Conference of the United Nations, like the Assembly of the League of Nations, is necessary to furnish a public forum for the discussion of major problems. This is the only way to prevent the interplay of national interests from sinking into the morass of intrigue which breeds suspicion and hostility among rival groups. Diplomacy will still remain the main instrument of inter-government dealings, but in the enlarged contacts of the modern world it must renounce the old methods of secrecy which opened the door to so much misunderstanding. This is especially necessary in multilateral negotiations and becomes imperative when all the nations of the world are concerned. But the conference method does not call for the full discussion of every point at issue in the whole public assembly. No conference has ever been a success which attempted to deal with delicate international problems by improvising solutions in the presence of many delegates. The solutions must be thought through and the proposals checked against each other in committees or smaller meetings. That is the way the Assembly of the League carried on its business, and it is the inevitable form for the organization of all major international conferences. The efficiency of the international conference, like that of a legislative body of any constitutional government, will depend upon the efficiency of its committees and its civil service fully as much as upon the capacity of the statesmen who address it in public sessions. All this is, or should be, commonplace, but it is often forgotten.

The smaller body in the central political organization of the United Nations presents far greater difficulties than the general Conference. Its task will be less that of planning long-range projects than of meeting the insistent problems of current politics. On the one hand, it must not be a super-government, and on the other hand it must be able to secure action when delay may prove dangerous. The model offered by the Council of the League of Nations has not been improved upon in any theoretic planning of recent years, although it may be bettered in detail. The history of the Council is its best justification. A wholly new experiment, it met the tests of the minor international crises surprisingly well, and if it failed when the Great Powers were involved we should learn from those failures how to make it more effective.

This brings us to the very heart of the problem of world organization. This is not so much the setting up of machinery for the transaction of international affairs as it is setting the machinery going, so that it turns out more than mere debates and documents. It must work in ways which will be accepted and applied by the governments concerned. More important than what the representatives of a nation say in an international body, is the extent to which their votes bind the governments which sent them there. It is here that we come upon the problem of a super-state; for if the votes are binding and cannot be vetoed by the national governments, the nations lose their freedom to that extent. On the other hand, if the votes are merely expressions of opinion and good will, like the resolutions in a public meeting, the whole organization will fall to pieces in time of crisis. The compromise which will secure real vitality for an international organization and yet not rob the constituent nations of any vitality of their own is the most difficult problem in all the history of politics. It cannot be sidestepped, however, by a generation which has witnessed the consequences of evasion in the second World War.

There is no perfect solution for this problem. Some doctrinaire minds attempt to work out mathematical percentages of voting so that the procedure would be settled beforehand automatically. But the great creations of politics have not developed according to the law of logic; those which have been most successful are the result of practical adjustments to real situations. In the international organization the problem of voting should therefore be settled with reference to the subject of the vote on the one hand, and the nations affected by it on the other. Both these qualifications would limit it so that the world organization would not have all nations voting on everything, for that could result in the greatest miscellany and confusion possible to conceive in the whole history of politics. Upon the whole, it stands to reason that the great powers are interested in practically everything the world over because questions of peace as well as those of war are bound to touch them sooner or later. The smaller powers have, upon the whole, more local interests, although some of them, like Canada, Norway, the Netherlands and Belgium, have wide international interests in shipping, commerce, or commercial enterprises. Within these fields the international community should have at least enough authority to call to account a nation which misuses its privileged position either for the establishment of monopolies that seriously cripple other countries or for the exploitation of colonial labor. Such matters can safely be left to the international organization itself to work out its own rules of procedure; it is more likely to under-stress, rather than to over-stress, its prerogatives. There will not likely be much reason to fear a lessening of sovereignty in the economic sphere.

Quite different, however, is the situation with reference to national security. Unless the machinery of peace enforcement will work swiftly and efficiently in the hour of crisis, it will not work at all; for the deadly timetable of the general staff of a military government will anticipate the forces of peace. Therefore, the obligation to aid in maintaining peace cannot be left to haphazard. On the other hand, no greater concession of sovereignty could be made than to permit an international body to order governments to take up arms for the sake of preserving the world community. So long as this problem was viewed as one of the kind of collective security that forced an equal obligation upon all nations members of the League, it failed; and it will be bound to fail in any future international organization. The second World War has, however, shown that the Great Powers can take over the task of restoring and preserving peace, not just in their own name, but in that of the United Nations. The Quadruple Alliance, established to maintain concert of Europe after the Napoleonic Wars, is now repeated in the Four-Nation compact of Moscow, Cairo and Teheran. It therefore assumes the quality of an institution and should be recognized as such in the international organization. Only in this way is it kept free from developing into a corporate international dictatorship of the Great Powers.

The way in which the Four-Nation Agreement can fit into the permanent organization of peace still lies in the field of conjecture and surmise. But it can be safely assumed that none of its members, certainly not the United States of America, would accept as binding any vote of the other governments with which it disagreed. This means that the rule of unanimity would prevail in the executive sessions whenever the Great Powers would be facing the major issues of security. We should then be able to impose our veto when our government was opposed to the proposals of that body.

It will at once be evident that this method of reserving national sovereignty on the vital issue of peace enforcement lessens in theory its inevitability. But, on the other hand, the written obligation, set forth in the constitution of the nations, should not go beyond the possibility of fulfillment. If peace enforcement were only a matter of police, this proposal to reserve unanimity in votes on peace enforcement would really undermine the whole structure but, as we have argued throughout the preceding pages, peace is not merely the absence of war, but the condition which offers mankind the only enduring values, economic prosperity and spiritual, moral and intellectual freedom. Unless these values are enhanced by the parallel action of other sections of the international organization, the police action against violence will not have enough support to be effective.

Summing up this short survey of the greatest of all political problems, we come to the following conclusions. The detailed development of the international organization is a matter for negotiation by the United Nations. The arrangement should be such as to prevent obstruction by either recalcitrant governments or those indifferent to the general welfare. The central organization, in providing a proper place for the Great Powers, must at the same time take the necessary precaution against allowing the international body to become an instrument of imperialism. This is not a mere counsel of perfection; for in proportion as the threat of war is eliminated by the increased efficiency of the operations of peace, political negotiations and arrangements among nations will tend to lose the sinister aspect of power politics and international relations acquire more of the character of politics within the state. Everything will depend, at first, upon the completeness of the pacification at the end of the war; then it will depend upon the strength of the guarantee against new outbreaks of violence. The provision for security in the Constitution of the United Nations is therefore as essential for the smaller as for the more powerful nations.

The functions of the central organization naturally fall into two main divisions. In the first place, it would deal with current questions brought to it by governments. In the second place, it would have general supervision of the activities of the various bodies associated with it. The first of these functions would also be of two kinds, those which could be dealt with in a single session of either Assembly or Council or both, and those which call for more mature consideration. Temporary or permanent committees could deal speedily with some of the more pressing problems. But the major issues of international affairs are too far-reaching and intricate for disposal in a single hurried conference. Therefore the central organization should be served by a whole series of permanent technical bodies, some of them general in character like the secretariat of the League, and others highly specialized, composed of technical experts as well as experienced administrators. These continuing activities fall within the three or four major categories mentioned above, under which they should be grouped structurally for their adequate performance. Each of these calls for its own specialization, and the whole group of institutions must be held together by an administrative organization which would at the same time be at the immediate service of Assembly and Council.

The problem of administration is very important. The success or failure of the whole enterprise will largely depend upon the wisdom and efficiency of its administrators. Every effort should be made to avoid the creation of a large, unwieldy international bureaucracy filled with office-seekers of all the participating countries. On the other hand there must be a competent secretariat under the direction of experienced and capable chiefs who in turn would have the confidence of those in every country who can speak with authority on the subject matter in hand. The administration should be planned not only with reference to the competent handling of each special subject but also with reference to the interrelation of these subjects in a political sense. It would be largely through the administrative machinery, for which the League of Nations Secretariat might well serve as a model, that the essential unity could be kept.

(c) *Regional and Other Organizations: Graded Responsibilities*

Although the organization of the United Nations must be world-wide, it should not be highly centralized. International cooperation, especially in matters of welfare and health may, in some instances, be more effectively administered from other centers than that of the political organization. Similarly in the field of security, regional organizations might constitute a first line of defense against local wars arising out of the quarrels of neighboring nations because they would be based upon the direct interest of each state in both its own immediate safety and in its intercourse with nations close at hand. Care should be taken, however, to ensure the proper articulation of these special and regional organizations with the central one. They should all subscribe to the same fundamental purposes and cooperate in their fulfillment.

The basis for the Constitution of the United Nations is enlightened national interest. The organization of peace will neither function nor survive except as it provides the promise of greater security and increased welfare for each member state. The obligations incurred by membership in the United Nations ought therefore to be recognized as differing according to the situation of the country concerned and its relation to the particular questions involved. Nations close at hand have a more immediate interest in maintaining a good neighborhood than those at great distances from the locality in which disturbances are threatened. But the measures which they may take for their welfare or self-protection must be in harmony with those of the United Nations as a whole, for otherwise the entire structure is weakened in proportion as the regional arrangements tend to supersede it. The only solution lies in a form of federal structure which provides for varied responsibilities according to the nature of each nation's problems.

This principle of varied responsibility in the Constitution of the United Nations is a major departure from that of the Covenant of the League of Nations, which was based upon the traditional theory of the equality of all states and the universality of obligation. Throughout the history of the League there was much debate upon this point. To some extent the acceptance of the principles that the Great Powers should have permanent membership in the Council was a recognition of the fact of their preponderant interest in world affairs as well as of their power. But the formation of local organizations or arrangements went on outside the League, although, for the most part, coordinated with it. The outstanding examples in Europe were the Little Entente and the Treaties of Locarno, but there were many other measures to safeguard peace and further economic cooperation, such as the Treaties of Arbitration and of Non-Aggression and the arrangements made by the smaller powers of Northern Europe. The League sought to take this process under its aegis even before the Treaties of Locarno were signed, by recognizing it in the Protocol of Geneva, and in the General Act of 1928, which was prepared as a guide for similar negotiations in the future so as to ensure their coordination with the Covenant. Nevertheless, the General Act seemed to realistic negotiators to present something in the nature of an afterthought in support of the Covenant at a time when it seemed as if the local arrangements were bearing the chief burden of war prevention.

This record calls attention to a danger inherent in the growth of regional organizations, that they may weaken, instead of strengthen, the general system upon which the peace of the world finally depends. So far as security measures are concerned, the problem, however, is only a variation presented by the need for adjusting the individual sovereignty of each nation to the needs of the United Nations as a whole. The solution in both cases lies in the acceptance of the principle of graded responsibility, and the historical precedent is that of the Federal State, especially as worked out in the Constitution of the United States of America and widely emulated in South America, in the provision for law and order in municipalities by the local police, in the States by the National Guard, and for the nation as a whole by its total armed strength. The parallel should not be pressed too far, for there are other forms of association than that created in the Constitution of the United States. The British Commonwealth of Nations and the Soviet Union present highly variant forms. Continental Europe, however, has, upon the whole, followed the trend toward centralization of power, and the experience of President Masaryk, an apostle of Jeffersonian democracy, showed that the smaller nations of Eastern and Central Europe have little appreciation of the possibilities of Federalism, having been schooled in Germanic concepts of sovereignty. Nevertheless, the Little Entente was a beginning in this regard and for a time there seemed to be possibilities of Balkan Federation similar to the Locarno Treaties. The entire situation of Continental Europe will be changed, however, at the close of this war and no one can foretell what it will be like.

The regional arrangements of the Americas are already well under way in the fulfillment of the good neighbor policies, not only those so notably sponsored by President Roosevelt and the State Department, but also those sponsored by Latin American countries themselves.

The regional organizations for the other areas of the world raise questions of a different character, especially those of the backward areas. For them a revised form of the mandate system of the League of Nations will be an essential, in order to fulfill the purposes set forth in the Atlantic Charter and the Declaration of the United Nations. These arrangements, however, will be necessarily more directly under the aegis of the central organization than in the case of groupings of sovereign powers outlined above. One reason for this closer association with the Central Organization is the fact that these backward areas will need help in improving health and eliminating contagious diseases as well as in securing adequate protection against economic exploitation. The details of such an organization do not present insuperable difficulties provided that the fundamental principle of the interest of the natives is accepted by the United Nations. The ultimate aim of self-government in these areas should be constantly kept in mind together with the trusteeship character of the United Nations Administration.

The need for other organizations of a limited character for other purposes has already been indicated in connection with proposals for welfare, human rights, and public health. In order for representation on these bodies to be real and not fictitious it should be made with reference to the ends sought, and not with reference to the prestige or political interests of nations not primarily concerned with the subjects in question.

VIII

The United States in World Organization

(a) *General Statement*

WE HAVE now reached the end of our journey through the world of tomorrow and must come back to the world of today. We have seen how science, henceforth the imperious master of human destiny, is forcing mankind to give up war by making it an all-pervading instrument of destruction so vast and complicated as to escape control. On the other hand, during this journey, we have never let ourselves be blinded to the fact that the forces of science are so new that the full extent of the revolution caused by them in human affairs is only beginning to be apprehended even by thoughtful people. The policies of nations do not quickly respond to the dictates of reason; they are much more responsive to the time-honored slogans which history provides. It is hard to realize that civilization is now passing over the great divide from its barbaric past to a future in which intelligence will slowly but inevitably assume the mastery over the remnants of the savage mind which still linger on in all of us.

War is not the only technique of savagery which remains with us. Taboos still survive to darken the conscience of the most civilized societies. Justice is an aspiration never wholly realized, but the war system is the outstanding symbol and fullest embodiment of all the remnants of brutish life. The extent to which it has been suppressed and forced to yield to the organized peace has been the measure of the progress of civilization in the successive stages of political evolution, first within the settled communities of cities, states or kingdoms, and finally within the nations of the modern world. As the haunting fear of danger was removed, the spiritual life of mankind blossomed with new ideals of justice and new creations of beauty in the field of art. Now, with the advent of science, other and still finer visions of justice and strange, new creations of art beckon at the door of the future. For science, by making industries interdependent, challenges old taboos and outworn customs with new demands for social justice, and in the field of art its creations are not limited to the copy of form and color, but move with the power of nature itself.

But all this mounting triumph of mind only increases the danger from the war system in the new era, a danger greater than ever threatened any previous stage of human history. It is hard to realize that "total war" is a wholly new thing. Even the caveman never practiced it. In savage life the world over war has been the monopoly of the warrior class. As we have seen above, the distinction between civilian life and the profession of arms was maintained and developed by States and strengthened by international law. From now on all this will be increasingly changed. Science throws into the crucible of war all the resources which it can reach in every land. Even in the troubled intervals of peace, so long as the threat of war exists, it will cut at the heart of peacetime prosperity, not merely by the increased cost of war establishments, but by turning the creative energy of science itself to the instruments of destruction. Therefore if the war system persists we have before us the possibility of a new dark age like that which happened at the close of the history of the ancient world. To most people this parallel will seem extravagantly overdrawn, but not to historians who have studied the way in which successive civilizations have perished. There is, if anything, less guaranty of the permanence of our own than of those of Greece and Rome, because the war-lords of today can master a force of destruction infinitely greater than that of the poorly armed barbarians who sacked the cities of the ancient world.

Fortunately the Tamerlane of scientific militarism can be met on its own terms and overthrown. The time to do so is now. Later may be too late, for if, dreading an uncertain future, the nations that have suffered the inescapable horrors of the second World War turn in their uncertainty to an almost convulsive resort to the same methods of defense as failed them in the past, the resulting anarchy will promise no security for anyone, but will block the path to the only real solution, which is the recognition that war itself is a supreme enemy of civilization and that it must be put down by whatever means are necessary, not merely moral suasion and economic pressure but, in the last resort, joint international police action including the exercise of force. All history shows that there is only one way to ensure lasting peace. It is by asserting the authority of the law. In the international community there is one law upon which all can agree, and that is that the resort to "war as an instrument of national policy" is a crime against mankind. The Paris Peace Pact of 1928 (the Briand-Kellogg Pact), which set forth this moral principle, must now be supplied with its missing article, that which provides for its enforcement against the aggressor.

There is no escaping the issue which is here presented. The choice which lies before the world can no longer be evaded by one nation placing the responsibility upon another. The time has gone by for that commonest of all practices of hypocrisy. We of the United States are face to face with the question whether we shall play our part in the elimination of war and the organization of peace, or whether we shall by attempting to stand aside become the unconscious accomplice of the future aggressor. The power which we have shown in this war is a measure of our responsibility in the making of the peace. It is equally true that this responsibility must be shared with the United Nations, and more especially Soviet Russia and Great Britain. The military prestige of the U.S.S.R. at present outshines that of all other warring Powers, and Great Britain is still a bulwark of freedom for Western Europe; but without the embattled power of the United States the war could never have run its full tide of victory over the Axis Powers. We have therefore an opportunity as well as a duty for exercising a decisive influence upon the final settlement.

No one questions our right to participate in the making of the peace any more than in the making of the war. No one questioned it even at the time the Atlantic Charter was drawn up, although that was months before Pearl Harbor. But there is widespread doubt as to whether we shall make good the promises implied in our statement of the fundamental principles of a lasting peace. That doubt is not merely based upon our past history. It is also due to the fact that we have not apparently clarified the issue in our own minds with reference to the one fundamental thing, namely, what is the extent of the commitment necessary if the "general international organization, to maintain peace and security" of the Moscow Agreement is to be made good. Let us therefore, at the close of this survey, come squarely to grips with this fundamental question of what would be the place of the United States in the organization of peace. Would it involve a lessening of its sovereignty? Or would it only be using its sovereign powers to preserve its freedom among other nations and the freedom of its citizens at home?

These questions cannot be answered by vague generalities but only by coming to grips with realities. We start with the established and accepted fact that "the general international organization to maintain peace and security" of the Moscow Declaration will not be able to exist without the participation of the United States. But that participation will in turn depend upon something less august than the high moral purposes which have inspired the movement for international peace. The question will have to be brought down from this high plane to the level of practical politics, of how and on what the international body shall vote. If that body should take on the character of a super-government, the United States would not participate or would only participate under reservations which would largely nullify the powers of the international organization. On the other hand, if the action of the central body is subject to the veto of each and every member, it has no power at all. Unless there is a way to escape from both horns of this dilemma, we shall, when the test comes, be faced with disillusionment in our planning fully as much as in the 1920's, if not more.

Fortunately, with the experience of history to guide us, we can escape the dilemma by avoiding past mistakes. We know now, or should know, that the plan of the international organization of the future is an engineering rather than an architectural job. The political forces of today are vital and ever changing, and the instruments for dealing with them must not be too rigid but constantly adjustable to their task. This is what we mean when we say that they must be functional and practical. While this has always been more or less true of politics, its institutions have been so largely conceived in terms of power that they impress the imagination and are cloaked with the majesty of law. It was in this setting that the League of Nations was conceived like a Temple of Concord set alongside the capitals of sovereign States. Today we are building differently. Instead of drafting a constitution for the world in broad, firm outlines, leaving it for the future to fill in the details, the United Nations are already at work, as the body of this book has shown, carrying on activities of common interest by the creation of U.N.R.R.A., the Food and Agriculture Organization, and other international bodies, and by the support given the work of the International Labor Organization. This is the functional method of international cooperation, thinking first of the job to be done and then of the best means for doing it. No impairment of sovereignty is necessary when nations cooperate with each other on these terms, provided that the scope and the procedure of their cooperation are both consonant with the fundamental interests of the participating State.

The contrast between the method being pursued today and that which was followed in the creation of the League of Nations is surely evident without going back into a detailed analysis of history. It is no derogation of Woodrow Wilson's statesmanship to assert that the method of today is a sounder one; for in those pioneering days it was necessary to concentrate the attention and stir the imagination of the nations by an architectural creation without parallel in history. Even that challenge to the imagination, daring as it was, did not win sufficient support to overcome nationalist opposition in the succeeding years. The functional method of setting up the international organization keeps closer to realities. It is designed to meet inescapable problems and to deal with them in the most effective way. Therefore its organs will be varied according to the tasks which they have to perform. Ultimately the whole assemblage of its functions will require a central structure like that of the League of Nations, for without a coordinating center the activities of the various parts would become confusing and contradictory. But the chief purpose in the making of the new international organization will not be the creation of a magnificent symbol of world unity, inspiring as that ideal is; it will be the erection of a working instrument to guarantee peace and justice between nations and to help in securing better conditions of living for the common man the world over.

Stated in these terms, and they are the only real terms of an enduring organization of peace, it will be seen that they are but the fulfillment of the aims of the Founding Fathers, as set forth both in the Declaration of Independence and the Constitution of the United States. The task which they faced, that of uniting the Colonies into a confederation and then "a more perfect union" of states to form a single nation, was fundamentally a domestic problem and it is doubtful whether the great experiment of federalism could have been carried through successfully if the United States had had to enter at once upon the stage of world affairs and had not been protected by distance from the danger of foreign wars. But it is a wholly false interpretation of American history to conceive of the political doctrines of the Revolution and the Constitution as constituting a kind of Chinese wall of political isolation from the rest of the world for all time to come. Washington's neutrality proclamation of 1793 and his Farewell Address of 1796 are often referred to as though they had set a permanent pattern for American foreign policy, whereas both were conditioned by the fact that Europe was engaged in the wars of the French Revolution which were fought on issues that did not involve the vital interest of the United States. Nothing could be farther from the truth than to interpret these documents as indicating that Washington's view of world affairs was that of narrow, self-centered nationalism. On the contrary, several passages in his writings show the breadth of his vision and should rank alongside of the Farewell Address as a guide for American thinking. One of these occurs in a letter to Lafayette, written in 1786, in which he spoke of all mankind as one family, with world peace as its ideal.[1] The thought is on the same high plane as the teachings of the two sages of the East and West, Confucius and Immanuel Kant. Nor was Washington alone among his contemporaries in basing national polity upon the broader concepts of a universal humanity. There can be no doubt that if the statesmen who presided over the destinies of the United States at its beginning were to face the problems of the present, they would look not backward to an isolation of which science has robbed us forever but forward to the real issues of the present and future.

The argument of the foregoing pages may be summed up in a few words. We have to apply the functional methods to the three great fields of international relations: security, justice and livelihood. In each field appropriate methods and instruments must be applied, and naturally they will differ according to the problems with which they have to deal. In the field of security, the need is for an arrangement which can be counted upon to work quickly and effectively in times of crisis. In the field of justice, the need is for impartial judgment based upon wide experience as well as knowledge of law. In the field of livelihood, provisions shall be made for conciliation and conference, leaving the ultimate responsibility for action upon the governments concerned. At the risk of repetition we shall run over each of these problems once more.

[1] "On these occasions I consider how mankind may be connected like one great family in fraternal ties. I indulge a fond, perhaps an enthusiastic idea, that, as the world is evidently much less barbarous than it has been, its melioration must still be progressive; that nations are becoming more humanized in their policy, that the subjects of ambition and causes for hostility are daily diminishing; and, in fine, that the period is not very remote, when the benefits of a liberal and free commerce will pretty generally succeed to the devastations and horrors of war." *From Washington's letter to Lafayette, August 15, 1786.*

In this connection it is surely fitting to recall the following passage from Washington's last letter to Lafayette, written on Christmas Day, 1798, only a few months before his death: "My politics are plain and simple. I think every nation has a Right to establish that form of Government under which It conceives It shall live most happy, provided it infracts no Right or is not dangerous to others." The qualifying clause is fully as important as the general principle which it modifies.

(b) *Security*

It is only in the field of security that this multiple organization approaches the nature of a super-government; for that reason the safeguards against too great a commitment are as important as the maintenance of peace itself. The proposal is that the four nations which signed the Moscow Declaration, the United States, Great Britain, the U.S.S.R., and China, along with such others of the United Nations as are available and qualified for the purpose, should form a trusteeship for the maintenance of peace, thus making good the promise in that Declaration that they would "consult with one another and as occasion requires with other members of the United Nations with a view to joint action on behalf of the community of nations." This formula of the Moscow Agreement bears all the marks of careful drafting. The trusteeship which the signatories announced is not even an alliance at the start. The statement that they will "consult with one another and . . . with other members of the United Nations with a view to joint action," is a cautious diplomatic phrase which does not bind any of the nations against its will. It is wholly in harmony with an earlier phrase in the same document that the "General International Organization [is to be] based on the principle of the sovereign equality of all peace-loving states." While the details of this organization have yet to be worked out, the idea which has gained the widest acceptance in unofficial discussions is that the signatories of the Moscow Pact should form a unitary, initial organization which could readily take the form of a Defense Committee of the General International Organization. Under this arrangement there could be joint police measures to preserve the peace, but action would only be taken by the unanimous consent of the participating powers. In other words, no nation would be called upon to act against its will. When, however, joint agreement was reached that a case had arisen which called for the use of force to maintain peace the members of the Defense Committee, having "consulted together with a view to joint action," could in all likelihood rely upon the signatory nations fulfilling their duty quite as much as if they had given a hard and fast commitment. It should not be forgotten that the treaties which bound France to come to the aid of Czechoslovakia and Poland were no more effective in the hour of crisis than the more general obligations of the Covenant of the League. The really compelling fact which will make nations live up to a commitment to cooperate in the prevention of war is the danger to themselves if they do not do so. We therefore come back to the fundamental thesis of this book: that war under the conditions of modern science cannot be permitted anywhere in the world without endangering the peace of nations not parties to the dispute. Once that truth is driven home it will be a stronger guarantee for the preservation of peace than treaties which nations may seek to evade.

With this provision it could never be claimed that the United States could be dragged into the wars of other countries against its will. On the other hand it would not deny to the Defense Committee a vast and, in most cases, an overwhelming influence against the outbreak of war. It is of tremendous importance to have the Great Powers coordinate their efforts to maintain the peace in an institution dedicated to that purpose. The Defense Committee would be constantly at work in the quiet times of peace as well as in the crises which might breed war. Through such cooperative effort the will to peace would be immeasurably strengthened. The Defense Committee would therefore function as an executive committee of a slightly larger council resembling very much the Council of the League of Nations, the chief duty of which would be not merely to prevent war but to prevent provocative conditions from arising between nations. Alongside this executive body the Assembly of the United Nations would both strengthen the moral purpose and supply the added instruments for carrying it out. Thus the "General International Organization" would take the form of a revived and revised League of Nations, with the commitment to maintain peace "by whatever force is necessary" strengthened by both the experience of history and the needs of the future.

There has been too great a tendency in international planning to provide an iron-clad constitution which would, on paper at least, meet all emergencies. This tendency is especially noticeable in the plans for world peace drawn up in the United States. The reason is that our federal system of government teaches us to think in legal terms, to seek definite written guarantees in the constitution and the law to such an extent that we are not properly mindful of the great tides of political forces which may either reinterpret the texts or sweep them away. The "General International Organization" will be either better or worse than its constitution according to the development of sound public opinion and the contribution of statesmanship in the countries concerned. It cannot be repeated too often that the organization of peace will ultimately depend less upon the safeguards of a constitutional nature and more upon the moral purpose to make those safeguards work.

(c) *Justice*

The path which Germany took leading to the second World War was by the violation of treaties. The forceful recovery of the Rhineland was a violation of the Treaty of Locarno, which provided pacific means of settlement for that dispute. Each successive step after that, in Austria, Czechoslovakia and Poland, tested the international legal structure of the European State System until finally, and too late, its defenders came to its rescue under the most unfavorable conditions possible.

No greater mistake could be made, however, than to conclude from this tragic page of history or from the nature of the war that followed, that international law is no longer important or valid. On the contrary, it must be strengthened and reformed as the safeguard for those stable relations between nations which are necessary for their prosperity.

The World Court is the keystone of the arch of international law and order. It should be re-established. Necessary reforms should be studied and applied, and its jurisdiction accepted within the limits set forth in the court statute, covering, in general, the interpretation of treaties and the application of accepted rules of international law.

The argument that it would lessen our freedom of action in dealing with other nations if we were to enter the World Court is based upon the same kind of theory of irresponsibility to the community of nations which underlies the argument of the Nazis that they alone are to be the judges of their own action. It is unthinkable that we should any longer hesitate in regard to our relations to the World Court.

The Permanent Court of International Justice, to give the World Court its full name, deals only with governments in their relation with each other. The Nazis, however, have taught us that the violation of human rights within a nation may create sufficient disorder in the world to be an underlying cause of war. There should be an international institute either attached to the World Court or separate from it, to study the problem of human rights in all nations and the possible guarantees of freedom everywhere. Its recommendations should be referred to the governments of all nations, either separately or in joint conference.

(d) *Livelihood*

There can be no doubt that the problems of livelihood or welfare are chiefly domestic. They have to do with the day's work and the conditions of living in home and city and countryside. It is only with the growth of modern industry that the international aspects of economics have come so largely to the fore. It is but natural therefore that the growth of international bodies to deal with the problems of human welfare should be subject to very close, critical scrutiny because of the fear that they may infringe upon the sphere of domestic legislation. The apprehension lest governments should attempt to legislate by way of treaties is not limited to conservatives; it is widely shared by liberals who are jealous of the growth of executive prerogatives. The problem of setting up international economic organizations in harmony with the constitutions of sovereign states is a real one and must be faced in definite terms.

The answer to the problem lies readily at hand. It is that the international economic organization should, upon the whole, be limited to conference and consultation. The model to be followed is that of the International Labor Organization. While there would naturally be variations in details, in view of the fact that the whole structure rests upon a functional basis, the I.L.O. is the pioneering body which points the way to securing consultation under the best possible conditions.

As outlined above, the I.L.O. is composed of national delegations upon which non-governmental representatives are officially recognized alongside those of governments. On each national delegation there are two government representatives and one each from the employers and the workers. A Governing Body on which the countries of "chief industrial importance" are represented prepares the material. Thus the I.L.O. works by weighted majorities designed to secure adequate representation for the countries and the interests within the countries which are chiefly concerned with the question on the agenda. When agreement is finally reached it is embodied in a "draft convention" which is submitted to the member governments for ratification, or in the parallel form of a recommendation, for legislation. All questions are prepared by a highly qualified technical staff which sometimes works for one or two years on the details.

This procedure furnishes a helpful suggestion for the methods to be employed in other economic bodies which deal with questions of legislation. It is a procedure which must be limited either by holding it down to a recommendation for legislation or by circumscribing the field so as not to interfere too largely in domestic affairs. The final decision of acceptance or rejection would rest with the national government. Once again there is no superstate envisaged in such a program.

So far we have been dealing with the major organization designed for what has been termed "international legislation". There are others which are primarily administrative in function, the most recent example of which is the United Nations Relief and Rehabilitation Administration. An organization for action cannot refer each item in its program back to its constituent governments. Once its budget is voted, its responsibility for the effective discharge of its program must be left to its own officers. The outlines of its program are prepared by its own deliberative body because they must be adaptable to changing conditions. A national government like that of the United States will naturally be careful to delimit the field of activity of such international administrative bodies; but once having accepted the principle that a given organization is necessary and that we should participate in it, we should maintain that participation loyally until the structure itself is changed by agreement.

In actual practice these problems of international administration will undoubtedly prove less difficult than may be anticipated in theoretical discussions. In any case, there is no evidence of reluctance upon the part of American public opinion to fulfill our national obligations in all those activities which have to do with the pressing need of relief or reform in dealing with the less fortunate peoples of the world.

(e) *Central or Political Organization*

The functional method of organization is sound so far as it goes. But none of it will work satisfactorily unless the central political issue of war and peace is adequately dealt with. It is not only the question of security which makes the creation of a central international body essential, although that by itself would be enough. There is the added need of preventing overlapping or contradictory action by functional bodies of limited jurisdiction. It is self-evident that none of these functional bodies can operate without reference to others. None of them can work without money. The coordination of activities in a central political clearing house or in a central economic commission is essential. There is ample lesson in this regard in our own wartime government as it has been improvised to meet changing situations.

The need for this central international body is clear enough, but there is no precedent either in international or national political experience which is wholly applicable to it. The structure of the League of Nations offers valuable suggestions which we must feel free to use without prejudice or without even a reminder of past controversies. The test is whether an institution will work, not what has happened under other conditions in the past. We can only repeat here what we have said throughout this survey, that we must first consider the kinds of problems which will be met in the future, and plan accordingly.

(f) *The Constitution and World Organization*

We come now to the final problem in the minds of all thoughtful Americans. How can the organization for international peace fit within the framework of the Constitution of the United States?

Fortunately this problem has recently been dealt with in an authoritative survey by one of the most competent students of American constitutional law, Professor Edward S. Corwin, of Princeton University. In his recent volume entitled "The Constitution and World Organization," Professor Corwin surveys the problems of sovereignty, of constitutional limitations, and of the Senate's role in the conduct of foreign affairs. The impact of the problems of war and peace upon the Constitution is summed up at the close in an *Epilogue* which is so pertinent to the argument of this volume that, with the consent of the author and of the publisher, I have decided to close this discussion by quoting it in full:

> With the possible exception of the Civil War, the impact of World War II upon our institutions is the most massive force to which they have ever been subjected, and the shape which they will assume after they finally emerge from that unparalleled pressure is still to be determined. One thing, nevertheless, can be said at once. The chief beneficiary of the current war effort will be, in terms of governing power, the Presidency, as ultimately it has been of every great war in which this country has taken part in the past.
>
> We have thus shared in some measure, and are destined to share further, in a movement which has elsewhere attained the dimensions of disaster, and the results of which we are today combatting on a dozen fronts scattered over the globe. Throughout the greater part of the nineteenth century the strong flow of power was from the executive to the legislative. That is what the spread of political liberalism signified. So far this century this flow has been sharply reversed and before the resurging current constitutional governments have toppled even in some countries where they had long seemed part of a solidly established order.

What was the cause of this reactionary movement, so disappointing to the prophecies of less than a generation ago, when the world was being made safe for democracy, so calamitous to human freedom? First and last, the most efficient cause was war actual or threatened, and the necessity which states have been under not only of conducting their foreign relations, but also of planning their domestic economics, in the shadow of this constant menace, which has progressively deepened as war has become more terrible.

So today the maintenance of constitutional government in the United States becomes linked with the broader cause of its restoration and preservation elsewhere. This broader cause is, however, one which we can aid in the long run only collaterally, through the foreign policies we choose to pursue. Time was when our dominant position in the Western Hemisphere and the Monroe Doctrine, which vocalized this dominance, assured us against becoming involved in extra-continental wars, and thereby protected free institutions among us. Unfortunately that assurance no longer holds, a fact of which our entry into two world wars within a generation is certainly sufficient proof.

What choices, then, are left us in the realm of foreign policy? I see only two: *imperialistic adventuring* and *the active promotion of world peace,* and which of these alternatives is likely to supply the more favorable conditions for the continuance of constitutional democracy among us is hardly open to reasonable doubt. Yet even wars fought for the most generous ends can still spell disaster for that complex set of values which our Constitution aims to uphold and promote. In World War I we sought no territorial or other gains for ourselves except some guarantee that the peace following it would be a lasting one. Nevertheless, it was following this war that so sober and conservative a thinker as former Chief Justice Hughes raised the question whether, "in view of the precedents now established . . . constitutional government as heretofore maintained in this Republic would survive another great war even victoriously waged."

That question is still unanswered and, as I implied above, will probably remain unanswered for some time to come. But the question itself bears witness to the fact that the *cause of peace abroad and the cause of constitutional democracy at home are allied causes,* and must be so treated by those whose lot it will be to forge our foreign policies in the years to come.

And as this study shows, there are no substantial constitutional obstacles to the pursuit by our government of a foreign policy which has as its main objective the maintenance of international peace, while as to Sovereignty I repeat: *When Total War is the price of Total Sovereignty,* the price is too high. What, indeed, is "Sovereignty," as we see it daily at work, except the freedom of decision and action with which the Constitution and laws endow our governing agencies; and always the important question is: How can this freedom of decision and action be exercised by such agencies so as to serve best the real freedom of the American People, their "Unalienable right" to "life, liberty and the pursuit of happiness"?[*]

[*] Quoted by permission of the publishers, Princeton University Press.

The conclusion is that only through the organization of peace can our constitutional liberties be preserved. The alternative is some form of militarism, for that would be the only safety for our country if confronted with the danger of a third World War. But to keep the ramparts of freedom manned, with the necessary support from sea and air, we should have to meet the menace of total war with plans for the total conversion of our economic strength, thus denaturing our whole social and political life. The only way of escape from this dangerous trend in the history of a democracy, a trend which has betrayed other nations in the past, is through the organization of peace.

It would be over-dramatizing the decision which the American people must now make, between the continuance of international anarchy and support for the rule of law throughout the world, to think of the army and navy headquarters in the great Pentagon building across the Potomac from the White House as the center for a future Praetorian Guard crushing underfoot the provision of the Constitution. Such a development in the United States of America is unthinkable. But it is only unthinkable because of our confidence that peace will be the normal relationship between nations. In the nineteenth century we cherished the hope that war would be narrowed to a vanishing point, and yet maintained it as an institution for the final settlement of international disputes. Two world wars have shown us the fallacy of that theory of international relations, the one upon which we have hitherto relied. We know now that permanent peace cannot be assured by a do-nothing policy, but that we must build the structure of international relationships to prevent the danger of war arising and supply that structure with sufficient force to keep the lawless nations within the law. If at the same time full provision is made for peaceful change and the redressing of out-worn or oppressive conditions, the sword which Justice holds need never be sullied.

So far we have been dealing with the structure of economic organizations within the "general international organization" rather than with their functions. To stop at this point would be especially fallacious in the economic field. More than once in the course of this volume we have emphasized the strength and vitality of economic forces as the real, creative, energizing elements in international relations as well as within the state. We must therefore turn from the agencies for doing things to the problems themselves.

A good illustration of the way in which political planning in the economic sphere is obliged to meet the tests of reality is offered by the reaction of the world of business and banking to the plans for establishing an international stabilization fund, described in an earlier chapter. The resistance of banks to the proposal that an international fund of eight billion dollars should, directly or indirectly, be placed at the disposal of governments, is based upon concern for the maintenance of the credit structure which has been built up by modern banking in the course of its entire history, fearing transference of financial trusteeships to agencies dominated by political considerations. The attitude of the world of trade is also somewhat hesitant; for it holds strongly to the thesis that national currencies cannot be stabilized with reference to each other without regard to the movement of those goods and services which money can buy. Here we come back to the argument of the earlier chapter, that the solution for international economic maladjustments, as well as for prosperity at home, lies in the lowering of barriers to trade, if that policy be combined with domestic fiscal policies designed to make taxation an instrument for preventing exploitation.

None of these problems can be settled at once. There will therefore be need for continuing discussion and planning in international bodies. The one thing that is perfectly clear is that they cannot be left to the hazard of sudden improvisation in hours of crises. Hardly less important than the prevention of a third world war is the prevention of a second world economic depression, for in the disorders which it would breed lie the roots of war itself. These are sobering thoughts, but they are the inescapable conclusions of any serious consideration of world economics.

Appendices

THE ATLANTIC CHARTER

As promulgated by PRESIDENT ROOSEVELT *and*
PRIME MINISTER CHURCHILL *on August 14, 1941:*

THE President of the United States of America and the Prime Minister, Mr. Churchill, representing His Majesty's Government in the United Kingdom, being met together, deem it right to make known certain common principles in the national policies of their respective countries on which they base their hopes for a better future for the world.

1. Their countries seek no aggrandizement, territorial or other.
2. They desire to see no territorial changes that do not accord with the freely expressed wishes of the peoples concerned.
3. They respect the right of all peoples to choose the form of government under which they will live; and they wish to see sovereign rights and self-government restored to those who have been forcibly deprived of them.
4. They will endeavor, with due respect for their existing obligations, to further the enjoyment by all States, great or small, victor or vanquished, of access, on equal terms, to the trade and to the raw materials of the world which are needed for their economic prosperity.
5. They desire to bring about the fullest collaboration between all nations in the economic field with the object of securing, for all, improved labor standards, economic advancement and social security.
6. After the final destruction of the Nazi tyranny, they hope to see established a peace which will afford to all nations the means of dwelling in safety within their own boundaries, and which will afford assurance that all the men in all the lands may live out their lives in freedom from fear and want.
7. Such a peace should enable all men to traverse the high seas and oceans without hindrance.
8. They believe that all of the nations of the world, for realistic, as well as spiritual reasons must come to the abandonment of the use of force. Since no future peace can be maintained if land, sea or air armaments continue to be employed by nations which threaten, or may threaten, aggression outside of their frontiers, they believe, pending the establishment of a wider and permanent system of general security, that the disarmament of such nations is essential. They will likewise aid and encourage all other practicable measures which will lighten for peace-loving peoples the crushing burden of armaments.

FRANKLIN D. ROOSEVELT.
WINSTON S. CHURCHILL.

ARTICLE VII OF THE MUTUAL-AID AGREEMENT

In the final determination of the benefits to be provided to the United States of America by the Government of the United Kingdom in return for aid furnished under the Act of Congress of March 11, 1941, the terms and conditions thereof shall be such as not to burden commerce between the two countries, but to promote mutually advantageous economic relations between them and the betterment of world-wide economic relations. To that end, they shall include provision for agreed action by the United States of America and the United Kingdom, open to participation by all other countries of like mind, directed to the expansion, by appropriate international and domestic measures, of production, employment, and the exchange and consumption of goods, which are the material foundations of the liberty and welfare of all peoples; to the elimination of all forms of discriminatory treatment in international commerce, and to the reduction of tariffs and other trade barriers; and, in general to the attainment of all the economic objectives set forth in the Joint Declaration made on August 12, 1941, by the President of the United States of America and the Prime Minister of the United Kingdom.

At an early convenient date, conversations shall be begun between the two governments with a view to determining, in the light of governing economic conditions, the best means of attaining the above-stated objectives by their own agreed action and of seeking the agreed action of other like-minded governments.

THE THREE-POWER CONFERENCE AT MOSCOW

Text of the Agreements

JOINT COMMUNIQUE OF TRIPARTITE CONFERENCE.

The conference of Foreign Secretaries of the United States of America, Mr. Cordell Hull; of the United Kingdom, Mr. Anthony Eden; and of the Soviet Union, Mr. V. M. Molotoff, took place at Moscow from the nineteenth to the thirtieth of October, 1943. There were twelve meetings. In addition to the Foreign Secretaries, the following took part in the conference:

For the United States of America: Mr. W. Averell Harriman, Ambassador of the United States; Maj. Gen. John R. Deane, United States Army; Mr. H. Hackworth, Mr. James C. Dunn and experts.

For the United Kingdom: Sir Archibald Clark Kerr, Ambassador; Mr. William Strang, Lieut. Gen. Sir Hastings Ismay and experts.

For the Soviet Union: Marshal K. E. Voroshiloff, Marshal of the Soviet Union; Mr. A. Y. Vyshinski and Mr. M. Litvinoff, Deputy People's Commissars for Foreign Affairs; Mr. V. A. Sergeyeff, Deputy People's Commissar for Foreign Trade; Maj. Gen. A. A. Gryzloff of the General Staff, Mr. G. F. Saksin, senior official for People's Commissariat for Foreign Affairs, and experts.

Some Decisions Taken

The agenda included all questions submitted for discussion by the three Governments. Some of the questions called for final decisions, and these were taken. On other questions, after discussion, decisions of principle were taken. These questions were referred for detailed consideration to commissions specially set up for the purpose, or reserved for treatment through diplomatic channels. Other questions again were disposed of by an exchange of views. The Governments of the United States, the United Kingdom and the Soviet Union have been in close cooperation in all matters concerning the common war effort, but this is the first time that the Foreign Secretaries of the three Governments have been able to meet together in conference.

In the first place there were frank and exhaustive discussions of the measures to be taken to shorten the war against Germany and her satellites in Europe. Advantage was taken of the presence of military advisers representing the respective Chiefs of Staff in order to discuss definite military operations with regard to which decisions had been taken and which are already being prepared in order to create a basis for the closest military cooperation in the future between the three countries.

Second only to the importance of hastening the end of the war was the recognition by the three Governments that it was essential in their own national interests and in the interests of all peace-loving nations to continue the present close collaboration and cooperation in the conduct of the war into the period following the end of hostilities, and that only in this way could peace be maintained and the political, economic and social welfare of their peoples be fully promoted.

China Is Joint Signer

This conviction is expressed in a declaration in which the Chinese Government joined during the conference and which was signed by the three Foreign Secretaries and the Chinese Ambassador at Moscow on behalf of their Governments. This declaration published today provides for even closer collaboration in the prosecution of the war and in all matters pertaining to the surrender and disarmament of the enemies with which the four countries are, respectively, at war. It set forth the principles upon which the four Governments agree that a broad system of international cooperation and security should be based. Provision is made for the inclusion of all other peace-loving nations, great and small, in this system.

The conference agreed to set up machinery for ensuring the closest cooperation between the three Governments in the examination of European questions arising as the war develops. For this purpose the conference decided to establish in London a European advisory commission to study these questions and to make joint recommendations to the three Governments.

Provision was made for continuing, when necessary, the tripartite consultations of representatives of the three Governments in the respective capitals through the existing diplomatic channels.

The conference also agreed to establish an advisory council for matters relating to Italy, to be composed in the first instance of representatives of their three Governments and of the French Committee of National Liberation. Provision is made for addition to this council of representatives of Greece and Yugoslavia in view of their special interests arising out of aggressions of Fascist Italy upon their territory during the present war. This council will deal with day-to-day questions other than military preparations and will make recommendations designed to coordinate Allied policy with regard to Italy.

Affirm Stand on Italy

The three Foreign Secretaries considered it appropriate to reaffirm, by a declaration published today, the attitude of the Allied Governments in favor of the restoration of democracy in Italy.

The three Foreign Secretaries declared it to be the purpose of their Governments to restore the independence of Austria. At the same time they reminded Austria that in the final settlement account will be taken of efforts that Austria may make toward its own liberation. The declaration on Austria is published today.

The Foreign Secretaries issued at the conference a declaration by President Roosevelt, Prime Minister Churchill and Premier Stalin containing a solemn warning that at the time of granting any armistice to any German Government, those German officers and men and members of the Nazi party who have had any connection with atrocities and executions in countries overrun by German forces will be taken back to the countries in which their abominable crimes were committed to be charged and punished according to the laws of those countries.

In an atmosphere of mutual confidence and understanding which characterized all the work of the conference, consideration was also given to other important questions. These included not only questions of a current nature but also questions concerning treatment of Hitlerite Germany and its satellites, economic cooperation and assurance of general peace.

JOINT FOUR-NATION DECLARATION

The governments of the United States of America, the United Kingdom, the Soviet Union and China:

United in their determination, in accordance with the declaration by the United Nations of Jan. 1, 1942, and subsequent declarations, to continue hostilities against those Axis powers with which they respectively are at war until such powers have laid down their arms on the basis of unconditional surrender;

Conscious of their responsibility to secure the liberation of themselves and the peoples allied with them from the menace of aggression;

Recognizing the necessity of ensuring a rapid and orderly transition from war to peace and of establishing and maintaining international peace and security with the least diversion of the world's human and economic resources for armaments;

Jointly declare:

1—That their united action, pledged for the prosecution of the war against their respective enemies, will be continued for the organization and maintenance of peace and security.

2—That those of them at war with a common enemy will act together in all matters relating to the surrender and disarmament of that enemy.

3—That they will take all measures deemed by them to be necessary to provide against any violation of the terms imposed upon the enemy.

4—That they recognize the necessity of establishing at the earliest practicable date a general international organization, based on the principle of the sovereign equality of all peace-loving States, and open to membership by all such States, large and small, for the maintenance of international peace and security.

5—That for the purpose of maintaining international peace and security pending the re-establishment of law and order and the inauguration of a system of general security, they will consult with one another and as occasion requires with other members of the United Nations with a view to joint action on behalf of the community of nations.

6—That after the termination of hostilities they will not employ their military forces within the territories of other States except for the purposes envisaged in this declaration and after joint consultation.

7—That they will confer and cooperate with one another and with other members of the United Nations to bring about a practicable general agreement with respect to the regulation of armaments in the post-war period.

Declaration Regarding Italy

The Foreign Secretaries of the United States, the United Kingdom and the Soviet Union have established that their three governments are in complete agreement that Allied policy toward Italy must be based upon the fundamental principle that fascism and all its evil influence and configuration shall be completely destroyed and that the Italian people shall be given every opportunity to establish governmental and other institutions based upon democratic principles.

The Foreign Secretaries of the United States and United Kingdom declare that the action of their governments from the inception of the invasion of Italian territory, in so far as paramount military requirements have permitted, has been based upon this policy.

In furtherance of this policy in the future the Foreign Secretaries of the three governments are agreed that the following measures are important and should be put into effect:

1—It is essential that the Italian Government should be made more democratic by inclusion of representatives of those sections of the Italian people who have always opposed fascism.

2—Freedom of speech, of religious worship, of political belief, of press and of public meeting shall be restored in full measure to the Italian people, who shall also be entitled to form anti-Fascist political groups.

3—All institutions and organizations created by the Fascist regime shall be suppressed.

4—All Fascist or pro-Fascist elements shall be removed from the administration and from institutions and organizations of a public character.

5—All political prisoners of the Fascist regime shall be released and accorded full amnesty.

6—Democratic organs of local government shall be created.

7—Fascist chiefs and army generals known or suspected to be war criminals shall be arrested and handed over to justice.

In making this declaration the three Foreign Secretaries recognize that so long as active military operations continue in Italy the time at which it is possible to give full effect to the principles stated above will be determined by the Commander-in-Chief on the basis of instructions received through the combined chiefs of staff.

The three governments, parties to this declaration, will, at the request of any one of them, consult on this matter. It is further understood that nothing in this resolution is to operate against the right of the Italian people ultimately to choose their own form of government.

Declaration on Austria

The governments of the United Kingdom, the Soviet Union and the United States of America are agreed that Austria, the first free country to fall a victim to Hitlerite aggression, shall be liberated from German domination.

They regard the annexation imposed on Austria by Germany on March 15, 1938, as null and void. They consider themselves as in no way bound by any changes effected in Austria since that date. They declare that they wish to see re-established a free and independent Austria and thereby to open the way for the Austrian people themselves, as well as those neighboring States which will be faced with similar problems, to find that political and economic security which is the only basis for lasting peace.

Austria is reminded, however, that she has a responsibility, which she cannot evade, for participation in the war at the side of Hitlerite Germany, and that in the final settlement account will inevitably be taken of her own contribution to her liberation.

Statement on Atrocities

Signed by President Roosevelt, Prime Minister Churchill *and* Premier Stalin

The United Kingdom, the United States and the Soviet Union have received from many quarters evidence of atrocities, massacres and cold-blooded mass executions which are being perpetrated by Hitlerite forces in many of the countries they have overrun and from which they are now being steadily expelled. The brutalities of Nazi domination are no new thing, and all peoples or territories in their grip have suffered from the worst form of government by terror. What is new is that many of these territories are now being redeemed by the advancing armies of the liberating powers and that in their desperation the recoiling Hitlerites and Huns are redoubling their ruthless cruelties. This is now evidenced with particular clearness by monstrous crimes on the territory of the Soviet Union which is being liberated from Hitlerites and on French and Italian territory.

Accordingly, the aforesaid three Allied powers, speaking in the interests of the thirty-two United Nations, hereby solemnly declare and give full warning of their declaration as follows:

At the time of granting of any armistice to any government which may be set up in Germany, those German officers and men and members of the Nazi party who have been responsible for or have taken a consenting part in the above atrocities, massacres and executions will be sent back to the countries in which their abominable deeds were done in order that they may be judged and punished according to the laws of these liberated countries and of the free governments which will be erected therein. Lists will be compiled in all possible detail from all these countries, having regard especially to invaded parts of the Soviet Union, to Poland and Czechoslovakia, to Yugoslavia and Greece, including Crete and other islands; to Norway, Denmark, the Netherlands, Belgium, Luxembourg, France and Italy.

Thus, Germans who take part in wholesale shooting of Polish officers or in the execution of French, Dutch, Belgian or Norwegian hostages or of Cretan peasants, or who have shared in slaughters inflicted on the people of Poland or in territories of the Soviet Union which are now being swept clear of the enemy, will know that they will be brought back to the scene of their crimes and judged on the spot by the peoples whom they have outraged. Let those who have hitherto not imbued their hands with innocent blood beware lest they join the ranks of the guilty, for most assuredly the three Allied powers will pursue them to the uttermost ends of the earth and will deliver them to their accusers in order that justice may be done.

The above declaration is without prejudice to the case of German criminals whose offenses have no particular geographical localization and who will be punished by joint decision of the governments of the Allies.

JOINT COMMUNIQUE ON CAIRO CONFERENCE
November 22-26, 1943

President Roosevelt, Generalissimo Chiang Kai-shek, and Prime Minister Churchill, together with their respective military and diplomatic advisers, have completed a conference in North Africa. The following general statement was issued:

The several military missions have agreed upon future military operations against Japan.

The three great Allies expressed their resolve to bring unrelenting pressure against their brutal enemies by sea, land, and air. This pressure is already rising.

The three great Allies are fighting this war to restrain and punish the aggression of Japan.

They covet no gain for themselves and have no thought of territorial expansion.

It is their purpose that Japan shall be stripped of all the islands in the Pacific which she has seized or occupied since the beginning of the first World War in 1914, and that all the territories Japan has stolen from the Chinese, such as Manchuria, Formosa and the Pescadores, shall be restored to the Republic of China.

Japan will also be expelled from all other territories which she has taken by violence and greed.

The aforesaid three great powers, mindful of the enslavement of the people of Korea, are determined that in due course Korea shall become free and independent.

With these objects in view, the three Allies, in harmony with those of the United Nations at war with Japan, will continue to persevere in the serious and prolonged operations necessary to procure the unconditional surrender of Japan.

THE TEHERAN DECLARATION

We, the President of the United States of America, the Prime Minister of Great Britain, and the Premier of the Soviet Union, have met in these four days past in this the capital of our ally, Teheran, and have shaped and confirmed our common policy.

We express our determination that our nations shall work together in the war and in the peace that will follow.

As to the war, our military staffs have joined in our round-table discussions and we have concerted our plans for the destruction of the German forces. We have reached complete agreement as to the scope and timing of operations which will be undertaken from the east, west, and south. The common understanding which we have here reached guarantees that victory will be ours.

And as to the peace, we are sure that our concord will make it an enduring peace. We recognize fully the supreme responsibility resting upon us and all the United Nations to make a peace which will command good will from the overwhelming masses of the peoples of the world and banish the scourge and terror of war for many generations.

With our diplomatic advisers we have surveyed the problems of the future. We shall seek the cooperation and active participation of all nations, large and small, whose peoples in heart and in mind are dedicated, as are our own peoples, to the elimination of tyranny and slavery, oppression and intolerance.

We will welcome them as they may choose to come into the world family of democratic nations.

No power on earth can prevent our destroying the German armies by land, their U-boats by sea, and their war plants from the air. Our attacks will be relentless and increasing.

Emerging from these friendly conferences we look with confidence to the day when all the peoples of the world may live free lives untouched by tyranny and according to their varying desires and their own consciences.

We came here with hope and determination. We leave here friends in fact, in spirit, and in purpose.

Signed at Teheran, December 1, 1943.

ROOSEVELT, STALIN, CHURCHILL.

Index

Abyssinia, failure of the League to take action, 6, 37

Academy of International Law at The Hague, 199

Acheson, Dean G., Assistant Secretary of State, organization for food and agriculture, 168-169

Africa, Italian aggression, 6, 37

Aggression: American Committee's proposal for the test of aggression, *1924*, 5; use of defensive war, 6, 133; neutrality, a help to the aggressor, 6, 44, 134; protection of smaller powers, 26; condemnation of Russia's attack on Finland, 37; war of aggression a criminal act, 88, 220; quarantine against aggression, 95; test of aggression, 100-101; international measures for enforcement of obligation not to commit aggression, 123; air police, 130; domestic policy a clue to foreign relations, 195

Agriculture, international plans, 46, 51, 82, 156, 158, 159, 172; *see also* Hot Springs Conference

Air power: effect on isolation, 94; a preventive, in the increased fear of war, 129; need for international air-police force, 124, 125, 129; advantage of air police over naval and military forces, 130, 131; regulation of civil aviation by air police, 131

All Soviet Union Congress, *February 1, 1944*, announcement of Molotoff decrees, 74; *see also* Molotoff decrees

Allied Powers, first World War: waste of man power due to enlarged scope of war on the part of German War Office, 10; protests at continuing the post-armistice blockade of Germany, 20

American Association for the Advancement of Science, 192

American Committee, Geneva *1924*, test of aggression, 5

American States: Conference *1889* (Pan-American Congress), non-recognition of territory acquired by force, 127; reorganization of Intellectual Cooperation, 188

Anarchy, international: post-war prevention by cooperative action of United Nations, 17, 94, 198, 233; sovereign right of warfare, 85; reform of international law to prevent, 113; threat of third World War, 125, 220; safeguard of an effective international police force, 131; absolute sovereignty, a conception of anarchy, 202

Angell, Sir Norman, *The Great Illusion*, 7, 12

Appeasement, ineffective policies of, 20

Arbitration procedure for the settlement of disputes: device for political security, 90, 99, 146; a judicial method, 100; Paris Conference *1856*, 103; development of international law, 114; history, 114-116; a stricter method than conciliation, but not a substitute, 115, 116; United States Senate's prerogative to pass on terms, 115; first world court, a permanent court of arbitration, 116; *1887* British-American arbitration memorial, 116; Latin-American countries, 116; rules for systematizing, *1907*, 117; compulsory, 117; *see also* Hague Conferences; Permanent Court of Arbitration; Treaties

Armaments: race in rival armaments, 9, 86, 136; effect of the industrial revolution, 86; no longer a solution of the problem of security, 86; increase for defense, with the lowering of geographical barriers, 88; United Nations' lessened post-war need, 138, 141; post-war measures against rearmament by enemy states, 138; burden in cost, 139; engineering adaptations to increase amounts allowed under ratio agreements of Washington Conference, 143; constant increase not offset by periodic attempts at pacific settlement, 147; *see also* Disarmament; Inspection of armaments

Asia: initial successes of Japanese, 6;

245

American public opinion regarding British policy, 32; post-war problem of race and color, 32; priority of European war over that in Asia, 42; Soviet policy of federation, 80; League conferences on rural life, 161; increased interest on the part of the State Department, 189

Athens, ancient: unwillingness to form political union with other city-states, 30; advantage of naval power, 130

Atlantic Charter, *August 14, 1941:* freedom from want, 23; a declaration of general principles, not a structural document, 44, 45; formulated before United States's entrance into the War, 45, 200, 221; need for implementation, 54; guarantees reinforced, 65; definition of security, freedom from fear, 87; complete disarmament of Axis Powers, 132; acceptance, the test for membership in the post-war organization, 204-205; need for post-war organization leading to fulfillment of purposes, 216-217; *text,* 235; (joint declaration) cited in Lend-Lease agreement, Section VII, 236

Atlantic City, meeting of the UNRRA, *November 1943,* 47, 173

Atlantic Ocean, war in the, 29

Atrocities, statement at Moscow Conference on the punishment of war criminals, 50, 60; *text of agreement,* 238, 240

Augustine, doctrine of the just and the unjust war, 133

Australia, membership in the UNRRA, 173

Austria: Triple Alliance, 9; partition of Poland, 39; declaration by Moscow Conference, 60, *text,* 240; threat against Serbia *1914,* 105; Austrian Loan, 182; invasion by Germany, 227

Aviation, civil, regulation by international air police, 131; need for post-war communications organization, 159; *see also* Air power; Police

Axis and enemy Powers: unconditional surrender, 17-19, 132; need for martial law until revival of civil government, 17; warning on playing into the hands of militarists in peace negotiations, 19, 203; American tentative relationship prior to Pearl Harbor, 44; initial victories, 44; punishment of war criminals, 50, 60, 238, 240; policy of furthering mistrust between Western Powers and Soviet, 54, 64; United Nations decision forced, as to maintenance of peace, 125; complete disarmament, 132, 137, 138; neutrality an incentive to their aggression, 134; unilateral resort to armaments, 136, 138, 140; post-war inspection of armament, 138; need for re-education to recover freedom and lost decencies, 188-190; post-war need for cooperation by elements within enemy countries, 197, 203-204; disregard of human rights within their own countries, 198, 228; question of membership in international organization, 202; *see also* Occupation by United Nations; Germany; Japan

Backward peoples: problems of government, 32-33, 161, 217; from earliest times, a possible menace to security, 92-93; revised form of mandate, 216-217

Balance of Power: challenged by Louis XIV, Napoleon and Germany, 25; American reluctance at being drawn into European arena, 31; no longer necessary when Four-Nation Declaration is in effect, 59

Balkan States: possible effect of federation of Soviet Union, 80; investigating commission of the League, *1925,* 105; German attitude to Russia's interest *1914,* 105; League conferences on rural life, 161; one-time possibility of federation similar to Locarno Treaties, 216

Baltic Republics: Stalin's intention to incorporate in Soviet Republic, 36, 38; formerly a part of "Holy Russia", 37; *1939* treaties with Russia concerning naval bases, airdromes, etc., 37; British-American attitude, 65; transfer camouflaged by principle of local autonomy, 68

Bancor, suggested international unit of account, 179

Bank for reconstruction and develop-

ment of the United and Associated Nations: United States Treasury Proposal, 159, 181; to facilitate long-term international investment, 182
Baptists, opposition to use of force in world organization, 134
Battleships, ratio suggested at Washington Conference *1921-22*, 142; see also Naval power
Bayard, Thomas F., 115
Belgium, 8; man-power unit under Esher plan, 145; membership in UNRRA, 173, 174; Congo atrocities, 197; wide international, commercial interests, 211
Bergson, Henri, Chairman, first Committee on Intellectual Cooperation, 186
Bethmann-Hollweg, Chancellor, testimony before the Reichstag on the nature of war, 8
Beveridge, Sir William, Report on unemployment, 81
Bill of Rights, proposal of an international, 196, 198
Bismarck, Chancellor, 12; use of war as an instrument of policy, 5, 9, 71
Blaine, Secretary James G., first Conference of American States *1889*, 127
Bloch, Jean, *The Future of War, 1898*, 7, 12
Blockade of Germany, protests regarding the post-armistice, 19, 20
Bonnet, Henri, Director of the International Institute of Intellectual Cooperation, 187
Borah, Senator William E., 13
Bourgeois, Léon, on mutual understanding among League members, 186
Brazil, member of UNRRA, 173
Briand, Aristide: letter to the American people on the renunciation of war as an instrument of national policy, 12; Saar Administration incident, 106-108; on the organization of peace, after signing the Pact of Paris, 126-127, 147; see also Treaties: Pact of Paris (Kellogg-Briand treaty)
British Commonwealth of Nations, 130; relations with the United States, 29, 30, 31, 33; comparison of setup with that of the federated Soviet republics, 73, 76, 77, 216; final achievement of Dominions, maintenance of separate armed forces in first World War, 79; share in disposition of international monetary fund, 179
Bryan, William Jennings, Treaties for the Advancement of Peace, 104
Bulgaria, League Commission to investigate the threat of war with Greece *1925*, 105
Bureaucratic system, danger in the development of a, 81, 82, 130, 157-159, 172, 189, 214
Business: need for post-war establishment on sound principles of international cooperation, 22; response to the obligation for post-war cooperation, 63, 82, 166; representation in I.L.O., 156-157, 164, 192, 229 and in International Chamber of Commerce, 165; post-war strengthening and control, 175; see also Capital

Cairo, unfounded rumor, reported by Soviet press, of British-German peace negotiations, 67
Cairo Conference, *November 1943*, 211; priority of executive action, 48, 52; foundations laid at Moscow Conference, 53; joint communique, text, 241-242
Canada: protest at unification of her foreign affairs under British Foreign Office, 76; agent in British denunciation of alliance with Japan, 144; uncertainty regarding American stand on tariff, 154; membership in UNRRA, 173, 174; plans for international monetary reorganization, 177, 180; frontier problems, 206; statement on post-war international organization, 206-207; wide international interests, 211
Capital: post-war problems, 23, 166; Communist attitude toward capitalism, 34, 35, 81; share with labor in International Labor Organization, 164; national resistance to inflow of foreign capital, 181; see also Business; Monetary Organization, foreign investment
Carnegie Endowment for International Peace: *Economic and Social History of the World War*, 10-12; Academy of International Law at The Hague, 199
Chambers of Commerce: vote on refer-

248 INDEX

endum of the United States Chamber on post-war international cooperation, 63
Chemistry: a war potential, 139, 146; rapidity of mobilization, 145; *see also* Science
Chiang Kai-shek, 43; Cairo Conference, 53
China: position in wartime alignment of Great Powers, 29; relations with Russia in eastern Siberia, 40; pacific tradition a good basis for a new order in the Far East, 42; "Three principles", 42; mass education, 43; signer of Four-Nations Declaration of Moscow Conference, 51, 60, 225; Manchurian question, 127; Japanese aggression, the real beginning of the second World War, 127; ineffective pacts *1922* for pacific procedure, 144; membership in UNRRA, 172-174
Christianity: Fascist and Nazi challenge, 110; principle of universality, 111; teachings of the Christian Church, 132-135; literal conception of the Sermon on the Mount, 132, 133; war for a just cause permissible, 133; non-resistant pacifism, 134, 135; influence on Roman law, 193; reaction to oppression as policy of state, 196
Churchill, Winston: Harvard address, on unity and aims of Britain and the United States, 30, 31; Teheran Conference, 40; Moscow Conference, 53
City-state, 30, 111, 193, 218
Civil Service, need for an international, 199, 209
Clausewitz, General Karl von, "war a continuation of policy," 7, 14
Clearing Union, British plan for an international, 179
Cleveland, President Grover, presentation of British arbitration memorial, 116
Colonies, post-war aid, 23; responsibility of world community in the exploitation of labor, 32, 197, 211; *see also* Mandates; Backward areas
Commission to Study the Organization of the Peace: Second Report, problems of the transitional period, 22; Third Report, proposal of the United Nations Conference, 47; Fundamentals of the International Organization, 55
Committee on Intellectual Cooperation: appointed by the League Council to act in an advisory capacity to the Assembly, 186-187; relation to American body, 188
Committees on Intellectual Cooperation, National, 187; authorized to act as intermediaries with the International Committee, 187; Chairman of the American Committee a member of the Committee on Intellectual Cooperation, 188; coordination of Latin-American committees with American Committee, 188; Havana Conference, 188; American Committee and post-war cultural relations organization, 191
Commodity prices, post-war need for stabilization, 160
Communications, need of an international organization, 156, 159
Communism, and Communist Party: spread throughout the world, 28; fought by White Russians, 34; creed regarding capitalism and exploitation, 34, 81, 163; "the League of Nations a farce", 35; expulsion of Trotsky and Zinovieff from Central Committee, 35; fading dream of world Communism, 36; conviction that dislike of Communist State caused expulsion of Soviet Union from the League, 37, 38; attitude of Social Democrats and Social Revolutionaries toward strong central control, 69; *1919* convention: statements on local autonomy, 69; program in favor of Federative Union of States, 69; early Red Army, the instrument of the Party, 71; a unifying force in the Soviet system, 72; challenged by nationalist movement, 73; spread of Communism into federated border states, 80; challenge to American economic interests, 82; threat of world overturn *1918–1919*, 163; "Communist Manifesto", 163
Community life, breakdown in, a factor in post-war epidemics, 22
Compiègne, German surrender *1918*, 19
Compromis, technical operation of the law in settlement by arbitration, 115

INDEX

Concert of Europe, 211
Conciliation as a pacific means of settlement: a "political" procedure, 100-102, 105; Hague Peace Conferences, 103; "good neighbor" policy in action, 106; preventive value of the conference method, 107-108; compared with arbitration, 114, 116; suitability of American participation, 115-116; within an international organization, 121, 224; procedure leading to realized non-resistance, 135; see also Conference Method; Arbitration
Conference method of peaceful settlement: ancient Greece, 4; initial attempts by United Nations, 47; proposed by Commission to Study the Organization of the Peace, 47; UNRRA, 47; problem of wartime conference of United Nations, 48; relation to security, 90; necessity in post-war organization of United Nations, 100, 108, 157, 201, 209, 224; use in conciliation procedure, 105; a means of anticipating disputes, 108; alternative to a third World War, 109; in international juridical matters, 114-116; inadequacy of *ad hoc* conferences, 159; International Labor Organization, 165; a forum proposed for Food and Agriculture Organization, 170; need for consultation implicit in Paris Peace Pact, 148
Conference on Food and Agriculture, *see* Hot Springs Conference
Confucius, 42, 224
Congo, Belgian atrocities in the, 197
Congress of Berlin, 34
Connally, Senator Tom, Resolution on American interest in an international cooperative organization, and the maintenance of the peace, 55-56, 58, 59, 63
Constantine, recognition of Christianity as a state religion, 133
Consumption, capacity for, as well as production, a measure of prosperity, 153
Contraband articles, limited conception prior to the first World War, 149
Cooperative action of sovereign powers: necessary for security, 89, 94, 124, 226; cooperative or collective security, 93-99; "quarantine against aggression", 95; plans and contingents of armed force in readiness, 123; comparison of cooperative and joint action, 125; only use of warlike force to be permitted, 126
Corwin, Prof. Edward S., *The Constitution and World Organization*, 231
Council of Learned Societies, 192
Court of Arbitral Justice, failure because of demand by smaller states for equal representation, 118
Credit, continuing dislocation by war of world credit, 11; resulting depressions, 62; plans at present under negotiation, 159, 175-182; post-war control and strengthening to insure improved international business, 175-176; short-term credit, 176, 177, 182; British, American and Canadian plans, 176-182; pressure to keep balances at work, 180; recommendation, after examination of a nation's situation, 182
Crimean War: Russian drive for the Dardanelles, 34; Conference of Paris, a step toward future arbitration, 103
Cuba: oppression under Spain, 26, 197; *see also* Havana
Cultural relations, *see* International Cultural relations
Curie, Marie, 186
Curzon Line, Polish-Russian frontier, 39, 40, 63
Czechoslovakia: alliance with Soviet Union, 44, with France, 226; invasion by Germany, 227

Dafoe, John W., the British-Japanese alliance, 144
Danubian States, effect of possible federation with Soviet, 80
Dardanelles, Russia's XIXth century drive for the, 34
Davis, Norman, American policy in peace cooperation, 148
Declaration by the United Nations, *January 2, 1942*, see Treaties and agreements
De Gaulle, General Charles, 41
Demobilization: of men, and problem

of employment, 22; of war establishments, 138
Depression, post-war, 62; *1930*, 153
Diplomacy: a technique for peace preservation, 90, 92; settlement of disputes, 100-102, 117, 121; need for change of rules, when implied threat of use of power is no longer permitted, 103; recognition of culture as a national asset, 190; recognition of the right of the state to deal with its own citizens, 197; renunciation of secret methods in post-war dealings, 209
Disarmament, and reduction of armaments: Soviet suggestion at Genoa Conference *1922*, 35, by Litvinoff at Geneva Conference, 35; French need for security before disarmament, 87; post-war effort at progressive reduction and limitation of armaments, 124; provision for police, in relation to degree of disarmament, 126, 128; post-war disarmament of enemy states, 132, 137, 138; reduction and control of armaments, 136-151; reduction to lowest point consistent with national safety and international obligations, 136; post-war Commission, 137; following first World War, confusion of term "disarmament" with non-resistant pacificism, 137, 142-143; Hughes' challenge of a naval holiday and ratio, 142-143; search for ratios for armies, as well as navies, 145; French memorandum *November 1932*, 147-148; British plan *March 1933*, 148; United States' statement, 148-149; two activities of an international disarmament organization, proposal for the reduction of armaments, and inspection of armament, 150; *see also* Armaments; Hague Conferences; Inspection of Armaments; Geneva Disarmament Conferences; Washington Conference
Disarmament Conferences, 35, 140, 145, 148, 149; *see also* Genoa Conference
Drug Traffic, preventive measures, 156, 161
Dunkirk, the miracle of, 14

Economic action, obligation on the part of the United Nations, 123
Economic Conference *1933*, 35
Economic organization, international, limited to conference and consultation, 229
Economic warfare of the XXth century, 155, 166; post-war guard against economic relationships in disguised form, directed against other states, 205
Economic welfare: effects of total war, 10, 22, 219, 233; post-war depressions, 62; need for sound domestic economy in building up better international economic relations, 152; safeguarded by machinery for democratic legislation, 155; a condition of the peace, 212; *see also* Social and economic problems; Backward areas
Economics: problems brought within the scope of scientific analysis, 85; post-war police force, and provision for economic and political adjustment, 130; post-war chance for instituting policy of economic liberation, 156; proposal of an international advisory body for the whole field of economics, 160, 165; forum for the development of policy, 165; post-war interrelation with UNRRA, 174; post-war need for cooperation with enemy states, 204; influence of growth of modern industry, 228
Eden, Anthony, British Foreign Minister: Moscow Conference, 52, 62; tribute to Cordell Hull, 62
Education: re-starting in devastated areas, 172; work of International Intellectual Cooperation, 187; need for re-education of the Nazi mind, 188-190; domestic control, so long as education is not directed against interest of others, 190
Einstein, Albert, 186
Eisenhower, General Dwight D., 29
Employment, post-war provision for, 82
Engels, Frederick, *see* Marx, Karl, and Frederick Engels
Equality of states, doctrine of the: 26, 215; equality in sovereignty, 97; *see also* Universality, principle of
Esher, Lord, proposal of man-power unit, 145
Established Church, 134

Esthonia, in a Russian federation, 72; see also Baltic Republics

Far East: Russo-Japanese problem, 40; Japanese naval supremacy, 143; American cultural interests, 192

Fascist, the; post-war plans for areas liberated from, 18; challenge to Christianity, 110; degenerate leadership, 189; corruption of national culture, 190; oppression, a state policy, 196, 197

February decrees, see Molotoff decrees

Federalism: responsibilities of citizenship and the liberty of the citizen, 97; the United States, 98, 216, 223; form of federal structure for the United Nations, 215, 216; little appreciation by smaller European nations, 216; see also Molotoff decrees; Union of Soviet Socialist Republics

Finland: relations with Russia, 36; anti-Bolshevik Government, 37; attack by Russia, 37, and effect on world opinion, 38; Russification under the Czars, 68; Stalin, on possible federation, 70

Food supply, 51, 156, 158; see also Hot Springs Conference

Foreign Secretaries, Conference of, see Moscow Conference

Fort Knox, gold hoard, 179

Four-Nations Declaration, see Treaties; Moscow Conference

Fourteen Points, Woodrow Wilson's, *January 1918*, 200

France: Treaties of Locarno, 5-6; German invasion, 8, 14; Triple Entente, with Russia and Great Britain, 9; military maneuvers before first World War, 9; rapid conquest by Germany in second World War, 14; League membership, 27; French-British alliance prior to first World War, 31, and coalition after *1918*, 34, 35; relations with Soviet, 34-39; joins with Polish forces against Bolshevik, 39; underground movement, Fighting French, 41; effect of oppression on younger generation, 41, 197; French Committee of National Liberation, 61, 62, 173; *sécurité* and disarmament, 87, 145; attitude toward universal obligation of security, and a police force, 98; Germany's *1914* ultimatum a pretext, 105; Poland and the question of international law, 106, 226; Saar Administration incident, 106-108; Hague Conference *1899*, 117; the submarine, defense against navalism, 140; man-power unit under Esher plan, 145; willingness to accept pacific means of settlement, 147; memorandum of November *1932* on disarmament, "collective system of security", 147, 148; membership in UNRRA, 173, 174; International Institute of Intellectual Cooperation, 187; French Revolution, 223

Franco-Prussian War *1870*, 8

Frederick the Great, 129

Free enterprise of private, economic interests, necessity of safeguarding, 166

Freedom, safeguards of, 192-199; from fear, 87, 90; from want, 23; from hunger, 202; of the press, and speech, 98, 198; to think, 184; to listen, 199

Frontier problems, better understanding by national, than by local, governments, 206; see also Curzon line

Fulbright, Congressman, J. W., Resolution on post-war international organization, 55, 56, 63

Gallup poll, American public opinion as to an international organization, 54

Gandhi, Mahatma, 32

General Act of *1928*, see League of Nations

General Staff for War, deadly timetable, 11, 98

Geneva, see Disarmament Conferences

Geneva Protocol, *1924*: test of aggression, 5, 100, 101; provision for inspection of armaments, 150; safeguard of peace and economic cooperation, 215

Genoa Conference *1920*, Soviet suggestion of general disarmament, 35; see also Disarmament Conferences

Geographical barriers, and security, 88, 89

George III, 33

Georgia, the Caucasus: question of federation and Soviet Russia, 68; native place of Stalin, 69

Germany: signatory of the Treaty of Locarno, 6; violator of treaties, 6, 227; Division of Raw Materials, Ministry of War, 8, 9; Nazism a variant of Prussianism, 9; mass production for war, 8, 10, 112; alertness prior to first World War, 9; naval race with Great Britain, 9; Triple Alliance, 9; yearly maneuvers, 9; apparent control of war in early conquest of France, 14; British stand in second World War, 15; United Nations' administration of territories liberated from Nazis, 18; and occupation of German territory, 19, 197; lesson against playing into the hands of militarists after this war, 19, 203; objection to post-armistice blockade *1918*, 19, 20; used as propaganda by Nazi demagogues, 20; devastation by Nazis exceeds anything in history, 22; challenge to balance of power XXth century, 25; member of the League *1926*, 27, 35, 106; *1922* alliance with Russia, 34; *1926* treaty of mutual assistance with Soviet, 34-35; Moscow's attitude toward German treatment under Versailles Treaty, 34-35; Weimar Government, dream of coalition in Central Europe, 35; Reichstag fire, 35; withdrawal from League, 35, 140, 164; German culture traces in Baltic States, 37; Soviet federation, a buffer against future German invasions, 37; war with Russia, 40; coming allied settlement of Germany, an act of power, 41; mutual distrust between Western Powers and Soviet used by Germany for propaganda purposes, 54; charge of Soviet massacre of Polish patriots, 64; centralized tyranny of Nazi Government, 68; Stalin's idea of a soviet Germany, 70; Soviet's greater military strength, 81; absolute expression of nationalism, 93, 97; progressive weakening of the League used to Germany's advantage, 101, 108, 140; Saar Administration incident, 106-108; doctrine of complete freedom of action for a sovereign state, 110, 216; challenge to Christian morality, 110; initiator of total war, 112; "guns instead of butter", 126; horrors of war brought home to Germany in second World War, 129; militarization, and loss of civil liberty, 130; failure to throw off the yoke of Prussianism, 130; complete disarmament, 132, 137, 138; principle of state religion, 134; disarmament under Versailles Treaty, 138; agreement on the abolition of the submarine, 140; rearmament, 140, 141; resentment against non-recognition of equality, 147; secrecy in war preparations, 150; hostile economic alignment, 153, 155; attempt to propagandize the Paris International Institute of Intellectual Cooperation, 188; post-war recovery of a perverted generation, 188-190; subservience of culture to religion of nationalism, 190; military conception of peace, 194; oppression, a policy of state, 197; violation of human rights within the nation a cause of war, 198, 228; their concept of sovereignty, the right to judge their own actions, 228; *see also* Axis and enemy powers.

Gold: international standard after the Napoleonic Wars, 176; power to fix parity, an attitude of national sovereignty, 177; relation to Bancor, unit of account, 179

Golden Rule, the application of social justice to daily affairs, 162

Gompers, Samuel, Chairman of the Labor Committee at the Paris Peace Conference, 200

"Good neighbor", policy of the: Soviet Union's relationships, 40; mediation by good neighbors in settlement of disputes, 98; conciliation, 106; movement in Latin America, 116, 216; necessity of cultural relations, 191; hinderances, 206

Government, share with capital and labor in the International Labor Organization, 164

Great Britain, 208; definition of aggression in Geneva Protocol and the Treaties of Locarno, 5; race in sea power, 9; Triple Entente, 9; unsupported stand against Germany in second World War, 14, 15; member of the Council of the League, 27; British-American relations, 28-29, 30, 33, 45,

INDEX

54; alliance with France, 31; responsibility in post-war effort to suppress militarism, 32, 40, 51, 54, 220, 225; history of relations with Russia, 33-34, 38; imperiled pathway to India, 34; *1942* alliance with Soviet Union, 44; recognition of Polish Government-in-exile, 64; attitude toward Baltic and other Russian frontier states, 65, 73; problem of unemployment, Beveridge Report, 81; world of commerce, and British economic system, 85; challenge to former geographical isolation, 89; reaction to Germany's ultimatum to Serbia *1914*, 105; second World War begun in defense of international law, 106; Common Law, 111; arbitration memorial to the United States *1887*, 116; Hague Arbitration Conferences *1899* and *1907*, 117; advantage of naval power, 130; the Established Church, 134; policy of non-resistance of certain religious sects, 134; naval ratio at Washington Conference, 143; alliance with Japan denounced, 144; Esher plan for man-power ratio in standing armies, 145; attitude toward French plan of *sécurité*, 146; plans for disarmament, and Germany's resentment, 147; *1933* disarmament plan, 148; responsibilities in the UNRRA, 172-174; plan for monetary reorganization, 177, 180; International Clearing Union, 178-179; Bancor, unit of account, 179; suggestion that credit needs be adapted to trading needs of countries, 179; post-war program for education in invaded countries, 188; need for governmental recognition of movement for international intellectual cultural cooperation, 190, 191; suggestion of an international Bill of Rights, 198

Great Powers: military coalition in the United Nations, 17; new relationships, 25, 28; principle of the inviolability of sovereignty, 26; wider range of adjustment of policies, 27; compromise in the Constitution of the UNRRA, 27; responsibility of definite, coordinated leadership in peace preservation, 49, 205, 212, 226; potentialities in industrial mobilization for war, 89; shared authority in international interests, 206, 211; post-war organization, a guard against imperialism, 212, 213; permanent membership in League Council, 215

Greece, *ancient:* conference and diplomacy, 4; natural law, and the modern doctrine of "equality of states", 26; ineffective political union of city-states, 30, 111; re-discovery in the Middle Ages, 185; *modern,* membership in Advisory Council under the Moscow Declaration, 61; League Commission *1925* to investigate threat of war with Bulgaria, 105

Grey, Lord, of Fallodon, 142

Grotius, Hugo, *On the Law of War and Peace*, 85, 112

Habeas corpus, a safeguard to freedom, 196

Hague Conferences *1899* and *1907:* called by Nicholas II, 7, 117, 139; fact-finding, conciliation and arbitration, 103; international panels, 103-104, 117; attempted codification of laws of war, 113; Court of Arbitration, 116, 117; rules for systematizing arbitration, 117; proposed Court of Arbitral Justice, 118; influence in furthering mediation, 119; suggestion of international police force, 119; failure to limit military expenditure, 139, and to secure effective measures for disarmament, 142, 149

Hale, G. E., 186

Halifax, Lord, suggestion of unification of Dominion foreign affairs under the British Foreign Office, 76

Havana: conference for the organization of intellectual cooperation in the Americas, creation of a provisional center, 188

Hay, John, Secretary of State, work for the settlement of international disputes, 115, 119

Health and welfare measures: prevention of disease and welfare improvement an obligation of the post-war international organization, 17, 22, 156, 160, 161, 214, 217; relation of welfare to security, 202

Hitler, 15, 68, 108, 185; war a fundamental condition of government, 6; in power by *1933*, 35; influence on acceptance of League membership by Russia, 35; temporary alliance with Stalin, 38; invasion of Poland, 39; attempt to propagandize the International Institute of Intellectual Cooperation in Paris, 188

Holy Alliance, 25

Hoover, President Herbert: doctrine of the non-recognition of territory obtained by aggressive action, 127; relief organization after the first World War, 171

Hot Springs Conference on Food and Agriculture *May-June 1943:* long-range program for nutrition and world agriculture, 46, 159, 166, 171, 222; proposed United Nations Organization for Food and Agriculture, 159, 169-171; closed to the Press, 166; attended by specialists, 167; Final Act, 167; Opening Declaration, 167; Interim Commission, 168

Hughes, Charles Evans: proposal of a naval ratio, 142, 143, 144; on the survival of Constitutional Government in the United States in the event of a second World War, 232

Hull, Cordell: Moscow Conference, 52; Four-Nations Declaration, 53, 61, 67, 74; careful planning for the organization of peace, 58; Report to Congress, 58, 59, 60, 62, 63; power of the people in peace guarantees, 60, 97; "Hull declaration", 62; doctrine of the "good neighbor", 116; reciprocal trade agreements, 153-155

Human relations, 183-199, 217

Human rights: provision for safeguarding, 96, 196; Roman law, 193; until the reaction of foreign governments to the Fascist-Nazi doctrine of force, treatment of the citizen a national affair, 197; disregard of rights, a real preparation for war, 198, 228; proposed International Institute to study, 228

Hungary, Stalin's statement regarding federalism, 70

Imperialism, a variation of nationalism, 91

India, problem of, 32-34

Industrial revolution, as applied to war, 9, 86, 89, 112, 145, 146

Inquiry (fact-finding), a method in pacific settlement of disputes, 99-105; provision for research, 157

Inspection of armaments, a peace precaution, 131, 137, 138, 149-151

Institute for Jurisprudence, proposal for a, 199

Intellectual cooperation, 187; *see also* Committee on Intellectual Cooperation, International Institute of Intellectual Cooperation

International Chamber of Commerce, 165

International Clearing House: British Proposal, 178-179; Bancor, unit of account, 179

International Cultural Relations Organization of the future, 191, 192

International Development Authority, for the development of countries lacking modern equipment, 160

International economic organizations: trade barriers, investment, commodity prices, and cartel agreements, 159, 160

International Institute of Agriculture, 170

International Institute of Intellectual Cooperation: secretariat in Paris, 187; Nazi attempt to propagandize, 188

International Intellectual Cooperation Organization: Section of the League of Nations, 186; activities, 187

International Labor Organization, 186; representatives of labor, industry, and government, 156-157, 164, 192, 229; a creation of the Labor Committee at the Paris Peace Conference, 158, 163, 200; a model for other international organizations, 162-166, 169, 229; its Constitution, *Article XIII* of the Treaty of Versailles, 162, 199; range of international conventions, 164, 229; General Conference, 164; International Labor Office, 165, 170; Governing Body, 165, 172, 229; support of UNRRA, 222

International Law: accepted theory that war is a continuation of policy, 7;

INDEX

validity of a continuing blockade, 20; changing principles in modern warfare, 20, 110, 113, 132; limits on international anarchy, 25, 113; attempt to link Russia in framework, 34; modern international law based in work of Grotius, 85; security under recognized rules of international law, 90; problem of nationalism and sovereignty, 91-92, 195, 203; Permanent Court a guardian, 102, 227-228; provision for fact-finding bodies, 104; denial of international law, the cause of the second World War, 106; juridical methods of pacific settlement, 109; maintenance of treaties, 110, 112; historic background, 111, 112, 193; inspired by Christian, Greek and Roman ethics, 111, 195, 196; effort to humanize war, 112; last great effort against war, 113; post-war task, the reform of safeguards, 113, 114; change of emphasis to laws of peace, 113, 116, 227; overlapping of Constitutional Law, 115; Wilson theory, international law too conservative a basis for association of nations, 119; contribution by World Court, 121; right of nations to deal with their own citizens, 197; distinction between civilian life and the profession of arms, 219

International Stabilization Fund: United States Treasury proposal, 178, 181, 182; accounting unit, 178; stabilization of exchange rates and provision for short-term credits, 182

Invaded and devastated areas, continued suffering before liberation, 3; industrial exploitation in modern war, 9; need of temporary civil administration under the United Nations, 18; relief and rehabilitation of victims, 23, 40, 172, 203; underground movement, 41; incautious idealism preceding invasion, 137; loans, 180; post-war plans of governments and groups-in-exile, 188, 197

Investment, foreign, *see* Monetary and financial organization

Iran (Persia), 40, 70

Isolation: swing in the United States away from, 15, 54, 92; ineffective in modern warfare, 49, 89-90, 91, 109; development of air power, 94; false interpretation of early American stand, 223; *see also* Neutrality

Italy: aggressive action under the weak authority of the League, 6, 37, 101; Moscow declaration regarding Italy, 60, 61, *text*, 238, 239; influence of Hitler, 108; man-power ratio under Esher plan, 145

Japan: initial successes of aggression, 6; problem of occupation by United Nations after surrender, 19, 197; voluntary withdrawal from the League of Nations, 37; Soviet problems in Siberia, 40; new order in Asia not that of militant Japan, 42; nationalism of war lords, 93; flouts League authority, 101, 108; Sino-Japanese war *1932*, 127; Japanese aggression, real beginning of second World War, 127; fear of bombing, an instrument for peace enforcement, 129; accepts naval ratio at Washington Conference, 143; British denunciation of alliance, 144; secrecy in preparation for war, 150; post-war planning, to defeat militarist elements, 203

Jews, treatment in Czarist Russia, 197

Judicial method of pacific settlement: arbitration and judicial decision, 100, 109, 123; Protocol of Geneva, 100; inadequacy, as a voluntary measure, 101; continuing conference of jurists and students of public affairs, 114, 199; advocated by Theodore Roosevelt, 119; United Nations' post-war plans, 123; *see also* Arbitration

Jus Gentium (Law of Nations): historic background for legal thought in Western World, 111-112; principle of universality, 111, 203, 205; comparison with international law, 114; fitting law of a world empire (Roman), 193; need for a new law of nations, 193; necessity for modern agreement on fundamental principles, 198, 199

Justice, a field of international relations, 224, 227-228; *see also* Human rights

Kant, Immanuel, 224

Karelo-Finnish Republic, 77

Kellogg, Secretary Frank B.: aggressive *vs.* defensive war, 13; consultation in

international peace system, 148; Kellogg-Briand Treaty, *see* Treaties, Paris Peace Pact
Kerensky Government, 34
Keynes, Lord, unit of account, Bancor, 179
Krakow, 39

Labor: post-war responsibility, 23, 82, 156; exploitation under old colonial system, 32; share with capital and government in International Labor Organization, 156, 157, 164, 192; legislation previous to I.L.O., 164; *see also* International Labor Organization
Lafayette, Marquess de, letters of George Washington on foreign relations, 224
La Fontaine, Senator Henri, Belgium, proposal at the League regarding the world of thought, 186
Latin-American states: equality of sovereignty, 97; movement for arbitration fostered by conferences, 116; work of the International Labor Organization, 164; Nazi attempt to take over the International Institute of Intellectual Cooperation for propaganda purposes, 188; reorganization of Intellectual Cooperation in the Americas, 188-189, 191, 192; security measures, and the principle of graded responsibility, 216
Latvia, in a Soviet federated system, 72
Law, growth of: English Common Law, 111, 196; Roman law, 111, 193, 196; Orient, 196; *see also* International Law: Judicial method of pacific settlement; Grotius; *Jus Gentium*
Law of Nations, *see Jus Gentium*
Law of Nature: ancient Greek and Roman ideas, 26; XIXth century hope for a solution of security, 86; Stoic idea, 111, 193; see also *Jus Gentium: Universality, principle of*
General Act of *1928*, a League guide for the negotiation of treaties, 215
League of Nations: a precedent for a post-war international organization, 27, 123, 207, 231; Germany becomes a member *1926*, withdraws *1933*, 35, 106; Russia becomes a member *1934*, 35, expelled *1939*, 37; Japan withdraws, 37; failure to provide bulwark of collective security against militant governments, 53, 86, 98, 108, 140, 207, 208; "neutrality" and non-membership of the United States, 54, 95, 124, 207; membership of British Dominions, 79; early American plans for a league of nations, 97; debate as to universal or regional application, 98; Commissions of Inquiry, 104; Investigating Commissions, 105; incident of the Saar Administration, 106-108; conference method, 108, 127, 209; Manchurian episode, 124, 127; Esher plan of comparative strength of standing armies, 145; international inspection of armaments, 150; technical organizations, 157, 161; Financial, Fiscal and Economic Committees, 160, 182; Economic Intelligence Service, 160; health sections, 161; social hygiene, 161; Austrian Loan, 182; recognition of world of thought, 186, 187, 189; League created by a committee of the Paris Conference, 200-201; Secretariat, 213; General Act of *1928*, 215; mandate system, 216; an "architectural" job, 222
Assembly, 172, 208; equal votes for all nations, 27, 97, 104, 118; rule of unanimity in voting, 97; *1924* attempt to close gap on resort to war, 100, 215; a public forum, 209
Council, 172, 208; dominated by the larger nations, 27, 97, 107, 118, 210, 215, 226
Covenant: 200; practical methods of peace enforcement, 6, 12, 116, 126; "war a matter of concern to all nations", 100; ultimate right to resort to arms, *Article 15, paragraph 7*, 100, 126; solidarity of nations to prevent war, *Article 11*, 104; establishment of World Court, *Article 14*, 118, 120; *Article 10*, 124; *Article 16*, 124; reduction and limitation of armaments, 136, 142; theory of the equality of states, and universality of obligation, 215
League to Enforce Peace, William Howard Taft's contribution to peace settlement, 119

INDEX

Lend-Lease Agreements, 44, 45
Lenin, Nikolai: local autonomy and federation, 69; Thesis on the Nationality Question, 70; leader of a Marxian crusade, 163
Leningrad, defense, and problem of security, 37, 38
Lippmann, Walter, *United States Foreign Policy*, 30
Lithuania, in a Soviet federation, 72
Little Entente, 215
Litvinoff, Maxim, challenge for general disarmament, 35
Livelihood, a field of international relations, 152, 224, 228-230; *see also* Health and welfare
Local autonomy, doctrine of, in the Soviet system, 68-70, 72
London, world's money market after the Napoleonic wars, 176
London Conference *1908*, survey of the nature of armaments, 149
London Imperial Conference *1920*, 144
Louis XIII, 85
Louis XIV, 25
Lutheran Church, Germany, principle of non-resistance, 134
Lytton Commission on Manchuria, 105

Machiavelli: "soldiers . . . the measure of a nation's power", 9, 14
Mackenzie King, William Lyon, Prime Minister of Canada, statement on an ultimate international organization, 206
Mackinac Conference of Republican Party, 55
Manchuria: Japanese aggression, 98, 105, 124, 127; Lytton Commission, 105; Russian aggression, 127
Mandate system for backward areas, a revised, 216-217
Man power: waste under conditions of total war, 10; Esher plan for ratio per nation in military strength, 145
Martial law, temporary post-war need, 23, 204
Marx, Karl, and Frederick Engels, *The Communist Manifesto*, 163
Masaryk, President, of Czechoslovakia, apostle of Jeffersonian democracy, 216
Mass education, China, 43

Mediation, procedure for peace enforcement, 99, 100, 101, 121; origin in diplomacy, 103
Meighen, Arthur, Prime Minister of Canada, British denunciation of the Japanese alliance, 144
Mennonites, principle of non-resistance, 134
Methodists, non-resistant pacificism, 134
Mexico, frontier problems, 206
Migration and settlement, post-war problem, 22, 161
Military measures and "militarism": results of military action in modern warfare, not the total effect of the war effort, 8, 11; preparedness, a constant preoccupation prior to *1914*, 9; "soldiers, the measure of the power of a nation", 9; use of massed forces of industry by militarists, 9-10; direct cause of the fall of Rome, 14, 93, 194; need for continuing a temporary military coalition prior to normal post-war relationships, 17; post-war maintenance of minor military establishments to offset possible renewal of militarism, 21, 128-129; suppression of militarism, a cure for dangers inherent in European balance of power, 31-32; a causative agent of the two World Wars, 86; military action, to restore peace under international law, 90, 92; menace of professional militarism all through history, 93; naval power compared to the militarism of land power, 130; false economic structure, 138, 141; confidence of the enemy states in the perfection of their military preparations at the beginning of the second World War, 198; warning against playing into the hands of enemy militarists during the peace conference, 19, 203; danger to constitutional liberties, 233
Millikan, Robert A., 186
Molotoff, V. M., Soviet Commissar: Moscow Conference, 52; address to All Soviet Union Congress, 67, 74
Molotoff decrees: revision of Constitution of 1936 to permit confederation of sixteen Soviet Republics, 86; proclaimed at All Soviet Union Congress,

February 1, 1944, 67; republics granted two symbols of sovereignty, 67; control of military forces, 67, 79, 80; control of limited foreign relations with foreign states, 67, 74, 78, 79; reaction of other nations, 67-68; local autonomy, 68-70, 72; background for an understanding of the decrees, 68, 71; Communist Party not dealt with, 73; *Articles 14 and 18* of the Constitution of *1936*, 75-76; relation of border states, 77, 80; economic and cultural contacts aided by reform, 205-206, 209

Moltke, Count von, 12

Monetary and Financial Organization, proposed international, 156, 175-182; currency problems, 46, 176, 177; stabilization of foreign exchange, 46, 176-178, 182; relation of financial matters to relief, 47; foreign investment, 154, 160, 180, 182; need for stable international policy, 159; short-term credit, 176-178; American, British, Canadian plans for monetary revision and international organization, 177-180; accounting units, Bancor, 179; necessary financial dealings with enemy states, 204; *see also* Credit; International Stabilization Fund; Bank for Reconstruction and Development

Money economy, present-day questioning of orthodox ideas, 175

Monroe Doctrine, 26, 30, 232

Montreal, Canada, wartime headquarters of International Labor Organization, 164

Moscow Conference *October 1943* (Tripartite Conference of Foreign Secretaries): general post-war international organization agreed upon, 37-38; priority of executive action, 48; declaration on atrocities and the treatment of war criminals, 50, 60, *text*, 240; communique on international organization (Joint Four-Nation Declaration, including China), 51, 52-53, 59, 60, *text*, 60-61, 71, 79, 238; long preparation by United States State Department, 52, 58; contribution by Mr. Hull, 53; United States Congressional and State Department action following declaration, 56-58; Hull's report to Congress, 58-60, 62, 63; "first peace conference" of second World War, 59; declaration concerning Italy, 60, *text*, 238, 239; declaration concerning Austria, 60, *text*, 240; Four-Nations declaration limited to problems of security, 61, 225; American public interest, 62, 63; attitude of United States Chamber of Commerce, 63; declaration tested by Russian action regarding frontier states, 63-66, 79; effect of Molotoff decrees, 67; forecast of an international organization, 221

Moscow decrees, *see* Molotoff decrees

Murray, Gilbert A., 186

Mussolini, Premier, 6, 14, 185

Napoleonic Wars, 25, 176, 197, 211

National Research Council, 192

Nationalism, 90-93; of smaller powers, 25; in Europe during the *1920's*, 27, 53; Soviet Union, 38, 73; conservative fumbling in the field of political security, 90, 91, 109; compared with isolation, 91; akin at times to imperialism, 91; its weakness based on emotion, 91; reliance on military strength, 92, 93; sovereignty, an absolute expression of nationalist terms, 97; fanatic nationalism a hindrance to effective international cooperation, 190

Naval power: race in armaments, 9, 140; advantage over militarism of land power, 130; mistaken belief regarding the submarine, 140; Washington Conference, disarmament, 142, 143; naval ratio, 143, 144, 145, 149

Nazi government, *see* Germany

Netherlands, the: protest of the smaller powers in the UNRRA, 27; wide international interests, 130, 211; independent war relief *1914–1918*, 171; membership in UNRRA, 173, 174

Neutrality: oftentimes of aid to the aggressor, 6, 134, 220; ineffectiveness under present wartime conditions, 49, 93

Neutrality legislation, United States, *1930's*, 44, 45, 95, 134, 220

Neutrality Proclamation, United States, *1793*, 223

New Deal, 81

INDEX

New York Times: comment on Moscow Conference, 59
New Zealand, 173
Nicholas II, call for the *1898* Hague Conference, 7, 117, 139
Nobel Peace Prize *1910*, awarded to Theodore Roosevelt, 119
Non-resistance, principle of: application by certain Christian sects, 133-134; leading to political opposition to international organization, 134; practical doctrine, if buttressed by international police, 135; association with "disarmament", 137
Norway, 174, 211
Nutrition, need for program improving post-war standards, 22, 46, 161

Occupation by the United Nations of enemy territory: restoration to law and order, 17, 18; temporary nature, 19, 197; Russian plans for administration, 66; post-war program of re-education, 188-190; need for cooperation from within enemy states, 197, 203-204
Opium Board, Central, League of Nations, 161; *see also* Drug traffic
Oppression as a state policy, 196, 197
Orient, the: theatre of war, 29, 42; in the post-war settlement, 42
Otlet, Professor, proposal that the world of thought be recognized at the League of Nations, 186
Ozorio de Almeida, Senhor, Chairman of Committee to reorganize Intellectual Cooperation in the Americas, 188

Pacific, America's interest in the war in the, 29
Pacific settlement of disputes, 100-122; obligation to accept, a revolutionary fact of modern times, 100, 101; need for adequate machinery, 101, 108; political settlement, 101-109; judicial methods, 109-122; increase in the importance of diplomacy, 102-103; operates well only in an atmosphere of international confidence, 146; *see also* Judicial Method; Politics
Pan-Slavism, used as a pretext by Germany in *1914*, 105

Paris: occupied by the Nazis, 3; secretariat of the International Institute of Intellectual Cooperation, 187, 188
Paris Conference *1856*, a step toward mediation, 103
Paris Peace Conference, 163; Poland's independence restored, 39; participation by British Dominions, 79; International Labor Organization established, 158, 162, 163, 186, 200
Pax Germanica, 194
Pax Romana, 194
Peace enforcement, 123-125; need for enforcement at close of second World War, 113; obligations, 123-126; services of the whole body of the United Nations, 123; police force, 124, 131; land, sea and air power, 126-132; concerted action against aggressor nations, 125, 127; distinction between police and military establishments of nations, 128; teachings of the Christian Churches, 132-135; need for swift and efficient work in time of crisis, 211
Peace organization: failure to understand the nature of war, 3; difficulty of distinguishing wars of aggression, 4; based on American-British understanding, 31; need for unequivocal statement by the United States, 58; drama at the Washington Conference in the proposal of a naval holiday, 35, 142; extent to which war has been suppressed, 218; only guarantee for the preservation of our constitutional liberties, 233
Pearl Harbor, 44, 45, 95, 221
Permanent Court of Arbitration, the Hague, 116, 117
Permanent Court of International Justice (the World Court), 99, 118, 228; guardian of international law and order, 102, 227-228; Statute of the Court, 120; satisfactory procedure since *1922*, 121-122; American responsibility, 228
Persian Gulf, Russia's outlet to, 40
Pitt, the elder, Earl of Chatham, 33
Poland: invasion by Germany and Russia, 38, 226, 227; frontiers and area of the old Kingdom, 39; three partitions by *1795*, 39; independence restored *1919*, 39; Curzon Line, 39; invaded by

INDEX

the Bolshevik, 39; Government-in-exile, 63, 64, 65; British position with regard to Polish invasion and international law, 64, 106; massacre of Polish patriots, 64; protest against Soviet claims, 64; British guarantee, 65; Polish occupation of White Russia and the Ukraine, 65; question of local autonomy under the Soviet Union, 68, 70; man-power unit under Esher plan, 145; ineffective treaties with France, 226

Police, international: attitude of the United States, 95; need for automatic and definite action, 99; *1910* suggestion to enforce peace work of the Hague Conference, 119; post-war need for international air police force, 124, 129, 132, 220; limited to air power, 125; dependence of effective police measures on progressive limitation of all armaments, 126, 130, 141; to be used only as war preventive, 128; comparison of police action with military establishments of nations, 128; size, 129; advantage of air police over transit of ground forces, 129; under direct authority of international organization, 130; limited to airplane and attendant equipment and bases, 130, 131; air police and relation to civil aviation, 131; non-resistance and conciliation buttressed by police force, 135; problems of policing, a continuing challenge, 141; not arranged for at *1922* Washington Conference or the Paris Peace Pact negotiations, 143, 147-148; necessity for parallel action by other sections of international organization, 212; unanimous consent for police action, 225

Politics: no adequate scientific analysis, 85; political methods for the settlement of disputes, as against judicial methods, 100, 101-109, 123, 213; efforts to eliminate power politics, 86, 154, 169, 213

Production: German mass production *1914*, 8; recuperative powers increased by scientific technique, 23; displacement by total war, 62; need for post-war increase with safeguards against exploitation, 82; challenge to Communism, 82; need for adequate consumption to bring about prosperity, 153; necessity for short-term credit, 176

Propaganda: loses force by development of international understanding, 184; effort of Nazis to take over International Institute of Intellectual Cooperation for purposes of propaganda, 188; interchange of international cultures not to be distorted into a medium of propaganda, 190

Protestant Churches, influence of the principle of non-resistance, 134

Prussia: partition of Poland, 39; military ambitions under Bismarck, 71; first Hague Conference, 117; a yoke on Germany, 130

Public opinion: *1941-1942* poll of United States' interest in a post-war international organization, 54; distrust in the United States of methods of molding public opinion, 185

Public utilities, post-war restoration, 172

Quadruple Alliance, to maintain the concert of Europe, 211

Quakers, doctrine of non-resistance, 134

"Quarantine against aggression," 95

Rathenau, Dr. Walther, Division of Raw Materials of the German War Ministry *1914*, mass production a phase of war, 8, 9

Red Cross, 171

Reichstag Fire *February 1933*, 35

Relief and rehabilitation, problems of, 21-24, 47-48, 202; present emphasis on relief, and interim rehabilitation, 172, 174; must follow in track of invading armies of United Nations, 203; *see also* United Nations Relief and Rehabilitation Administration

Republican Party, Mackinac Conference, 55

Responsibility, graded, in post-war organization, according to a nation's problems, 97, 99, 208, 214-215, 216

Rhineland, forceful recovery by Germany, 227

Rome: resort to war only after the

formalities of religion and law, 4; the Empire, the direct result of the wars, 14; cause of the fall of the Empire, 14, 93, 194; loss of civilian's freedom of action, 93, 130; equality of states, and Roman natural law, 26; federation by arrangements with "allies and friends", 111; influence of the Stoic idea of a natural law, 111; 193; *Jus Gentium*, a fusion of laws of peoples within the Roman State, 111; relation to international law, 114; distinction between just and unjust wars from the days of Augustine, 133-134; Roman law a noble expression of human rights, 193; *Pax Romana*, 194

Roosevelt, President Franklin Delano: at Teheran, 40; Moscow Conference a basis for the Cairo and Teheran Conferences, 53; "quarantine of the aggressor", 95; doctrine of the "good neighbor", 116, 216; UNRRA, 171

Roosevelt, President Theodore: mediator in Russo-Japanese War, 103, 119; awarded Nobel Peace Prize *1910*, 119; suggestion of international police force to implement the Hague Conferences, 119

Root, Elihu: effort to include Kerensky in the international law setup, 34; treaty-making, and the prerogative of Congress, 115; League of Nations and the World Court, 118; Hague Court, 119; Statute of the World Court, 120

Rural life, post-war conferences on, 161

Russo-Japanese War *1905*, 103, 119

Saar Valley Administration, incident concerning, 106-108

Sanction, or peace enforcement, 127

Scandinavian relief organization of the first World War, 171

Scialoja, Vittorio, Saar Administration incident, 106, 107

Science: mobilization for war, 7, 8, 11, 14, 87, 90, 112, 146; interdependence of nations under the regime of science, 13, 15, 192; challenge of scientific militarism, 13; the final and invincible ally of peace, 15, 194, 219; aid to recuperative powers of national life, 23; overrides isolation, 89; invention of airplane, an effective police force, 129; progress of scientific discovery, and need for continuing provisions for disarmament, 136, 149; instrument of destruction, 218; *see also* Chemistry

Sécurité, French conception, 87, 145, 148

Security, and collective security, 82, 85-99; need of smaller nations, and their responsibility in attaining it, 28, 49, 205; responsibility of the Great Powers, 49, 205, 207, 212; failure of the League of Nations, 53, 86, 98, 108, 140, 207, 208; vote of Congress, 57; Four-Nations Declaration, 61, 62; definition of national security, 85, 87-88; hope of the nineteenth century, through normal operation of natural laws, 86, 155; effect of armaments race, 84, 140; failure of statesmanship after the first World War, 87; a needed forerunner to disarmament, 87; "freedom from fear", 87; three foundations for security: natural, military, and mutual action, 87-89, 146; open-minded consideration of changing conditions, 90, 146; political means for attaining security, 90; problem of "nationalism", 91; cooperative action, an alternative to international anarchy, 94; quarantine against aggression, 95; problem of national sovereignty, 95-97, 216; ineffective when universal in theory, but local in application, 98; post-war structure for cooperative defense, 123-124; *1933* efforts, 147-148; international system of inspection, 150; dependence of work for welfare, 202; varying degrees of post-war participation by nations, 205; need for swift and efficient operation of machinery, 211, 224; regional organization against local wars, 214; a trusteeship for the maintenance of peace, 225-227

Serbia *1914*, 105

Sermon on the Mount, 132-133

Shotwell, James T.: address before the *Hochschule für Politik, March 1927*, 12; American member of the Committee on Intellectual Cooperation, 186; member of the Labor Committee, Paris Peace Conference, 200

Siberia, problem of Far Eastern settle-

ment at the close of the war, 40
Slavery, industrial, in modern warfare, 23
Smaller Powers: sense of nationality, 25; new relationships, 25; equality of states, 26; inviolability of sovereignty, 26, 49; responsibility for international condition preceding the second World War, 26; protest on division of control in the UNRRA, 27; procedure for collective security, 28, 49, 205; defenseless under modern wartime conditions, 28, 49; disinclination to give up the submarine, 140; international and local interests, 211
Smith, Adam, *Inquiry into the Nature and Causes of the Wealth of Nations, 1776*, 85, 113, 153
Smuts, Marshal Jan, on the destiny of mankind, 193
Social and economic problems, and reconstruction, international machinery to deal with, 157, 158, 160-161, 201, 214
Social hygiene, 161
Social justice: Confucian ideal, 42; the basis for universal peace, 162, 163; work of the International Labor Organization, 164; justice within states, 198; post-war problem of international organization, 201; challenge of science, 219; *see also* Human rights
Social Science Research Council, 192
Social security, 156, 164
Socialism, international, 163
Sovereignty: invoked by smaller powers, 26, 49; Mr. Hull's report on the Moscow Conference: recognition of the principle of sovereign equality, 59; a possible modification in dealing with people across frontiers, 80; conflict with cooperative war prevention, 95, 96, 212; rôle of the citizen, 96; Wilson's conception of the equality in sovereignty, 97; mediation blocked by the XIXth century conception of absolute sovereignty, 103; German doctrine of the sovereign state, 110; right of warfare, 110; question as to how far sovereignty is limited by membership in the United Nations, 202, 210; absolute sovereignty a concept of anarchy, 202; possible concession to international body for the sake of world preservation, 211; no impairment in cooperation in matters of mutual interest, 222; survey by Professor Corwin, 231
Spanish Civil War, 37, 108
Spanish-American War, 26, 197
Sparta, ancient, 30
Stabilization Fund, International: United States Treasury plan, 178; establishment of Bank by member governments, 181
Stalin, Joseph: rejection of world revolution, trend toward nationalistic conception, 35, 36, 40; determination to incorporate the Baltic States within the Soviet Union, 36, 37; distaste for the League, 37-38; temporary Nazi alliance, 38; partition of Poland, 39-40; Teheran Conference, 40, 53; problem of security in the Four-Nation Declaration, 61; German statement on the massacre of the Polish patriots, 64; reaction to British-American attitude on frontier states, 65, 66; plans for the administration of occupied territories, 66; announcement of the confederation of sixteen Soviet Republics, 67-69, 71; Commissar of Nationalities, 69; *1920* letter to Lenin on federation of soviets, 70, 72, 76; policy with reference to the Red Army, 71-72; ruler of the state through the Communist Party, 72-73; development of the nation through federalism, 73-75; safeguard to the revised Constitution of the state, 76, 80; possible long-range use of policy of federation, 80
State, the, an international person, 26; *see also* Equality of States; Universality, principle of
States rights, under the Soviet confederation system, 68
Statute of Westminster, 79
Stimson, Secretary Henry L., conquest does not constitute title, 127; implication of consultation in Pact of Paris, 148
Stoic idea of a law of nature, 111, 193
Streseman, Gustav, Saar Administration incident, 106-108
Students, plight of, an interest of the

INDEX

Intellectual Cooperation Organization, 187
Submarines, Germany's agreement to the abolishment of, 140
Sun Yat-sen, "Three Principles", 42
Sweden, 49
Switzerland, 49, 69

Taft, William Howard, 115; League to Enforce Peace, 119
Tariff: tariff legislation, a prerogative of Congress, 152, 154; the Great Depression, 153; Canadian-American trade relations, 154; a form of economic warfare to be considered in post-war arrangements, 166; disastrous policy of a raised tariff and foreign investment, 180
Technical competence, aid to post-war international organization, 156, 161, 213
Teheran Conference *November-December 1943*, 211; Russian outlet to the Persian Gulf, 40; priority of executive action, 48; Declaration, *text*, 242-243
Teutonic Knights, cultural influence on Baltic States, 36-37
Thirty Years War, 129
Trade: need of a freer trade, 82, 152-153; growing interdependence of world commerce, 85; an enlarged market and domestic prosperity, 153, 156, 183; barrier to debtor nations in sale of their goods, 153; international agreements, 154; limitation of trade barriers, not total free trade, 155; need for international organization, 156, 160; need for new monetary mechanisms due to economic consequences of two World Wars, 177, 182
Treaties and agreements: British-American understanding without the need of treaties, 33, 45; on the value of post-war alliances, 59, 110; obligations under international law, 110, 112; control by the United States Senate, 115, and deadening effect on negotiation of arbitration treaties, 115, 119; movement toward general arbitration treaties at end of XIXth century, 116; arbitration treaties not a substitute for more practical methods of pacific settlement, 116; arrangement and application under World Court jurisdiction, and need to preserve this structure of treaty law, 121, 228; need for revision to preserve international goodwill, 146; problem of tariff agreements by the United States, 154; post-war registration and publication of cartel agreements, 160; international labor agreements prior to establishment of I.L.O., 164, 229; secret treaties of the first World War, 204; international agreements affecting daily life of common man, 206; treaties of arbitration and non-aggression, 215; regional agreements outside the League, 215; failure of French treaties with Czechoslovakia and Poland, 226; violation by Germany, 227; danger of legislation by way of treaties, 228

1902 January 30 Anglo-Japanese treaty (renewed *1905* and *1911*) denounced by England *1920*, 144
1905 August 23 Treaty of Portsmouth (Japan, Russia), 103
1913-1914 Bryan Treaties of Conciliation (30 nations), 104
1919 June 28 Treaty of Versailles (World War I), 163, 180; Russia's attitude toward British-French measures for fulfillment by Germany, 34-35; German disarmament, 138; *Article XIII*, the Constitution of the International Labor Organization, 162
1921 March 18 Treaty of Riga (Russia, Poland, the Ukraine), Polish frontiers, 39
1922 Four-Power Pact (United States, Great Britain, France and Japan), 144
1922 Nine-Power Treaty guaranteeing the integrity of China, 144
1922 April 16 Treaty of Rapallo (Germany-Russia), German help in building up Russian industry, 34
1925 Treaties of Locarno: built around formal definition of aggression, 5, 12-13; *Article 5*, British intervention in case of German attack on France, 5-6; violated by Germany,

6, 227; formation of regional arrangements outside the League, 215, 216

1926 April Treaty of Mutual Assistance (Germany-Russia), 34

1928 August Paris Peace Pact (Briand-Kellogg Pact): a pioneering gesture, 3; distinction between aggressive and defensive wars, 13; denial of war as instrument of national policy, 113, 220; no enforcement measures provided, 126, 147, 220; need for consultation implied, 148; United States' commitment on reduction of armaments, 149

1933 March British draft convention in preparation for the Disarmament Conference, 148

1939 August 23 Mutual non-aggression pact (Germany-Russia), a temporary deal, 38

1939 September and October Russian treaties with three Baltic States, concerning naval bases, airdromes, etc., 37

1941 August 14 Atlantic Charter (Great Britain-United States), *see* by name in body of index

— Lend-Lease agreements, 44, text, Section VII, 236

1942 January 2 Declaration of the United Nations (by 26 nations at war with the Axis Powers), 238; lack of implementation, 54

May Great Britain-Soviet Union, 44, 52

1943 October Four-nation Declaration (Great Britain, Russia, United States at the Moscow Conference, with China) containing statements on Austria and Italy, *text*, 238-240; *see also* Moscow Conference

Statement on Atrocities (Great Britain, Russia, United States) issued at Moscow Conference, 50, 60, 238, *text*, 240-241

Treaty between the Soviet Union and Czechoslovakia, held back until after the Moscow Conference, 44

November 9 Pact creating UNRRA, 47, 171

November 22-26 Joint Communique (United States, Great Britain, China) Cairo Conference, *text*, 241-242

1943 December 1 Teheran Declaration (Great Britain, Russia, United States), *text*, 242-243

Tripartite Conference of the Foreign Secretaries, *see* Moscow Conference
Triple Alliance, 9
Triple Entente, 9
Trotsky, Leon, expulsion from the Central Committee, 35
Turkey: British support at the Dardanelles, 33; Soviet diplomacy, 40; Stalin's statement regarding confederation, 70

Ukraine, the: Curzon Line, 39; peace treaty with Poland and Russia *1921*, 39; Polish occupation, 65; opposition to Russification under the Czars, 68; federation in Soviet Russia, 72, 76, 77
Unanimity, rule of, in issues of security, 97, 212, 225
Unemployment, problem of, after demobilization, 22, 82; Beveridge Report, 81
Union of Soviet Socialist Republics, and Russia: Triple Entente, 9; yearly military maneuvers previous to *1914*, 9; test of the nature of the state, 26; Red Army's victorious strength in second World War, 28, 40, 66, 71, 73, 81, 220; member of United Nations, 29; post-war leadership, 29; British XIXth century suspicions with regard to India and the Dardanelles, 33-34; American attitude toward old regime, 34; Revolution *1917*, 34, 40, 69, 77; Kerensky Government, 34; Root's attempt to bring into the field of international law, 34; German technical aid to industry and army, 34; German entente *1922* and *1926*, 34; attitude toward capitalistic nations, 34-35; enters League *1934*, 35; United States recognition *1933*, 35; challenge to nations to disarm, 35; Moscow Treason Trials, *1936*, 36; isolation, 36; a new nationalism, 36, 73, 77; Finland, the Baltic Republics, and border states, 36-38, 68, 80; agrarian reforms, 37; expelled

INDEX

from the League, 37; alliance with Germany, 38; partition of Poland, 38, 39, 40, 64; the western frontier and the Curzon Line, 39, 63, 64, 65, 71; Far East problems, 43; devastating invasion by Germany, and economic needs, 40-41; *1942* alliance with Great Britain, 44, 52; alliance with Czechoslovakia, 44; German propaganda statement of Russian massacre of Polish patriots, 64; Polish occupation of White Russia and the Ukraine, 65; refuses to deal with the Polish Government-in-exile, 65; revision of *1936* Constitution, and confederation of states (Molotoff decrees), 66-68, 71-73, 75, 76, 80, 205-206, 209; preparations for post-war period, 67-82; newspaper attacks on Wendell Willkie, the Vatican, and Cairo rumor of British-German negotiations, 67; states rights, Czarist policy of Russification, 68; local autonomy, 68-72; Constitutions of *1918*, *1923* and *1936*, 70, 72; right of secession, 72; army commands divided under the sixteen republics, 72, 79; rise of literacy, 72; foreign relations policy, 74, 75, 78; sixteen republics free to deal with foreign nations in economic and cultural matters, 67, 74, 78, 79, 205-206, 209; final sovereignty and control of major questions of national policy of central government, 74, 76; national anthem, 77, 78; dominance of "Great Russia" in the Union, 77; Germany's fear of pan-Slavism in the Balkans *1914*, 105; Manchuria *1929*, 127; membership in the UNRRA, 172, 173; pogroms of Jews in Czarist Russia, 197; responsibility in post-war international organization, 220, 225; *see also* Communist Party; Moscow Conference; Molotoff decrees; Hague Conference *1899*

United Nations: organized temporarily for war, in order to destroy the power of the enemy states, 16-18, 21; organized for peace for the welfare and security of nations and individuals, 16, 17, *see* United Nations: Permanent International Organization; post-war constructive measures, 17, 23; unconditional surrender of the enemy, 17-19; welfare work in liberated areas, 18; temporary occupation of enemy countries, 19; ticklish problems in peace construction, 21; health and welfare, 22; problem of uprooted peoples, 22, 23; colonies and dependencies, 23; disparity in size and outlook of members, 27; problem of adventurous Russian policy, 41; beginnings, 44-50; a coalition of leaders, 44; formation of the Atlantic Charter *August 1941*, 45; Hot Springs Conference on Food and Agriculture, 46; draft agreement for the UNRRA, 47; technique of conference, 47; problem of representation by Governments-in-exile, 48; exclusion of topics on actual conduct of the war, 48; dominant leadership of Great Powers, 49; Conference of Foreign Secretaries at Moscow, 51; Four-Power Declaration, 60; Advisory Committee, London, to study plans for a permanent organization, 61; Advisory Committee on Italy, 61; disarmament of Axis Powers, 137-138

United Nations Conference on Food and Agriculture, proposed, 159, 169-171; *see also* Hot Springs Conference

United Nations Permanent International Organization for the future, 16, 17, 18, 223; must be composed of free nations, 19; Three Principles of Sun Yat-sen, security, justice, welfare, 42; argument against war-time establishment, 45; American public opinion of a post-war peace organization, 54-56; report of Mr. Hull to Congress, 59; Advisory Commission, London, to study plans for a permanent organization, 61; participation by Russia, 71, 74; graded responsibility, 97, 99, 208, 214-215, 216; need for swift and efficient work for peace enforcement, 98, 211; adequate police action, 99; submission of disputes to political or judicial methods, 100, 101, 123; enhancement of each sovereign state, 102; development of respected systems of law and order, 110; obligations of peace enforcement, 123-126; responsibility of the organization for war prevention, in return for pledge of members not to resort to war, 123; emergency air police force for war prevention, 124, 125, 128, 130, 132; progressive reduction of armaments, 124, 149; civil aviation, 131; suggested commission on the reduction and control of armaments: inspection of armament, 137, 138, 150; retention of some military force for international policing, 141; political organization of the United Nations, 200-217; "United Nations of the World", 201; Central Body, 201; questions of membership of ex-enemy states and state sovereignty, 202; active participation by states winning the war, 203; Constitution, 204, 213-215; ultimately, membership compulsory, 204; test for membership, acceptance of Atlantic Charter, 205; Canadian statement on conception and authority, 206; central political organization, 207-214, 217, 230; formed similarly to the League, 207, 208; a public forum for the discussion of major problems, 209; smaller body to meet insistent problems of current politics, 209; question of votes and veto, 210-211; temporary and permanent committees, 213; permanent technical bodies, 213; problem of administration, 213; provision in the Constitution for security, 213; avoidance of an unwieldy bureaucracy, 214; secretariat, 214; regional and other organizations, 214-217; federal structure, 215; an engineering, not an architectural, job, 222; statement on the American Constitution, and membership in the organization, 231

United Nations Relief and Rehabilitation Administration (UNRRA), 158, 170, 171-175, 222; constituted by the United Nations, *November 9, 1943*, 27, 47; membership by small and Great Powers, 28; Council 27; Director General, 27; program of immediate matters of relief, 46; operations in the humanitarian field, only partly economic, 160, 172, 174, 201; pact signed by forty-four nations, 171; the Council, policy-making body, 172, 173; Central Committee to deal with emergencies, 172, 173; Director General to carry on relief operations, 172, 173; Committees on Supplies, Financial Control, Europe, the Far East, 173; two groups of members, those paying in foreign exchange and those in local currencies, 174; administrative in function, 229

United States of America: Paris Peace Pact, 3; entrance into first World War, 10; late arrival of armaments, 10; Briand letter asking to American People to join with France in renouncing war as an instrument of national policy, 12; isolation, and the swing away from it, 15, 54, 89-90, 92; sympathy for oppressed nations, 26; Monroe Doctrine, 26; relations with Great Britain, 28, 29, 30, 31, 33, 45, 116; effect on military forces in the field, 29; Mr. Churchill's address at Harvard, 30, 54, 97, 124, 142, 188, 207; a reasoning, not emotional, view of freedom for backward areas, 32, 33; the Revolution, a fight for the freedom of Englishmen, 33, 223; Declaration of Independence, 33, 111, 113, 223; English heritage of the Bill of Rights, 33; support of the White Russians, 34; recognition of Soviet Russia *1933*, 35; British-American cooperation with the Soviet Union, 40; attitude to De Gaulle and the Fighting French, 41; Lend-Lease Agreements, 44, 45, *text* of Section VII, 236; anomalous position before entry into war, 44; neutrality, 44, 45, 95, 134, 220, 223; declaration of war, 45; Moscow Conference, 51, 225; American attitude to the Four-Nations Declaration, 53; public opinion on implementation of Atlantic Charter, 54; United States in the world organization, 54, 55, 218-233; responsibility for post-war peace enforcement, 55, 56, 221, 225; Congressional vote on collective security, 57; State Department's study of the post-war situation, 57, 58; Hull's report to Congress on the Moscow Conference, 58, 59, 60, 62, 63; reaction to the Polish frontier problem, 64, and Russian frontier states, 65, 73; study of American Federation by

INDEX

Stalin, prior to revision of *1936* Constitution, 69, 77; unemployment and related problems, 81, 82; interest in post-war economics, 82; free trade, 82; nationalism, 92, 223; effect of modern war on isolation, 94; federal system under the Constitution, and division of powers, 96; Articles of Confederation, 98; influence on American education, of Germanic theory of complete freedom for a sovereign state, 110; "laws of nature," 111-112; conduct of foreign affairs, and effect of treaty-making control by the Senate, 115, 231; Hague Conferences *1899* and *1907*, 117; Hughes' challenge for a naval holiday, 142; naval ratio, 143; British-Japanese alliance, 144; attitude toward French conception of security, 146; *1933* Disarmament Conference, 148, 149; trade and tariff, 152, 154, 155; Canadian trade, 154; a chance to institute a policy of economic liberation, 156; Treasury monetary proposal, 159, 177, 178, 181, 182; membership in the International Labor Organization *1934*, 163, 164; policy on permanent body for food and agriculture, 169; membership in UNRRA, 171-174; first World War relief organization, 171; international credit, 179, 180; foreign investment, 180, 181; distaste for a planned public opinion, 185; international cultural cooperation, 187-192; plan for the reeducation of occupied enemy states, 188; Bill of Rights, a basis for an international Bill of Rights, 196; veto power, or the rule of unanimity, in international organization, 212, 225; principle of graded responsibility, 216; good neighbor policies, 216; World Court, 228

United States Chamber of Commerce, referendum on the Moscow Resolution, 63

Universality, principle of, see *Jus gentium*

Vatican policy in Europe, Soviet denunciation, 67

Wages, dependence on inter-nation purchases, 82, 183; matter of conflict, 162

War: nature and consequences, 3-15, 218; failure of peace movement to understand its nature, 3; outlawry of aggressive war, 4, 6; instrument of national policy, 5, 11-13, 18, 20, 49, 62, 99, 113, 129, 220; substitutes and procedures, 5, 87, 90, 102, 114; false idea that war is a fundamental condition of government, 6, 14; defensive war, 6, 13; German theory that war is a continuation of policy, 7, 8, 14; accepted by international law, 7, 113; cost to the victorious nation, 8; an engineering operation, 9-10, 14, 15, 89, 112, 132, 138, 143, 219, 226; effect on whole economic life, 10, 11, 19, 22, 62, 94; no longer directable or controllable, 11, 12; failure to distinguish between aggression and defense, 13, 86; problem of liquidation, 16-24, 25, 51, 203; distinction between organizing for war or for peace, 16-19; necessity for the complete denial of its legitimacy, 20, 114; total war must be followed by total peace, 20, 162; economic and social problems left in the wake of war, 22, 23; punishment of war criminals, 50, 60, 240; international action for the prevention of war, 96, 99; attempt to humanize, in international law, 112; devolution of war, 112; preventive force, 128, 135; recognition by the Church fathers of a just war, 133; war potentials in chemistry and industry, 139; violation of human rights within a nation, a contributing cause of war, 198, 228

Warsaw, occupation by the Nazis, 39

Washington, President George: fight for the liberties of an Englishman, 33; Neutrality Proclamation of *1793*, 223; Farewell Address *1796*, 223; view of world affairs and world peace, 223, 224; letters to Lafayette, 224

Washington Conference on the Limitation of Armaments *1921–22*, proposal for naval disarmament and capital-ship ratio, 142-145

Weimar Government, *see* Germany

Welfare, *see* Health and Welfare; Livelihood; Human rights

Welles, Sumner, Undersecretary of State:

preparation for post-war settlement, 58; statement in support of Baltic States, 65

White Russia: Curzon Line, 39; Polish occupation, 65; place in Soviet federation, 72

"White" Russians, American support for British forces aiding in fight against the Communist Government, 34

Wilhelm II, 9

Willkie, Wendell, attack by Soviet press, 67

Wilson, Woodrow: request for American support of the League of Nations, 30; reconsideration by Americans of *1919* attitude, 55; conception of the sovereignty of states, 97; the World Court, 118; inherits Hague Conference tradition, 119; attitude toward a league to enforce peace, and international law as a basis for an association of nations, 119, 120; Fourteen Points, 200; League of Nations, a compact pioneering effort, 201, 222

Women and children, League work in behalf of, 161, 164

World Court, *see* Permanent Court of International Justice

World Court League, *see* League to Enforce Peace

World War I: initial successes of the aggressor, 8, 14; German mass production, 8-9; United States entry as an "associate", 10, 45, 200; Carnegie Endowment, *Social and Economic History*, 10; modern war no longer controllable, 11, 14; lesson on playing into the hands of the militarist element of the enemy at the peace negotiations, 19, 203; post-war disillusionment, 23, 53; independence of Baltic republics, 36; conflict in the United States between the Executive and Senate, 58; separate formations of the British Dominions, 79; problem of "national" security, 86, 87, 105; cause in the political field, 105; progress into total war, 112; armaments race, 136, 140, 142; amateurish post-war plans for armament reduction, 137, 145; movement for the reduction of armaments, 140; nature of contraband articles, 149; cost, and the Great Depression, 153; post-war threat of economic and social overturn, 163; relief organizations, 171; post-war interest in international affairs, 185; secret treaties, 204; international monetary reorganization a consequence of the war, 177; no territorial gains sought by the United States, 232

World War II: arousing of democratic peoples after act of aggression, 10; apparent control by the aggressor, 14, 138, 227; loss of control by the enemy, 15; tremendous cost, 21, 125-126; greatest catastrophe in history in terms of human misery, 22, 231; responsibility of smaller powers for present international conditions, 26; ultimate aims, 31, 54, 194, 198; division of war in Europe and Asia, 42; long term post-war liquidation, 50, 51; Moscow meeting, the "first peace conference", 59; statement on atrocities, 50, 60, *text*, 238, 240; political effect on Soviet, 71-73, 81; race in rival armaments, 86; security needed prior to disarmament, 87; pre-war disbelief in the United States, 95; causes in political field, 105, 195; in the denial of international law, 106, 108, 113; elimination of war as an instrument of national policy, 113; Germany's slogan: "guns instead of butter", 126; Japanese aggression, the real beginning, 127; Axis unilateral resort to arms, 136; post-war inspection of armaments, 137; post-war organizations, 158, 210, 220; cultural destruction and degradation, 189; British-American efforts toward international cultural cooperation, 191, 207-208; early beginning of peace machinery, 200-202; chief post-war burden on the Great Powers, 205, 211

World War III: need for preventive measures, 23, 109, 125-126, 132, 202, 220, 233

Yen, James Y. C., work for mass education in China, 43

Yugoslavia, 61

Zinovieff, Grigori, expulsion from Central Committee, 35